Artificial Intelligence and Global Society

Artificial Intelligence and Global Society

Impact and Practices

Edited by

Puneet Kumar, Vinod Kumar Jain, and Dharminder Kumar

CRC Press
Taylor & Francis Group
Boca Raton London New York

CRC Press is an imprint of the
Taylor & Francis Group, an **informa** business

A CHAPMAN & HALL BOOK

First edition published 2021
by CRC Press
6000 Broken Sound Parkway NW, Suite 300, Boca Raton, FL 33487-2742

and by CRC Press
2 Park Square, Milton Park, Abingdon, Oxon, OX14 4RN

ISBN: 978-0-367-43943-9 (hbk)
ISBN: 978-0-367-70465-0 (pbk)
ISBN: 978-1-003-00660-2 (ebk)

Typeset in Palatino
by MPS Limited, Dehradun

Printed in the United Kingdom
by Henry Ling Limited

Contents

Preface

In the chase between human intelligence and machine intelligence, machines are close to surpassing human intelligence in the current era. The profuse use of digital technologies in making the processes automated was one of the prime advantages of the Third Industrial Revolution. As a result, advanced and developing nations have started digitalization of their mundane tasks. Due to this, the digital technologies or ICT (Information and Communication Technologies) have exceedingly high market space in terms of infrastructure building, employment generation, education sector reforms, funds mobilization, electronic governance, hardware manufacturing, software development, etc. Hence, it is evident that ICT or digitalization was penetrating every segment of the society.

But with the advent of GPUs in the market, artificial intelligence technologies—along with IoT and big data analytics—have gotten an apt pace. As per Gartner, in the year 2017, the total market share of Business Intelligence and Data Analytics was 18.3 billion dollars, and it is expected to reach up to 25.3 billion dollars by the year 2021 with an 8.5% CAGR. It can be contemplated that machine learning is going to capture the whole society by providing a sense of machine intelligence in every mundane task. This is the beginning of the Fourth Industrial Revolution where society is relying more on machine decisions—manufacturing industries are approaching massive automation, e-commerce industries are giving personal attention to each consumer despite millions of customers, people are frequently using various wearable healthcare devices equipped with a variety of sensors, social media predictions are influencing political decisions, etc.

This book encompasses the novel AI practices being followed across the global community in various domains: security, health care, crime prevention and detection, education, etc. Furthermore, it also suggests innovative techniques which can be adopted in the future to ensure better delivery of services to the society. It's the sincere hope of the editors that the efforts of the academe and researchers contained in this book will be helpful to the society and open many avenues for further research.

Editors

Puneet Kumar is an Associate Professor in the Department of Computer Science and Engineering and Coordinator of Research and Development Cell at the School of Engineering and Technology, Mody University of Science and Technology, India. Though he has obtained his master's and PhD in computer science, he believes in the philosophy of interdisciplinary research. He has also completed a certificate course on intellectual property rights at WIPO Academy, Geneva. He has more than 17 years of teaching, research, and industrial experience. His major research interests are Machine Learning, Data Science and e-government. He has published various research papers and articles in national and international journals, and his papers are widely cited by various stakeholders across the world. He is the recipient of a software copyright from the Ministry of Human Resource and Development, Government of India. He has also published books on e-governance titled *"E-Governance in India: Problems, Prototypes and Prospects" and "Stances of e-Government: Policies, Processes and Technologies"* . He is a Life Member of CSI, IAENG, IET and a Professional Member of ACM.

Vinod Kumar Jain is Vice Chancellor at Sage University, Bhopal (MP). He earned an MBA, an MTech (CS), and a PhD in computer science at Devi Ahilya University, Indore. He has been involved in teaching, training, research, and administration for 25 years, which includes 15 years as vice chancellor, dean of academics, dean, director, or principal at various universities and institutions in India. He has a rich experience in autonomy implementation; the Accreditation Board for Engineering and Technology (ABET), US; IET Accreditation, UK; National Board of Accreditation (NBA), India; and National Assessment and Accreditation Council (NAAC), India. He received the Rashtriya Shiksha Gaurav Puruskar 2016 from the Center for Education, Growth, and Research (CEGR), New Delhi, the Academic Leader of the Year Award 2018 by ICCI, New Delhi, and Accredited Management Teacher by All India Management Association (AIMA), New Delhi. Dr. Jain has more than 220 publications to his credit, including books, monographs, research papers, and popular articles. He has organized many conferences, seminars, and QIPs and delivered more than 50 keynote and expert lectures. Dr. Jain is actively associated with professional and social organizations such as Institute of Electrical and Electronics Engineers (IEEE), Computer Society of India (CSI), Indian Society for Training and Development (ISTD), Indian Society for Technical Education (ISTE), Institute of Electronics and Telecommunication Engineering (IETE), Institution of Engineers -India (IEI), All India Management Association (AIMA), Association of Indian Management Schools (AIMS), Global Conference on Flexible Systems Management (GLOGIFT), Quality Circle Forum of India (QCFI), and Bharat Vikas Parishad (BVP). He is a PhD supervisor at Mody University Lakshmangarh and has guided 14 PhD scholars. He is a Fellow of IET -UK, IETE, and New Delhi and Institution of Engineers -India. His recent publications include *The Stances of E-Government: Policies, Processes and Technologies* (CRC Press).

 **Dharminder Kumar** is a Professor in the Department of Computer Science and Engineering and Director, PDU Innovation and Incubation Cell, Guru Jambheshwar University of Science and Technology, Hisar. Professor Kumar has been Founder Dean of Colleges, Dean of the Faculty of Engineering and Technology, Chairman of the Department of Computer Science and Engineering, Bio-Medical Engineering and Printing Technology, Coordinator of TEQIP (1.2 and 1.3) – a world bank project for improving quality in technical education.

More than 15 students have earned PhDs in computer science and engineering under his supervision or joint supervision. He has published more than 95 research papers in journals and national and international conferences/seminars. He has also written four books.

He has more than 30 years of teaching and research experience.

He has visited many countries. He is an expert member of many national-level committees of NBA, NAAC and UGC.

He has been nominated as Margdarshak by AICTE to help two technical institutions for their NBA purpose in the state of Haryana.

His areas of interest include data mining and communication networks.

Contributors

D. P. Acharjya
School of Computer Science
and Engineering VIT Vellore

Pankul Agarwal
Department of Computer Science
and Engineering
Amity School of Engineering and Technology
Amity University
Noida (U.P.), India

Simran Agarwal
Department of Biomedical Engineering
School of Engineering and Technology
Mody University of Science and
Technology
Laxmangarh, Sikar, Rajasthan

Himanshu Aggarwal
Department of Computer Science
and Engineering
Punjabi University
Patiala

Leena Bhole
School of Computer Science and IT
Devi Ahilya Vishwavidyalaya
Indore

Manojkumar Vilasrao Deshpande
Department of Computer Science
and Engineering, Prestige Institute of
Engineering Research and Management
Indore

Deepak Dudeja
CT University
Ludhiana, Punjab

Raghu Garg
Department of Computer Science
and Engineering
Punjabi University
Patiala

Rahul Gupta
Department of Computer Science
and Engineering
Amity School of Engineering and
Technology
Amity University
Noida (U.P.), India

Sangeeta Gupta
MERI
Delhi

Piali Haldar
School of Business Studies
Sharda University

Maya Ingle
School of Computer Science
and IT Devi Ahilya
Vishwavidyalaya
Indore

Somil Jain
Department of Computer Science and
Engineering School of Engineering
and Technology
Mody University
of Science and Technology
Rajasthan, India

Vinod Kumar Jain
SAGE University
Bhopal

Sunil Kumar Jangir
Department of Computer Science and
Engineering, School of Engineering
and Technology
Mody University of Science and
Technology
Laxmangarh, Sikar, Rajasthan

Aditi Kajala
Department of Computer Science and
   Engineering School of Engineering
   and Technology
Mody University of Science and
   Technology
Rajasthan, India

Raj Kamal
Department of Electronics and
   Communication Engineering
Prestige Institute of Engineering
   Research and Management
Indore, India

Babita G. Kataria
UIIC AKTU
Lucknow

Josyula Raja Kishore
CSC E-Governance Services
   India Pvt. Ltd.
Telangana and Andhra Pradesh

Dharminder Kumar
CSED GJUST
Hisar

Manish Kumar
Department of Biomedical Engineering
   School of Engineering and Technology
Mody University of Science and
   Technology
Laxmangarh, Sikar, Rajasthan

Puneet Kumar
Department of Computer Science
   and Engineering School of Engineering
   and Technology
Mody University of Science
   and Technology
Rajasthan, India

Sunil Kumar
Department of Computer and
   Communication Engineering, SCIT
Manipal University
Jaipur

Vijay Kumar
Computer Science and Engineering
Department National Institute of
   Technology Hamirpur
Himachal Pradesh

Singaraju Suguna Mallika
Department of CSE
CVR College of Engineering

Ramesh Narwal
Computer Engineering Department
Punjabi University
Patiala, Punjab

Vikas Raina
Department of Computer Science
   and Engineering School of
   Engineering and Technology
Mody University of Science and
   Technology
Rajasthan, India

Debashish Roy
University of Petroleum and
   Energy Studies Dehradun, India

Preeti Saxena
School of Computer Science and
   Information Technology
Devi Ahilya Vishwavidyalya
Indore

Deepak Sethi
Department of Computer Science and
   Engineering Amity
School of Engineering and Technology
Amity University
Noida (U.P.) India

Anand Sharma
Department of Computer Science and
   Engineering School of Engineering
   and Technology
Mody University of Science and
   Technology
Rajasthan, India

Chandraprakash Sharma
Wisflux Private Ltd.
Jaipur, Rajasthan

Jeetu Sharma
Department of Electronics and
    Communication Engineering School
    of Engineering and Technology
Mody University of Science
    and Technology
Rajasthan, India

Sahil Sharma
Computer Science and Engineering
Department Thapar Institute of
    Engineering and Technology
Patiala, Punjab

Vijay Prakash Sharma
Department of Information
    Technology SCIT Manipal University
Jaipur

Abhishek Singh
Computer Science and Technology
Galgotias University

Ashok Singh
School of Business Studies
Sharda University

Riyazveer Singh
Computer Science and Engineering
Department Thapar Institute of
    Engineering and Technology
Patiala, Punjab

Priyanshu Singhal
Department of Computer Science and
    Engineering Amity
School of Engineering and Technology
Amity University
Noida (U.P.)

Aakriti Singla
Department of Computer Science and
    Engineering School of Engineering
    and Technology
Mody University of Science and
    Technology
Rajasthan, India

R. Srivastava
University of Petroleum and
    Energy Studies
Dehradun

Satyajee Srivastava
Computer Science and Technology
Galgotias University

Sandeep Taumar
SME IBM
India

Ranjana Thalore
Department of Electronics and
    Communication Engineering
    School of Engineering and Technology
Mody University of Science
    and Technology
Rajasthan, India

Vandita Vyas
Department of Electronics and
    Communication Engineering
    School of Engineering and Technology
Mody University of Science and
    Technology Rajasthan, India

1

Artificial Intelligence: Revolution, Definitions, Ethics, and Foundation

Sandeep Taumar

CONTENTS

1.1 Revolution

Whenever a discussion comes to the revolution of artificial intelligence, I cannot restrict myself from stating key information on how big the AI revolution is set to bring in the next five to seven years. What is the broader historical setting from an industrial view-point that has led to the AI revolution?

Let's discuss the various reports that have been given by different organizations.

"By the year 2025, 95% of the customer interactions will be driven by Artificial intelligence."
— **Servion Report**

"By 2020 AI algorithms will positively change the behavior of most of the global workforce."
— **Gartner Report** [1].

"Closely links Internet of Things (IOT) with Artificial Intelligence '100% of all IOT initiatives will be supported by Artificial intelligence from 2019 onwards.'"
"At least 75% of all developers will include AI functionality in one or more of their business applications from 2018 onwards."
— *IDC* **report** [2].

"Artificial intelligence will add 14.5% to the GDP of North America and 26.1% to the GDP of China by 2035."
— **PWC studies** [3].

"AI will contribute to around 15% to India's GDP by 2035."
— **NitiAyog, India**

Even, as per the Tractica report which estimates that AI will grow approximately 15 times between 2016 and 2025 [4].

The artificial intelligence revolution is set to bring many changes in every industry for several factors like planning, communication, production, consumption, integration, etc. (Figure 1.1).

If we go through the timeline of the industrial revolution, we will find that each version is associated with a change in its overall functioning, resulting in the increased use of independent and self-sufficient machines and a decrease in human intervention.

In the early 1780s, the very first industrial revolution **(Industry 1.0)** took place when the invention of power looms, water and stream power invention occurred, and production shifted from handcrafted to mechanical (i.e. textile industry shifted from hand-woven to power loom; stream trains and ships in transportation helped increase communication [5]).

Then, in the early 1870s — almost 90 years after the second industrial revolution **(Industry 2.0)** took place where — electricity and conveyor belts were invented. With these, industries shifted from mechanical to mass production, the textile industry shifted

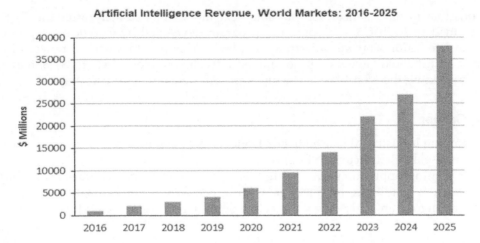

FIGURE 1.1
AI revenue in the world market.

from power looms to industrial sewing machines, and efficiency in communication industries increased with the help of the invention of the telegraph.

Further into the 1970s, the third industrial revolution **(industry 3.0)** took place, resulting in the invention of information technology and electronics, computer-aided designs, robots, and digital techniques that made it possible for industries to shift from mass to automated production. With this evolution, textile industries started digital printings on fabrics, and the invention of the internet and cellular phones led to remarkable changes in communication industries.

Presently, we, as humans, are taking our first steps in the world of artificial intelligence. Many researchers are also saying that we are in the fourth industrial revolution **(Industry 4.0)**, and we will witness the most advanced technologies to date (i.e. the invention of artificial intelligence, big data, and the internet of things).

With these technologies, industries will be able to shift from automated production to autonomous production, which will lead not only to a decrease in human intervention but also the implanting of intelligence into our systems. AI technologies can sense, analyze, and communicate (through IOT devices) better and perform real-time monitoring. For example, textile industries are doing personalized designing and 3D printing. Recently, the first smart factory, where post-order placement, production, and delivery happens without any human intervention, has been developed.

1.2 Applications

Since 1956, when it was first introduced, AI has achieved a lot one could have not thought of in the 50s. In 1950, Arthur Samuel created a checkers program that challenged amateurs; in 1994, Chinook became the first AI program that won a world championship against humans in a checkers game, and it was extremely popular with board games. In 1997, IBM's supercomputer creation — Deep Blue — defeated the chess legend Garry Kasparov. This was considered a great landmark in the field of AI and in the game, as it was possible to have almost 400 possible next moves immediately after the first two moves. In 2016 AlphaGo — a computer program developed by Google's Deepmind — defeated Lee Sedol, who was a leading Go player. This program was so powerfully developed that it could have thought of almost 130,000 possible moves. In 2018, the Dota2 game created by the Elon Mask's startup, OpenAI, defeated a human player.

1.2.1 Gaming

In the gaming industry, AI is used to create video games where basic methods are used to control non-player characters (NPCs).

Other gaming applications use AI to alter a player's emotional state by modifying environmental conditions, adding a new level, controlling music, analyzing a player's behavioral algorithm, and using GPS technologies (e.g. Pokémon GO) [6].

1.2.2 Technology

One of the applications of AI in the industry is the creation of AI personal assistants. To date, many industries have created major assistants like Siri by Apple, Alexa by Amazon, Duplex by Google, and Cortana by Microsoft. These assistants are used to reduce human workload and do simple tasks like fetching information from pages like IMDB and Wikipedia, pulling out suggestions for news websites, setting alarms, making lists, streaming videos and audios, and booking appointments, etc. [7].

1.2.3 Computer Vision

Visualizing objects using human power can be limited, so AI can be utilized to sense, analyze, understand, and aid several types of decision making. Using computer vision, AI can be used for scene reconstruction (filling the missing bits of an image or video), event detection (detecting a particular signal in the image or video), object recognition, 3D pose estimation, motion estimation, and image restoration.

Some of the real-life applications of computer vision are barcodes in supermarkets, financial data and business forms, computer-aided drawings, symbols and information from maps, x-rays and blood samples, traffic control cameras, geophysical imaging technologies, satellite imagery, image recognition, and rescue efforts.

Autonomous vehicles are the major application of computer vision, where they can navigate without human input. Self-driving cars can be beneficial in reducing collisions (and injuries), improving traffic due to reduced human errors (delayed reaction time, tailgating, distraction, aggressive or drunk driving), increased speed limits, and lower fuel consumption. It is also advantageous for people who cannot drive or cannot afford drivers.

Several automobile giants have already set their benchmark in terms of autonomous cars. In 2015, the states of Nevada, Florida, California, Virginia, Michigan, and Washington DC allowed the testing of autonomous cars on public roads. In 2017, Audi A8 became the first car to reach **level 3** of autonomous driving, where drivers can safely turn their attention away from driving. In 2018, Waymo announced that its test vehicles had traveled autonomously for over 8,000,000 miles without any issue; Starsky Robotics completed a 7-mile trip in Florida on self-driving trucks without any human.

By 2020, self-driving cars are expected to hit the roads. It is predicted that by 2040, 95% of new vehicles sold will be fully autonomous, and the technology is expected to expand to other vehicles such as trucks for the transport of goods.

1.2.4 Music Industry

In the music industry, AI is utilized to create and enhance music, personalize suggestions based on user activity data, and help artists monetize their music content and generate revenue. Magenta Project of Google is developing AI algorithms to generate songs, drawings, and other artworks — it is open-source, and real artists are using these tools to write their own songs.

Amper — a cloud-based, AI-driven music composition platform that generates unique musical selections based on the mood, style, and duration parameters selected by the user —is the first AI system to compose and produce an entire music album called "I AM AI". In collaboration with the artist Taryn, the first song composed with AI called "BreakFree" was released in 2017.

Spotify makes song recommendations with the help of Niland, an AI startup that improves the accuracy of music recommendations. With a variety of applications, AI is set to become an inherent part of the music generated in the near future.

1.2.5 Retail Industry

In the retail industry, automated out-of-stock scanning robots are the major application of AI. They make sure items are available on store shelves and replace them automatically, and check for items in the store (detect wrong name and wrong pricing on the items on the shelves and raise suitable alarms), which makes the entire process autonomous and more efficient.

Automatic checkouts are also becoming increasingly common in stores — computer vision algorithms scan the items in the bill payment section, detect the purchases, and send the bills to mobile devices.

Customer interests are also identified for better product recommendation (based on history and current trends), items are analyzed based on the positive or negative feedback, and virtual mirrors are used in apparel stores (so consumers can try on many clothes in a short period of time, without actually putting them on).

In the future of the retail industry, AI is expected to perform merchandising planning with executive oversight and forecast the sales of each product (with remarkably high accuracy) and direct activities autonomously.

1.2.6 Banking Industry

Banking institutions have started using AI to create conversational interfaces (financial data and accounting, AI-driven virtual assistants) to do general tasks like giving account balances, transferring and sending money between accounts, scheduling meetings with representatives, etc.

It also enables interaction with customers in the form of voice commands, texts, and pictures. It permits algorithmic trading — a method of executing a large trading order or a transaction too large to be filled out manually. There are some popular algorithms (like percentage of volume and target close) that enable automatic trading instructions and helps in sending small slices of the order out in the market. It was developed so that traders do not need to constantly watch over a stock and repeatedly send slices out manually.

Trading algorithms are widely used by investment banks, pension funds, mutual funds, hedge funds, etc. where large orders are executed in markets that cannot support all of the sizes. These algorithms are used to generate profits by the means of black-box trading

(trading strategies that are heavily reliant on algorithms and AI systems to generate profits by choosing the portfolio to invest in).

Apart from that, AI can be used in the banking industry to detect fraud (where historical and real-time data are analyzed and patterns that match fraud are identified). Fraud detection algorithms can identify whenever many transactions are carried out from a single card by verifying if they have been made by the owner or from a person who stole the card (by identifying the patterns of transaction, location, pin entry, etc.).

1.2.7 Agricultural Industry

AI is expected to bring a potential food revolution as it demands forecasting, lack of regular irrigation, fertilizer, and pesticide overuse, and improves crop yields through real-time advisory, advance detection of pest attacks, etc. Drones are also used to detect several factors that contribute to crop yield — weather, soil, rainfall, pests, etc. — and send real-time feedback on their status and suggest necessary actions to be taken. **Autonomous harvesting** (with the use of computer vision algorithms that automatically harvest fruits, vegetables, and other crops without human intervention) and **connected livestock programs** (where all animals are connected to a single system that can observe and monitor their food intake, GPS location, health records, stages in life, and take actions accordingly) are also utilized to improve agriculture experience.

1.2.8 Healthcare Industry

AI plays a vital role in the healthcare industry by detecting several diseases in their preliminary stages (e.g. cancer) and setting up virtual nurses (a system that monitors the health of the patients undergoing treatment and suggests treatment plans based on pattern recognition algorithms that can diagnose various ailments). AI Genetics — a major field that identifies genes responsible for hereditary diseases — identifies the genes responsible for a particular disease, which, in turn, helps edit the genes and eradicate their impact/effect. AI wearable devices can also help in the self-monitoring of health situations.

1.2.9 Sports Industry

In the sports industry, AI has become an integral part of sports training. It can help develop a chatbot for sites where sports teams can answer questions from their fanbase, including game and ticket information, team statistics, news, and logistics; monitor player health (remote activities of the player and send warnings to adhere to health regimen); and produce wearable technology (for performance monitoring and suggesting alternative movements that increase efficiency).

In recent events, the contributions of AI in sports have become evident. Wimbledon, in 2018, curated highlights for every game using AI based on important player movement and emotions in the game, crowd noise, and points. Ball tracking technology has also been used in cricket (where decisions for LBWs are made). The AI goal-line technology for the football world cup in 2018 was used to identify whether the ball has crossed the goal line (a special football was used that sent out a beep sound from an embedded microchip installed inside to the referee's watch to help him decide whether the ball has crossed the goal line), and cameras and wearable technologies that contain real-time data on the players' statistics were also used.

1.2.10 Definition Types

AI definitions are classified into four categories:
  Thinking like humans, acting like humans, thinking rationally, and acting rationally.

1.2.10.1 Thinking Like Humans

If a given artificial intelligence program thinks like a human, then the human brain's thought process needs to be understood 100%; producing AI that thinks like humans will not be possible for a while. Cognitive science, as a field, has tried to bring together techniques from psychology to model the human mind in the form of AI but it is still a developing field and the complete model of the human mind is still unknown [8].

1.2.10.2 Acting Like Humans

The Turing test, proposed by English mathematician, logician, and computer scientist **Alan Turing** in 1950, defined intelligent behavior as the ability to achieve human-level performance in all cognitive tasks, sufficient to fool an interrogator.
  The Turing test is defined as an AI system that is, while physically hidden, questioned by an interrogator. The AI system passes the test if the interrogator cannot tell whether it is a human or AI. To pass the Turing system an AI should:

- Understand its environment;
- Be able to reason; and
- Know natural language and possess learning capabilities.

An AI system performing activities on a narrow range of topics (like booking a haircut appointment) already exists, but it still has some distance to go in terms of passing a Turing test. AI systems that pass the Turing test (AI systems that act like humans are in progress) can narrow down conversations and communicate on any topic.

1.2.10.3 Thinking Rationally

Syllogisms — laws of thought, which govern the operation of the mind — initiated the field of logic and logical thinking (rational thinking). The development of formal logic in the late 19th and 20th centuries provided precise notations to solve logical problems. Logical tradition in artificial intelligence uses these foundations to build AI systems.
  Aristotle believed one can differentiate the right concepts from the wrong.

- **Problems in Thinking Rationally:** What is rational and what is not is subjective, therefore, quantifying real-world knowledge into rational inference can be daunting: what is rational for a vacuum cleaner is straightforward — it must clean the dirt — but what is rational for an autonomous driving car when faced with an accident situation? Who gets to decide on whether it is less ethical for five people on the road to die instead of one person inside a car?
  Initially, the emphasis was on drawing correct inferences; however, it is understood from the autonomous car case that there are situations where there are no absolutes, and something needs to be done about it.

1.2.10.4 Acting Rationally

There are situations where we act rationally without thinking rationally, like pulling one's hand off the hot stove — a **reflex action** that does not involve deliberation. Thinking and acting human-like are a bit futuristic for AIs (being rational involves acting according to one's beliefs, but it does not cover aspects such as reflex actions), and resulting actions according to the belief system is defined as rational here without questioning the beliefs in the AI system.

1.2.11 Definition Comparison

In this section, we will see an overview of the definition comparison of AI with regard to other related terms like **Machine Learning (ML) and Deep Learning (DL).**

Artificial Intelligence is a broad field that includes machine learning, representation learning, deep learning, logicism, robotics, linguistics, etc. (Figure 1.2) [9].

Machine Learning involves deep and representation learning together with the use designed feature-selection process.

Representation Learning and Deep Learning together with the automatic representation of features without abstract layers.

Deep Learning is the automatic representation of features in abstract layers.

1.2.12 Foundation Fields

The foundations of Artificial Intelligence are needed to be understood as they provide an idea about the fields that influenced — and are currently influencing — AI development. AI is a relatively new field and its basis comes from many fields that go as far as the roots of philosophy. It includes sectors like philosophy, mathematics, statistics, economics, neuroscience, psychology, control theory, computer engineering, linguistics, etc. Let us now discuss how each field contributed to the foundation of Artificial Intelligence [10].

1.2.12.1 Philosophy

Ancient Indian philosophy studies regarding the model of consciousness and AI research is also explored in the same field. Greek philosopher Aristotle discussed the **laws governing**

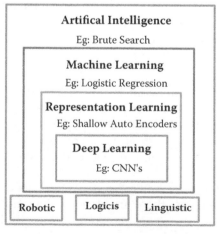

FIGURE 1.2
Classification of artificial intelligence techniques.

rationality, which form the foundations of rational artificial intelligent agents and digital binary computing. **Bertrand Russel** in the 1900s also discussed **logical positivism,** which considers that all knowledge can be developed into logical theories — thus, what is knowledge and what is not is defined by the information's ability to take shape into logical theories.

1.2.12.2 Mathematics

With the help of mathematics, logic was introduced by Aristotle, but it was made mathematical by George Boole. He introduced formal mathematical language (to make logical inferences in 1847), also known as **Boolean logic (where every information is reduced to 1s and 0s**), which is the foundation of digital computing that aids Artificial Intelligence today.

Apart from this, the **lncompleteness theorems** by **Gödel** established a limit on the algorithms and identified statements that, in any formal system, are unresolved or cannot be established as true in an algorithm. Lately, Turing Machine (developed by Alan Turing) helped in identifying statements that cannot be computed by an algorithm, and where probability plays a vital role.

1.2.12.3 Statistics

Artificial Intelligence agents require analysis of large amounts of data, hence, statistics play a critical role in converting information in the data to pragmatic intelligence using learning (like how **statistical hypothesis testing** helps draw inferences from data to make decisions for AI agents). In many problems of artificial intelligence, uncertainty is a factor that cannot be ignored, and **Bayesian statistical models** are used to deal with that.

1.2.12.4 Economics

Utility theory of economics, along with probability results in the decision theory, help identify whether an action is good or bad. AI borrows **rational agents** from economics that describe the autonomous programs capable of goal-directed behavior.

1.2.12.5 Neuroscience

So far, the human brain is the best-known example of intelligence and is being imitated by researchers through neuroscience (which provides a rich source of inspiration for new types of algorithms and architectures independent of mathematical and logic-based methods, and ideas that have largely dominated traditional approaches to AI). Neuroscience can provide validation for existing AI techniques. If a known algorithm is found to be implemented in the brain through neuroscience, then there is strong support for its possibility as an integral component of a system that could resemble the human brain.

1.2.12.6 Psychology

Psychology answers questions regarding people's behavior, perception, and cognition. Knowledge in artificial psychology involves research on understanding how machines (should) think; while, consumer psychology plays a role in answering questions regarding its form, size, color, tone, accent, gender, and many more. The results are becoming relevant especially in its application for humanoid robots as assistants.

1.2.12.7 Computer Engineering

For AI to succeed, **information** and **hardware** are needed — **computer** (acclaimed as the machine that best displays intelligence) and **computer engineering** (operating systems, programming languages, and tools needed to write programs).

1.2.12.8 Control Theory

Control Theory is about rationally perceiving, reasoning, and behaving in an environment; it defines the kinematic and dynamic of a robot. In Artificial Intelligence, a control system is the core of an intelligent agent that decides how it behaves. A robot has a body that feels the environment through sensors, actuators that obtain instructions and carry out movement, and a brain that acts as a controller that facilitates actions (as it references past experiences and improves its service by comparing the environment feedback with a goal).

1.2.12.9 Linguistics

Noam Chomsky, an American linguist, proposed structures based on syntactic models of language that explain creativity in language (e.g. how a child makes up sentences never heard before). AI and linguistics come together in the field of Natural Language Processing (NLP), which is the current focus of AI research.

1.3 Ethics of Artificial Intelligence

1.3.1 Unemployment

AI is expected to replace humans in many jobs — starting from translation services, legal research, etc., to complex ones like design, programming, etc. — and this makes everyone concerned about the future of mass unemployment. However, counterarguments have also been made:

- Our needs will evolve into complex forms that will require actual humans.
- AI will ultimately employ humans with a different set of capabilities.

And the **challenge** is to find suitable alternative jobs for humans who are replaced by AI.

1.3.2 Distribution of Wealth

Machines create an enormous amount of autonomous wealth, now the question is:

- Who will own these machines?
- How will the wealth be distributed and consumed?
- Will the wealth created to be distributed based on needs, capacity, information, or overall wellbeing [11]?

1.3.3 Influence of AI on Human Evolution

1.3.3.1 Argument

As machines progress in intelligence, it will develop a complex world beyond human intelligence. This may lead to the incorporation of machines into human systems, moving from a biological to technological evolution. If the AI system can comprehend its environmental details in a fraction of a second, it is near impossible for humans to match with an AI's capabilities. Looking forward, the integration of humans and AI will potentially alter human evolution.

1.3.3.2 Racism

When AI is fed with information like race, gender, or language, AI learns to give differential treatment based on these features. For example: on average, men between 20–40 years old are expected to take lesser leaves than women because of pregnancy, therefore, AI might learn to suggest employing more men in the future — this makes AI **sexist**.

The field of AI ethics is expected to mitigate similar racial conclusions drawn by AI.

1.3.3.3 Evil AI

Rogue AI could be harmful to humans. Military robots are equipped with an increasing ability to kill humans; their capacity to make autonomous decisions are being questioned. Rouge AI, with such power, could seriously harm human civilization.

Superintelligent AI might question the existence of humans because of less intelligence — similar to how humans perceive animal potential to be evil — and may decide to eliminate humans altogether.

1.3.3.4 Singularity

Hypothesis: an agent that automatically and constantly upgrades causes an intelligent explosion (resulting in **superintelligence**) that is impossible to predict as beneficial to humans.

There is a possibility of AI singularity wiping out humans, therefore, the need for a friendly artificial intelligence is a growing research topic in AI ethics.

1.3.3.5 Rights and Identity

With increasing intelligence, there is a potential for AI to acquire emotions, raising questions about its identity and rights. On one hand, the lack of AI rights allows for its possible abuse by humans; on the other, giving AI too many rights might result in an overwhelming control of AI over humans. Now, the questions that arise are:

- What kind of rights should be given to a machine that is more intelligent than humans?
- Will those with higher intelligence respect and live within those rights?

1.3.3.6 Sentient AI

A sentient AI is one that is capable of experiencing emotions, and when one becomes possible, decisions regarding its physical, mental, social, and intellectual capabilities — including subsequent interactions with its surroundings — will rest on humans.
Now questions arise like:

- How to treat a sentient AI?
- What kind of emotion should it go through in its lifetime?

So ethical questions need to be addressed by humans before creating sentient AI.

AI Consciousness includes areas of awareness, memory, learning, anticipation, subjective experience, etc., and leads to a few questions like:

- Is it possible to create a conscious AI considering the lack of scientific understanding about human consciousness?
- Is it okay to create AI without consciousness — a fundamental quality of humans given by nature — and render an incomplete being not in tune with its natural surroundings?
- Should humans hand themselves over to a more intelligent being (i.e. conscious AI)?
- What if an AI automatically becomes conscious?

AI Ethics deals with:

- How humans can treat AI ethically.
- How AI can treat humans ethically.

There are plenty of questions that need to be answered in this field.

References

1. Costello K., 2020. Gartner Predicts the Future of AI Technologies. https://www.gartner.com/smarterwithgartner/gartner-predicts-the-future-of-ai-technologies/.
2. FRAMINGHAM, Mass., March 11, 2019, IDC Predicts AI Spending to Close in on $100 Billion within Five Years. https://www.idc.com/getdoc.jsp?containerId=prUS44911419.
3. PricewaterhouseCoopers LLP, 2017, PwC's Global Artificial Intelligence Study – Sizing the Prize. https://www.pwc.com/gx/en/issues/data-and-analytics/publications/artificial-intelligence-study.html.
4. A. Kaul, C. Wheelock, Artificial Intelligence Market Forecasts (Tractica), 2016.
5. Desoutter, Industrial Revolution – From Industry 1.0 to Industry 4.0. https://www.desouttertools.com/industry-4-0/news/503/industrial-revolution-from-industry-1-0-to-industry-4-0.
6. Statt N. 2019. How Artificial Intelligence Will Revolutionize the Way Video Games Are Developed and Played. https://www.theverge.com/2019/3/6/18222203/video-game-ai-future-procedural-generation-deep-learning.

7. Takyar A. CEO LeewayHertz AI Applications across Major Industries. https://www.leewayhertz.com/ai-applications-across-major-industries/.
8. Russell S. Norvig P. 2020. Artificial Intelligence a modern approach, Fourth Edition. https://people.eecs.berkeley.edu/~russell/intro.html.
9. Jeffcock P. July 2018. Difference between Machine Learning, and Deep Learning. https://blogs.oracle.com/bigdata/difference-ai-machine-learning-deep-learning.
10. Lind N. 2019: Foundations of Artificial Intelligence. https://towardsdatascience.com/foundations-of-ai-b11d6ad7ce6f.
11. Alumni J. B. Global Shapers Community, Fathom Computing, Oct 2016: Top 9 Ethical Issues in Artificial Intelligence. https://www.weforum.org/agenda/2016/10/top-10-ethical-issues-in-artificial-intelligence/.

2

Impact of Digitization of Governance on Society

J. Raja Kishore and S. Suguna Mallika

CONTENTS

2.1 Introduction

Digital Literacy is the "ability of individuals and communities to understand and use digital technologies for meaningful actions within life situations." The Department of Electronics and Information Technology (DeitY) and Department of Administrative Reforms and Public Grievances (DARPG) formulated the National E-Governance Plan (NeGP) with the vision to *"Make all Government services accessible to the common man in his locality, through common service delivery outlets, and ensure efficiency, transparency, and reliability of such services at affordable costs to realize the basic needs of the common man."* According to the National IT Policy of 2012, every household in India must have at least one digitally literate person [1]. If the program is successfully rolled out into society, there shall be an improvement in people's standard of living, having government services more accessible and easier to use.

The objective of the National Digital Literacy Mission (NDLM) and Digital Saksharata Abhyaan (DISHA) is to ptovide digital literacy training to 52.5 lakh persons in every eligible household in all states and UTs. Common Service Centers have been established across the country to enable Government to Citizen (G2C) and Business to Consumer (B2C) services like banking, healthcare, etc. Each CSC is managed by a Village-Level Entrepreneur (VLE) with facilities like a computer, scanner, printer, and internet connection. As per the NLDM curriculum, the training is composed of introduction to digital devices, internet, and communication applications (email, WhatsApp, online booking of tickets, etc.). The VLEs are given incentives based on the number of citizens trained and certified in their center. 250 CSCs are currently implementing this program across Telangana in rural areas [2].

2.2 Proposed Model for Digital Literacy Training

The digital literacy training commences after the registration of the citizens, done by Aadhar-based biometric authentication. The registered citizens are trained on digital literacy; an assessment is conducted towards the end of the program through the Remote Proctor Monitoring System by DeitY and approved agencies like NIELIT and NIOS. The advantage of the program is that citizens can take the assessment in their NDLM Center. Currently, two implementation models are used to examine desired outcomes:

- VLE Model
- Educational Institution Model

2.2.1 VLE Model

In this model, VLEs conduct a survey of the village and categorize beneficiaries according to their convenient time. For instance, if the beneficiary is a farmer or daily wage worker, then they would prefer to have the trainings in the evening; if the beneficiary was a homemaker, she would prefer to have it in the afternoon. The VLE identifies the needs of the beneficiaries and the schedule for their training, motivating them towards completion. In this model, the training is conducted at a CSC NDLM center, and an assessment is conducted at the end of the training. Figure 2.1 shows the approach of a VLE for the digital literacy training program.

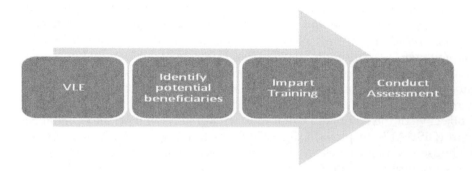

FIGURE 2.1
VLE model.

2.2.1.1 Case Study of Akoli Village

Under the NDLM-DISHA project, Akoli Village and Jainathmandal of Adilabad District became a 100% digitally literate village in Telangana State. Mr. Gajanan Nivalkar VLE of Akoli convinced Village Sarpanch and the youth association to support this program, and carried out a door-to-door survey of the village. He convinced and motivated the villagers to undergo NDLM training, set up computers and internet connectivity at his own cost, and conducted the training for three months in the village, catering to the varied times and needs of the villagers. He successfully completed the program to make Akoli a 100% digitally literate village. Figure 2.2 shows the NDLM training at Akoli Village in progress.

After the NDLM training, the villagers are now able to browse the internet for information. They constructed digital lockers by themselves, created IDs and communicated over email and WhatsApp, and sought information regarding policies, job notifications, and farming advice from government portals. All the farmers also registered for MKisan portal and are receiving various tips on farming and agriculture on their phone. The success story of Akoli have been published in media and the same may be referred to in [3, 4] standing as an inspiration for many other VLE's. Figure 2.3. Shows the

Motivating Citizens towards Digital Literacy Training by VLE Gajanan

Registration of the Citizens to the Digital Literacy Training Program

Digital Literacy Training in Progress at Akoli, Adilabad District

Certified Citizens who completed Assessment on Digital Literacy

FIGURE 2.2
Snapshots of NDLM training at Akoli village.

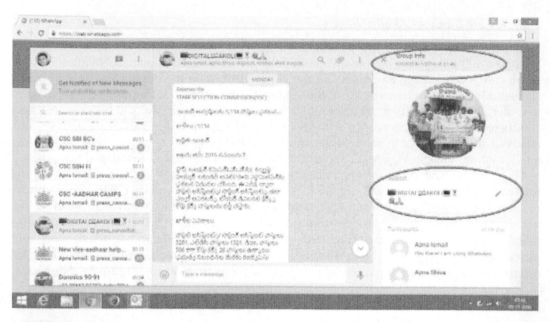

FIGURE 2.3
WhatsApp group created by Akoli villagers currently active.

snapshot of the WhatsApp group created by Akoli villagers to communicate. This is a classic case study where officials directly intervene and communicate with the citizens for direct transfer of benefits, broadcast of vital information and schemes launched especially for specific groups (farmers, self-help groups, etc.).

2.2.2 Educational Institution Model

In this model, an educational institution adopts a village for digital literacy. Volunteers from the educational institution are trained by the Telangana IT Association (TITA) and the Common Service Center (CSC) staff. This model is a support by institutions towards the construction of a Digital India. After the completion of the "training of the trainer" (TOT) program, the volunteers interact with the Sarpanch of the adopted village and identify the beneficiaries for the digital literacy training. Infrastructure arrangements like computers, internet connectivity, and other requirements for the training process are arranged by the volunteer institution. Figure 2.4. presents the educational institution model for the digital literacy training program.

A survey to identify the target group (i.e. beneficiaries of general and underprivileged categories) would be conducted in the adopted village. A household becomes eligible for the training offered if none of the members from that household, ages 14-60, are digitally literate. If someone from a household is eligible, members can nominate them. Once the target beneficiary list is finalized, the trainers coach the villagers for 20 hours across a span of 4-5 weeks, typically on Sundays. The roles and responsibilities played by each stakeholder is highlighted in Table 2.1. The state government of Telangana is aggressively promoting and supporting digital literacy initiatives.

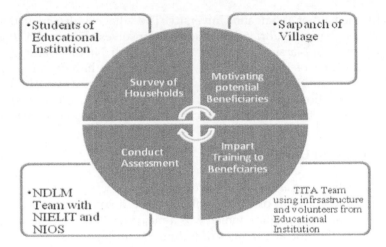

FIGURE 2.4
Educational institution trainer partnership model.

TABLE 2.1

Roles of Various Stakeholders in the First Model

Stakeholder	Role
Volunteering Educational Institution	Infrastructure, students, program support, registrations and training
Village Sarpanch	Citizens sensitization and mobilization, transportation of citizens to IIIT, support for door-to-door survey
TITA Team	Overall program implementation, training of citizens during Sundays supporting students
NDLM Team	Training of trainers, program support and assessments
ITE&C Government of Telangana	Overall support

2.2.2.1 Case Study of Narsingapur Village

Telangana IT Association (TITA) works with NDLM Team and Telangana University in implementing a gigital literacy program at Narsingapur Village, Dichpally Mandal, Nizamabad District, Telangana. The NDLM Team has trained student volunteers from Telangana University along with TITA team members through the TOT program. The NDLM-TITA team trained the students of Telangana University and coordinated with Sarpanch Mrs. Suvarna Murali in mobilizing and motivating citizens to attend the program at Telangana University. Students conducted household surveys, identified 155 households that are digitally illiterate. They trained them under the digital literacy program every Sunday from March 1 to April 30 at Telangana University. The Sarpanch arranged transportation for the citizens and ensured the attendance of the citizens through her constant motivation.

Citizens who have completed the course are awarded certificates. As a token of appreciation, four Chrome books were given to Sarpanch to be kept at the Panchayat for browsing and further training of others on digital literacy. Now, the village also got WiFi connection with the help of Telangana University. The villagers also created a WhatsApp group and started sharing information among themselves. Figure 2.5. highlights the events that took place at Narsingapur Village during their NDLM training.

With the liberalization of India after 1991, technology has become more user-friendly regardless of literacy rate. The arrival of the internet will enhance availability of personal computers and smartphones in rural areas, which may result into a knowledge-based economy—empowering the citizens with a citizen-centric governance [5–8].

2.2.3 Challenges Faced During Training

a. *Convincing the Citizens about Digital Literacy*
   People who are unaware of the benefits of using a computer did not show interest in the training program, which was a major challenge. A lot of effort went into demonstrating the advantages of technology in life situations.

b. *The Beneficiaries Are not Keyboard Comfortable*
   To overcome this challenge, the team conducted an exercise of dictating to the trainees every day for half an hour, to get their hands on with the keyboard typing and accustomed to the QWERTY layout of the keyboard.

c. *Internet Connectivity*
   Internet was a real challenge in villages like Akoli, because it does not have any connection. Hotspots were setup using 3G/4G dongle for internet availability.

Program Launch at Narsingapur

Training Program

Certificate Distribution

Celebrating Success with TITA members

FIGURE 2.5
Photos at Narsingapur digital literacy training.

d. *Investment*
   Investment in Computers and internet connectivity.

e. *Resistance from Citizens*

Among the citizens, the farmers were very resistant of the training because of their hectic farming schedules.

2.3 Impact Stories of Digitization of Governance on Society

In a village near Korutla, one of the beneficiaries, Mrs. Sattemma, was 58 years old—a female tobacco worker (beedi rolling)—joined the training program to be able to talk to her son (who is a plumber in Dubai) through Skype. Now, she has her own email ID that she uses to communicate with her son. Seeing her commitment and enthusiasm in the training despite all factors, motivated their entire family and the village itself into getting trained for digital literacy. The Union Minister for Electronics & Information Technology, Shri. Ravi Shankar Prasad, congratulated Sattemma for this incredible achievement and for being a role model to others. Similarly, Mrs. Bharathamma of AshwaraoPet Village, Khammam, 53 years old, created her own email ID and is now using the computer with ease. Another example is that of Mr. Bhaskar Reddy, a farmer by profession, who expressed his interest in digital literacy program, and is now able to receive tips related to farming. He now browses the internet and shares some of the advice to his fellow farmers. The increasing awareness of people exhibits the growing importance of the digital literacy program and its immense benefits.

Mr. B. Venkanna (33 years old), a small farmer from Kapprla village, Tamsi Block of Adilabad district in Telangana who cultivates chilli and cotton in his three-acre land. He enrolled himself under the NDLM scheme in June 2015 and is now certified. When all the farmers in his area began losing their crops and his chilli crop got infected with pests and other diseases, Venkanna realized the need for advanced methods and opted for better agricultural practices. During the training, Venkanna had learned to operate search engines and browse the internet. After, he started to look for farming-related information online. Venkanna now browses for innovative methods on YouTube and Google, and cultivates his chilli crop with bio-pesticides and fertilizers to prevent regular pests and diseases [9]. Figure 2.6. Shows the pictures of some of the aforementioned citizens who took benefit of the NDLM training program.

One digitally literate shepherd, Mr. Sai Kumar, posted a photo of the horrible roads in his village on the WhatsApp number published by the newspaper daily Eenadu. The photos of were subsequently published. As a response, the concerned officials responded and immediately got the road repaired; a new road was laid within two days. Figure 2.7 shows Saikumar, his WhatsApp posting on Eenadu reporting the terrible state of the road, and the repaired road after the officials responded to the situation.

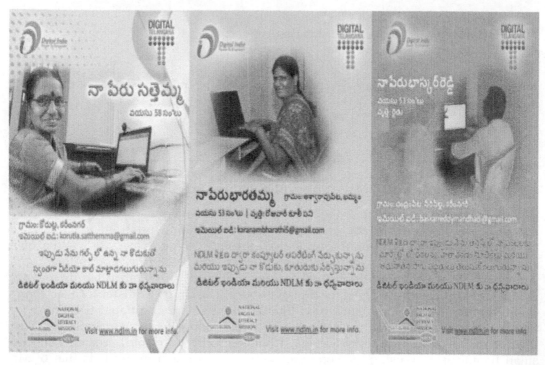

FIGURE 2.6
Impact stories.

2.4 Growing Trends in Telangana

In the state of Telangana, a total of 346,281 beneficiaries have been identified and registered for the training program, out of which 320,808 have been trained and 179,185 people have completed their digital training certification [2]. A total of ten villages became 100% digitally literates—Basara, Akoli, Narsingapur, Mukhra, Andharbandh, Mallellamadugu, Gopalpuram, mandagada, Sirsonna, Kowtha.

The training statistics of the ten villages are presented in Figure 2.8. It is observed that women are getting more enthusiastic and motivated towards digital literacy in some of the places. It is a thing of great pride that women are now able to realize the benefits of digital literacy and are proactively participating in the digital revolution. This would further the empowerment of women towards a brighter tomorrow.

The village sarpanch and local community youth played a vital role in motivating the citizens through their personal interaction daily. Villages where the Sarpanch recognized digital literacy as beneficial saw massive participation from the citizens. The program also saw women empowerment as an important outcome of the digital literacy training, where more and more women were motivated to become digitally literate and utilize the benefits of technology in their day-to-day activities (Figure 2.9).

In the future, a special training campaign for village sarpanches may be conducted to motivate them regarding the rewards of digital literacy and its current relevance to society. This will enhance the likelihood of a digitally literate state.

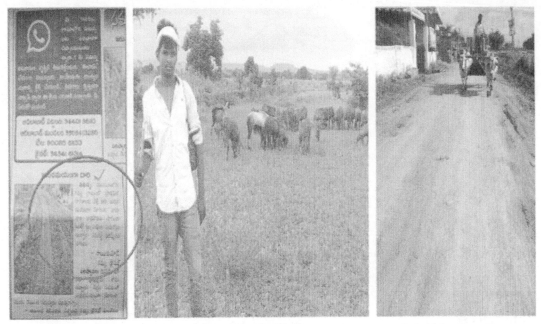

WhatsApp posting of Road with pits | Saikumar with his goats tendering them | Road repaired post the complaint

FIGURE 2.7
Impact story of Saikumar.

Telangana- NDLM DISHA

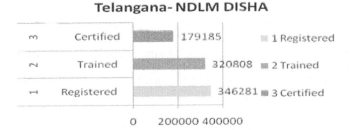

3	Certified	179185 ▪ 1 Registered
2	Trained	320808 ▪ 2 Trained
1	Registered	346281 ▪ 3 Certified

0   200000 400000

FIGURE 2.8
Telangana digital literacy status as of 30 October 2016.

The digital literacy program helps transform India by empowering citizens browse for government schemes, know about transforming policies, perform online transactions and further reduce the digital divide that exists in the society. . Governance becomes easy and flexible with digital literacy; society will witness radical changes such as the ones experienced in Aakoli, Narsingapur in the days to come.

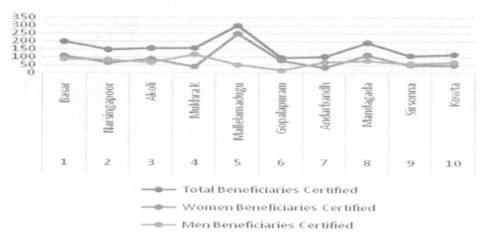

FIGURE 2.9
Statistics of digital literacy in Telangana state.

References

1. National Policy on Information Technology, 2012, Ministry of Electronics and Information Technology, http://meity.gov.in/content/national-information-technology-policy-2012.
2. Ministry of Electronics and Information Technology(Meity), Implementation process, https://www.pmgdisha.in/implementation-process/ (accessed on July 31, 2020).
3. S. Harpal Singh, Adilabad youth makes an entire village digitally literate, http://www.thehindu.com/news/national/telangana/adilabad-youthmakes-an-entire-village-digitally-literate/article8889237.ece (accessed July 23, 2014).
4. A. Jumde, Meet the man who single-handedly brought digital literacy to an entire Telangana village, http://www.thebetterindia.com/62180/nivalkar-gajanan-100-digital-literacy-akoli-telangana/ (accessed July 19, 2016).
5. Purushothaman, Aparna. (2011). Role of ICT in the educational upliftment of women - Indian scenario. Proceedings of the 2011 World Congress on Information and Communication Technologies, WICT 2011. 10.1109/WICT.2011.6141256.
6. S. Dutta, R. Mathur, "EPICS High: Digital Literacy Project in India", 4th IEEE Integrated STEM Education Conference, March 8, 2014, Princeton, NJ.
7. P. Malik, V. Gupta and P. Dhillon, "Citizen centric approach for E-Governance: looking at the service delivery through the eyes of the citizens," Wireless Engineering and Technology, 2011, 2, 212–220.
8. K. Chaudhari, U. Dalal, R. Jha, "E-Governance in rural India: need of broadband connectivity using wireless technology," Wireless Engineering and Technology, 2011, 2, 212–220.
9. ManaCSC, https://youtu.be/WcQ4Tc1HSI0 (accessed July11, 2016).

3

The Impact of AI on World Economy

Debashish Roy and R. Srivastava

CONTENTS

3.1 The Evolved World Economy

In this section, we will discuss the economic impact of AI across the world along with the discourse on how several countries have taken initiatives and plans to improve their economy with the use of AI [1–6].

The adoption of AI by different countries are at different levels as each has a distinct strategy; advanced countries are leading this movement. Countries that adopted technology earlier are expected to benefit 20-25% of its economic benefits, while developing countries are expected to benefit around 5–15%.

Many developed countries push for AI to enhance productivity and increase the momentum of their GDP. The aging population is also another reason for the adoption of AI. High wage rates are also factored in. These are few of the reasons developed countries adopt AI for their economy enhancement.

Developing countries have the options of restructuring and using the best practices to improve their economy; therefore, the adoption of AI is less. Several countries have expressed their initiative to adopt AI to help boost their economy. Some of the plans for those countries are:

China: The government of China is prioritizing AI. In their 13th five-year plan (2016 to 2020), they declared various plans such as "Internet Plus and AI Plans" and "New Generation AI Plan." China is expected to become the world-leading center for AI by 2030. Three internet giants of China (Tencent, Baidu, and Alibaba) have joined as a "national team" and are planning to develop AI in areas such as smart cities, imaging, and autonomous vehicles.

Europe: Europe has also taken initiatives to adopt AI; the government announced a double increase in the people involved in the AI project. The UK has published a plan to strengthen the AI foundation in an "Artificial Intelligence Sector Deal," aiming to be a leader in AI ethics.

Canada: Canada has established three new institutes of AI named the "Alberta intelligence institute" in Edmonton, the "Vector institute" in Toronto, and "MILA" in Montreal—a declaration that these three cities of Canada will be the main centers of AI.

3.2 The Ongoing Evolution

Firstly, it's important to understand that we cannot assume AI to be a single technology; AI is a group of technologies. Broadly, AI can be divided into five categories—natural language, computer vision, robotic process automation, virtual assistants, and machine learning. Companies are utilizing these technologies based on their needs, but there is variation in the degree of usage. Few are focusing on an opportunistic approach and are trying to use a single technology as a pilot project for specific function. Some companies have taken bold steps and utilize all five technologies across the whole organization.

The first approach can be called "adoption" and the second one can be called "absorption". There are many companies that are between the adoption and absorption approach.

A study predicts that by 2030, more than 70% of companies will adopt at least one technology of AI and many will fully absorb all the five technologies of AI.

AI is moving forward, and many best and large companies have already started huge investments in it. The investment and initiatives of a few of these companies are:

Amazon: This company has invested in the consumer-oriented side as well as the application for companies and processes related to them. Alexa, an AI computer assistant, is one of the well-known in the world. Application like AWS (Amazon Web Services) has already been adopted by various companies like Netflix and Siemens.

Apple: This company has invested in various AI start-ups in recent years. They have developed products like Siri and machine learning tools, which are used by macOS and iOS.

Facebook: The AI research group of Facebook, known as FAIR, has already committed to developing ML technology to serve better communication to customers.

Google: The CEO of Google, Sundar Pichai, has already announced that in the coming years, it will be evolving from a "mobile first" to an "Artificial Intelligence first" across the world in the industry of computers.

IBM: IBM has already developed a platform for machine learning named "Watson" used to integrate artificial intelligence into various process of businesses. For example, developing a chatbot for customer support.

3.3 The Substitutes and Complements

A hype for the world is just a demand and supply problem for the economists—that's how they see the world (Source: Prediction Machines: The Simple Economics of Artificial Intelligence). A rise in the price of goods lead to a fall in demand; a fall in the price of a good leads to a rise in its demand. We all know that the substitute goods' demand is directly proportional to its competitor's price; however, there may be some exceptions.

The main substitute for artificial intelligence is human intelligence. Human intelligence is capable of sound judgment without the need for massive amounts of data to be fed. Where the computer stops, a human intervenes. Previously, the gap between human and computer capabilities were huge. With time, we can see this gap getting smaller. The horse pulled carriages became obsolete with the emergence of cars. In the past few years, driverless cars are becoming the "in" thing for the wealthy. History has witnessed the decline in the price of what was once expensive.

Therefore, the future where many driverless cars (as their prices go down) will be on the road is not far. In that future, a human-driven car will stand as an obsolete substitute for driverless cars. In addition, there will be a decline, not only in human-driven cars, but in drivers.

3.4 Moving Lock Stock and Barrel

Humans have always migrated for better job opportunities—they are always in search of something better which often lead to discovery and invention. Several countries are equipped with resources to advance in the field of artificial intelligence, and situations there are getting better in that area.

A time may come where countries are exponentially evolved in the field of artificial intelligence. These countries will embrace technology in their day-to-day life—jobs in factories, mills, and offices will be fully-automated. In such scenario, the competition for job will increase.

Such event may cause the first migration of humans to a less-developed country in search of work—a country where humans are needed to operate machines, AI do not drive cars, and hands do the packing and storing in warehouses.

This migration may be international or local. A time when the government intervenes and restricts corporations from certain AI functions to revive their state is not far.

Relating this situation to the rural-urban classification of migration may be erroneous; people may not necessarily move to rural areas from the urban. They may move to urban areas, which are less developed in terms of AI, therefore, less competition for jobs. One can classify this type of migration under forced displacement (man-made), as a wider acceptance of manufacturing technology (AI) will displace the people.

TABLE 3.1

Top Twenty-Two Government AI Readiness

Ranking	Country	Score
1	Singapore	9.186
2	United Kingdom	9.069
3	Germany	8.810
4	United States of America	8.804
5	Finland	8.772
6	Sweden	8.674
6	Canada	8.674
8	France	8.608
9	Denmark	8.601
10	Japan	8.582
11	Australia	8.126
12	Norway	8.079
13	New Zealand	7.876
14	Netherlands	7.659
15	Italy	7.533
16	Austria	7.527
17	India	7.515
18	Switzerland	7.461
19	United Arab Emirates	7.445
20	China	7.370
21	Israel	7.348
22	Malaysia	7.108

Source: https://ai4d.ai/wp-content/uploads/2019/05/ai-gov-readiness-report_v08.pdf

The table above shows the AI Readiness Index of some countries in 2019. It shows the top 22 out of 194 countries. Singapore tops the list while India is emerging on 17. Though this index, the AI readiness index of a country, with respect to public service, is shown. This proves that some nations are better (or worse) with technology.

This means that the feared AI-related migrations in the future may not be true. If the government restrict certain AI functions to prevent job competition, that area may be attractive for migrant workers.

3.5 The Impact: In a Nutshell

Pioneers of AI (in advanced nations) could expand their lead over economically progressing nations, while many developing nations have no real option aside of pushing AI for a higher GDP.

This may also reflect maturing populace. In these economies, the high rates for wages can be a motivation to substitute the work force with machines. This can result in a broader divide between nations, further widening technological distance. Nations may require various dynamic plans as AI reception rates shift.

Interestingly, economically progressing nations, have diverse ways of finding the best practice in rebuilding their businesses to improve efficiency. In this manner, they may have less impetus to push for AI (which may offer them a lesser financial advantage than it does with economically advanced states). Some progressing nations may end up being exceptional cases in such situations.

The possibilities with AI are vast; however, its infiltration may cause disturbance. The profitability of AI will not emerge right away, and its effect will develop quickly only after some time. The advantages of introductory speculation will not be noticeable for the time being.

Authentic patterns should be utilized and modified for a lower worker-output ratio to consider work apart from automation. The all-out efficiency impact could have a positive commitment to work.

Governing bodies will be forced to demonstrate administration to beat distress among the working population about the apparent risk to their employments as AI takes over. Corporate leaders will play a significant role in arranging updates for employees when it comes to AI work.

People should be able to adjust at the beginning of the new era (job turnover could increase). They may need to progress to new kinds of roles, and they should persistently invigorate and refresh their abilities to coordinate with the necessities of a progressively changing working environment.

References

1. Executive office of the President, "AI, automation, and the economy," December 2016, pp. 27–28.
2. Mozur, P. "China sets goal to lead in AI," *New York Times*, July 21, 2017.
3. Maddox, T. "66% of US cities are investing in smart city technology," *TechRepublic*, November 6, 2017. //www.techrepublic.com/article/66-of-us-cities-are-investing-in-smart-city-technology/#:~:text=A%20report%20from%20the%20National,the%20plan%20for%20many%20municipalities.
4. Barton D. et al., AI: Implications for China (New York: McKinsey Global Institute, April 2017), p. 7.
5. Purdy, M., Daugherty, P. "Why AI is the future of growth," Canada, Accenture, 2017.
6. Jaana. R. 2018. Solving The Productivity Puzzle: The Role of Demand and The Promise of Digitization. San Francisco: McKinsey Global Institute.

4

Human Behavior Prediction and Artificial Intelligence

Ramesh Narwal and Himanshu Aggarwal

CONTENTS

4.1 Introduction

John McCarthy in 1956 coined the term Artificial Intelligence (AI) and is the buzz word of the 21st century. AI has wide applications in domains like Chatbots, eCommerce, Human Resource Management, Healthcare, Intelligent Cybersecurity, Supply Chain Management, Hotels, etc. Large IT industries are analyzing how AI can solve most complicated problems and improve the quality of life [2]. Deep and Machine Learnings are the core areas of artificial intelligence. Deep Learning is working as an engine and Machine Learning is the science behind the AI supreme power. Although AI is quite an old concept, it is gaining popularity very rapidly. Several of these reasons are illustrated in Figure 4.1.

4.1.1 Enhanced Computing Power

A lot of computation is required to run AI systems or Deep Learning Models. Advancements in GPU technology made it possible to run these systems, as there is a lack in computing power before.

4.1.2 Huge Data

Huge data is required by AI systems to find important patterns. Humans and machines generate a lot of data and data size doubles annually.

AI systems use an enormous amount of data to make smart decisions. Data size is directly propositional to the patterns hidden inside the data. The more data we collect, the more hidden patterns are accumulated.

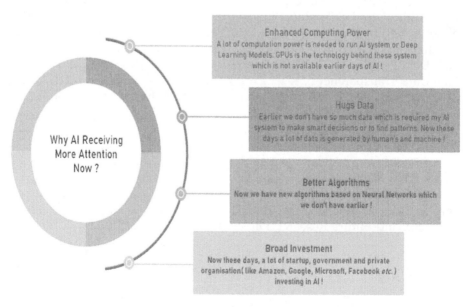

FIGURE 4.1
Why is AI receiving more attention now?

4.1.3 Better Algorithms

Now, better algorithms are used to cope with Big Data and fetch out significant insights. Advanced neural network algorithms are used these days to solve real-life problems.

4.1.4 Broad Investment

Investment has an important role in research. Due to wide applications of AI in various areas, startups, government and private organizations have started to invest in it more.

AI helps to solve complicated problems. One of them is the prediction of human behavior. This chapter will discuss the current research in human prediction and AI. In this section, questions like, "How are machine and deep learning associated with each other? Why is AI receiving more attention these days?" are answered. The next portion will discuss the significance of Human Behavior Research (HBR) in different areas.

4.2 Why Human Behavior Prediction?

When we start reading about Human Behavior, one question always arises in our brain: what is behavior? In simple terms, it is an active movement—visible actions like reading a book, talking, texting on the phone, etc.

For a long time, predicting and understanding human behavior have been the primary concern of researchers and social media companies. For consumer and social media research, attitude is the main key to predict human behavior. Our attitude has a significant role in the theory of human behavior prediction, as it is an important link between what we think and what we do.

Biosensor inventions increase the rate of research in human behavior, as they have a wide area of application in capturing events. These events help us collect data about human beings, which later helps in the prediction of human behavior signatures. With the help of biosensors, new data related to human behavior can be collected. Some of the application areas of biosensors that help capture events relating to human behavior signatures are illustrated below:

4.2.1 Medical Diagnostics and Health

There are biosensors available to diagnose several types of diseases [3]. Using biosensors such as GSR (Galvanic Skin Response) and ECG (Electrocardiogram) help in diagnosing PTSD (Post-Traumatic Stress Disorder). EEG (Electroencephalography), surveys, and eye-tracking sensors can be used to measure the decline in cognitive ability and localize epileptic seizures to diagnose and assess brain injuries and head traumas. We can also use an EEG biosensor to diagnose early-stage ADHD (Attention-Deficit and Hyperactivity Disorder).

4.2.2 Education and Training

Biosensors can also be utilized in learning technologies to identify how students learn in the classroom and online. Online course efficiency can be checked with the help of bio-sensors in eLearning [4]. In special operations and training, biosensors are utilized in a virtual reality environment to check for success of military training and identify the learning process of cadets.

4.2.3 Workplace and Product Testing

Human behavior and biosensors can be used to understand the workspace setup in different organizations to optimize employee's engagement and performance. It can also be used in human-robot interactions, eye-tracking (using biosensor like electromyography or EMG), to identify eye-hand coordination during assembly of parts and products.

Product usability examination is used to test whether the product is easy for first-time users. The biosensors specify the aspects that provoke annoyance and suspicion in the product; evaluate sentimental responses while the tester interacts with the product and test the comprehensive events.

4.2.4 Advertisement and Media

For TV commercial testing, trailer testing, general advertisement testing, static vs dynamic testing, outdoor commercial testing, and website testing, biosensors are used to identify the impact of advertisements on people.

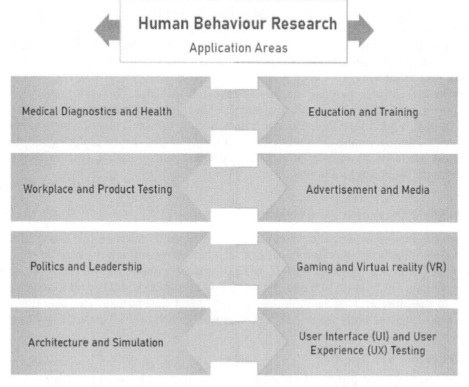

FIGURE 4.2
Application areas of human behavior research.

For media, it calculates the bit-by-bit response to videos [5] to identify which scenes trigger emotional response. Biosensors are used in the film industry to test TV programs and assess the success rate of new seasons or episodes.

4.2.5 User Interface (UI) and User Experience (UX) Testing

For websites, biosensors are used to test the usability effect of a website and contrast it with contending variants. For software testing, biosensors are used to examine the usability and identify block points of software applications [6]. Mobile platform testing can be done with the help of biosensors; usability of apps on mobile devices and tablets can also be identified.

4.2.6 Gaming and Virtual reality (VR)

With these biosensors, eye tracking measurement within a game environment can be combined with divine play actions before actual performance. For successful predictions of the games, in-market players' emotional reactions during play can be tested [7]. VR (Virtual Reality) can be used as a training environment for support for phobia [8].

4.2.7 Architecture and Simulation

Before construction of buildings or any other projects, you can draw and test every module of the architecture. Structure biosensors can used to access attention and emotion to the building. For design, EEG biosensors can test positive and impactful draft before mass production. For emergency and specialized training in air traffic controller, monitoring simulation is used.

4.2.8 Politics and Leadership

In politics, biosensors can be used to test how speeches impact the crowd. During campaign, the pictures, videos, and material present the influenced audience [9]. Clothing and posture are used to test the political candidate's behavior while appealing to the audience.

In leadership training, biosensors can be used to analyze the behavioral effect of leadership [10]. These sensors can be used to test the emotional impact on the audience and enhance the backer's ability to pitch effectively. Social groups can be analyzed to test and judge leaders and non-leaders [11]. In the next section, the online and offline behavior of people is discussed. Things such as how digital behavior is related to real behavior are also discussed in the next section.

4.3 Online vs. Offline Behavior

There is a discussion on the internet on whether the online and offline behavior of people is real. In my opinion both behaviors are real [12]; one just cannot be validated by others. For example, if someone says that they love you, how would you know if those sentiments are real? We look for patterns or consistency. Patterns are the key to knowing if the behavior is real, and our minds are wired to perceive these sentiments as real or not.

One of the best examples of this is the movie Mission Impossible starring Tom Cruise who is on a mission, with his team members, to replace high profile people. Before the swap, they analyzed all details of the person, and they noticed repeated patterns.

Even country security agencies use honey trapping to collect secrete information from an individual. In the latest news, some naval personnel were found to be guilty of online honey trapping by a neighboring country's intelligence agency. The same thing is happening in different countries.

In online behavior, our voice and body language play minor roles, and we are not able to predict how they react to us. However, in offline interaction, we can predict how people react to through voice and body language [13]. We behave differently for every situation; we show different sides of ourselves. All of these are part of us. We must play various roles in our like being a father, a musician, a poet, and a public speaker. Our offline behavior changes from role to role. So, we can say that offline behavior is a superset of online behavior.

Various systems in the market recommend products, hotels, restaurants, foods based on prior behavioral patterns recorded by social media companies when we surf for products we need (and want) to buy. This is how these online industries find out signatures related to our behavior.

In the next section, major challenges in Human Behavior Research (HBR) are discussed. Data privacy and data transparency are key issues in HBR.

4.4 Challenges in Human Behavior Prediction

Nations defend their physical borders, but digital borders are still open, which can be used to make changes in any country. The scandal of Cambridge Analytica is an example of this; UK-based Cambridge Analytica analyzed every citizen of the USA. They have more than 400 data points on every citizen. They collected their data from data points, predicted their political behavior, and molded it. This is how open digital borders can make changes in another country.

Human behavior prediction is like two sides of a coin: it can both be profoundly problematic hugely beneficial. There are various challenges in the prediction of human behavior, and some of them are explained below:

4.4.1 Data Privacy

When surfing the internet, a lot of our behavior trace are left behind. There are several types of data collected in terms of health, consumption, location, history, etc. This can be used for social benefits but can also be problematic. For example, users health can be collected to predict national health. Preventive measures must be taken to address these.

The Department of Chicago police developed a new technique that generates a heat map when a person is identified as dangerous, even if that person has no history of criminal record. This led to the creation of a heat list, where these people are tracked. Is that legal?

In the Cambridge Analytica Scandal, personal data was used without consent to alter votes. Digital giants need to take care of their users' data; they cannot share it without permission. Data privacy is a major concern, and all of us need to be aware when giving permissions to online applications.

4.4.2 Data Transparency

After the Cambridge Analytica Scandal, people became aware of their data privacy rights. Social media companies (like Facebook) do not allow their users to download data; even consumers have no idea which information social media companies are collecting and how they are being used. After a revolution on data rights, companies changed their terms to having consent as a prerequisite for data collection. However, citizens still have no idea how these companies use their data. Personality traits, human personality, and behavior relationships are discussed in the next section.

4.5 How Is Personality Prediction Related to Human Behavior Prediction?

Personality is defined as what we are, while behavior is what we do; personality cannot be changed while behavior can be changed.

Personality is a stable, consistent form of thought, emotion, and behavior. Behavior is an expression of personality in context [14]. According to Robin Stuart-Kotze, the personality of a person is virtually fixed at about the age of five.

4.5.1 Big 5 Personality Traits

These big five personality traits are also called the Five-Factor Model (FFM) and Ocean Model [8]. The five factors are:

4.5.1.1 Openness

People who like to learn and experience new things come under openness. Openness also includes traits like being intuitive, creative, and having a wide variety of interests.

4.5.1.2 Conscientiousness

People who have high degree of conscientiousness are more reliable and prompter. This includes being orderly, methodic, and rigorous.

4.5.1.3 Neuroticism

It relates to one's emotional stability and degree of negative emotions. A high score in neuroticism means emotional instability and negatively emotional. Traits include being unpredictable and stiff.

4.5.1.4 Agreeableness

These individuals are friendly, collaborative, and sympathetic. People who are less agreeable may be more reserved; some traits include kindness, admiration, and pleasantness.

4.5.1.5 Extraversion

Extraverts get their energy from interacting with others, while the reserved get their energy from themselves. Extraversion includes the traits of being energetic and assertive.

We can say that the collection of traits makes the personality of a person. In the past decades, experiments to predict human behavior from personality traits were not satisfactory. Even in the 1970s, some psychologists such as Walter Mischel and Daryl Bem were starting to consider personality traits as delusions. They kept thinking that strength of situations controls the behavior of a person, not personality (Figure 4.4).

When more research is done on the field, scientists found that personality traits are a good interpreter of human behavior. Predicting human behavior in a particular situation and over an extended period is advantageous.

The traits that are critical for our behavior prediction is known as Self-Schematic; other traits that are less vital are called as Aschematic Traits.

The diagram above shows that by using personality traits, personality can be classified into the Five-Factor Model (FFM), which will help us predict human behavior. For example, an extrovert may be prone to smartphone addiction or social media addiction. In the next section of this chapter, the negative side of human behavior research is discussed.

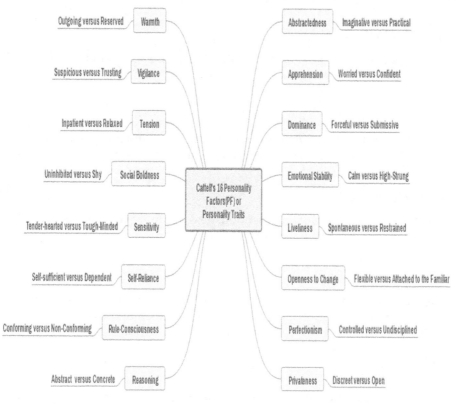

FIGURE 4.3
Cattell's 16 personality factors (PF) or personality traits.

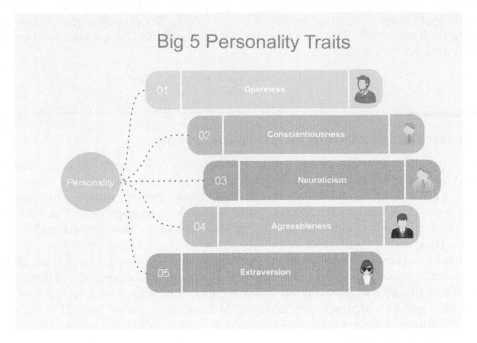

FIGURE 4.4
"Big 5" personality traits.

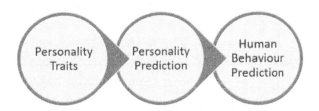

FIGURE 4.5
Personality for human behavior prediction.

4.6 Negative Side of the Coin

Currently, scientists are trying to replicate human behavior through AI and computer vision, but the uncertainty of it means it is impossible to predict. If we assume to forecast behavior, there will no longer be freewill for us—we will be surrounded by a mechanical universe. A small aspect of human can currently be predicted with the help of high computing power and better algorithm.

The problem with these predictions is that if we can predict it, we can alter it. For example, through social media we can predict the political party of a person [15]. Social media companies and researchers have already been doing this for political parties—they continue tracking a person to prevent other parties from changing their behavior. If they see someone who does not belong to their group, they will alter the news visible to that person so that negative ones will be shown. This is how political parties manipulate people and data for their benefit. In the next section, we conclude this chapter and describe future research direction.

4.7 Conclusion and Future Research Directions

Artificial intelligence and machine learning scientists modify the machine to learn from the past and to predict the future (like how we predict the next part of a movie in a theater). In our mind, do we match the patterns in the present movie with that of the past? If a match is found, then we can predict what will happen next. The same thing can be said with what scientists are doing with machines through AI and Machine Learning [10].

In the future, video will be ubiquitous and capturing everything will be a trend. MIT's CSAIL team is already working on a project that can predict a person's next move [16]. They built a model that was trained using 600 hours of videos and tested it on latest videos; they got 43% accuracy—there's a lot of room to improve that. This project can help in the future when everything is recorded in the camera (like in smart city projects) to predict people's next move.

Biosensor wearables in the market can help with the collection of new data, aiding in the prediction of a person's next move. Merging new data with the old can produce more behavioral insight; new algorithms can be developed with the help of AI, Deep Learning, and Machine Learning to predict human behavior more accurately.

References

1. Han, J., Zhang, Z., Cummins, N., and Schuller, B. (2019) Adversarial training in affective computing and sentiment analysis: recent advances and perspectives [Review Article]. *IEEE Computational Intelligence Magazine*, vol. **14** no. (2), pp. 68–81.
2. Miller, T. (2019) Explanation in artificial intelligence: Insights from the social sciences. *Artificial Intelligence*, vol. **267** no. (July), pp. 1–38.
3. G. Rong, A. Mendez, E. Bou Assi, B. Zhao and M. Sawan. (2020) , "Artificial intelligence in healthcare: review and prediction case studies". *Engineering* vol. 6 no. (6), 291–301.
4. Chassignol, M., Khoroshavin, A., Klimova, A., and Bilyatdinova, A. (2018) Artificial intelligence trends in education: a narrative overview. *Procedia Computer Science*, vol. **136**, pp. 16–24.
5. Ozbay, F. A., and Alatas, B. (2020) Fake news detection within online social media using supervised artificial intelligence algorithms. *Physica A Statistical Mechanics and Its Applications*, vol. **540**, pp. 123174.
6. McCreery, M. P., Kathleen Krach, S., Schrader, P. G., and Boone, R. (2012) Defining the virtual self: personality, behavior, and the psychology of embodiment. *Computers in Human Behavior*, vol. **28** no. (3), pp. 976–983.
7. Bard, N., Foerster, J. N., Chandar, S., Burch, N., Lanctot, M., Song, H. F., Parisotto, E., Dumoulin, V., Moitra, S., Hughes, E., Dunning, I., Mourad, S., Larochelle, H., Bellemare, M. G., and Bowling, M. (2020) The Hanabi challenge: a new frontier for AI research. *Artificial Intelligence*, vol. **280**, pp. 103216.

8. Hong, T., Chen, C. f., Wang, Z., and Xu, X. (2020) Linking human-building interactions in shared offices with personality traits. *Building and Environment*, vol. **170** no. (September 2019), pp. 106602.

9. Kaplan, A., and Haenlein, M. (2019) Rulers of the world, unite! The challenges and opportunities of artificial intelligence. *Business Horizons*, vol. **63** no. (1), pp. 37–50.

10. Michie, S., Thomas, J., Johnston, M., Aonghusa, P. M., Shawe-Taylor, J., Kelly, M. P., Deleris, L. A., Finnerty, A. N., Marques, M. M., Norris, E., O'Mara-Eves, A., and West, R. (2017) The human behaviour-change project: harnessing the power of artificial intelligence and machine learning for evidence synthesis and interpretation. *Implementation Science*, vol. **12** no. (1), pp. 1–12.

11. Khashman, Z., and Khashman, A. (2016) Anticipation of political party voting using Artificial Intelligence. *Procedia Computer Science*, vol. **102** no. (August), pp. 611–616.

12. Emanuel, L., Neil, G. J., Bevan, C., Fraser, D. S., Stevenage, S. V., Whitty, M. T., and Jamison-Powell, S. (2014) Who am I? Representing the self offline and in different online contexts. *Computers in Human Behavior*, vol. **41**, pp. 146–152.

13. Mirlohi Falavarjani, S. A., Zarrinkalam, F., Jovanovic, J., Bagheri, E., and Ghorbani, A. A. (2019) The reflection of offline activities on users' online social behavior: an observational study. *Information, Processing & Management*, vol. **56** no. (6), pp. 102070.

14. Robinson, M. D., Klein, R. J., and Persich, M. R. (2019) Personality traits in action: a cognitive behavioral version of the social cognitive paradigm. *Personality and Individual Differences*, vol. **147** no. (May), pp. 214–222.

15. S. Han, H. Huang and Y. Tang, "Knowledge of words: an interpretable approach for personality recognition from social media." *Knowledge-Based Systems*, vol. **194**, pp. 105550, 2020.

16. Papangelis, A., and Georgila, K. (2015) Reinforcement learning of multi-issue negotiation dialogue policies. *SIGDIAL 2015 - Proceedings of the 16th Annual Meeting of the Special Interest Group on Discourse and Dialogue* (September), 154–158.

5

Emotion Recognition for Human Machine Interaction

Maya Ingle and Leena Bhole

CONTENTS

5.1 Introduction

Emotion is one of the vital elements that control human intelligence and changes many aspects of human life. The importance of emotional aspects in Human Computer Interaction (HCI) paved the way for the development of emotion recognition research [1]. Emotion recognition is a widely accepted concept to communicate with machines using adjustable, capable, and instinctive way. It is envisioned that emotional intelligence will be a significant part of forthcoming intelligent HCI. Human, robots, and digital twins will be able to recognize and respond to human emotions. The context where computers detect, recognize, and respond to a user's emotional state is referred to as Affective Computing (AC). The purpose of AC is to minimize the communication gap between human, robots, and industrial machines. It is essential to incorporate the elements of rational and emotional intelligence into the functionality of impassive computer systems [2].

Integrating emotional intelligence in computer applications is anticipated to contribute towards enhancement in their effectiveness and convenience. Although emotions have been studied extensively for previously mentioned purposes, the underlying neural mechanisms (especially in response to expression in terms of emotional stimuli) are not [3]. Various techniques use the face, speech, gestures, body movement, and physiological signals. Further, technological advancements in designing computer applications motivate researchers to investigate the approaches for integrating emotion recognition and analyze ability in computers.

5.2 Emotion Representation Models

Emotions are intricate states of feelings that result in physical and psychological changes—they are observable facts that are difficult to grasp due to complexity. The emotion models deal with the way emotions can be described for computational purposes. Emotion models contribute to analyze human emotions for the integration of emotion recognition ability in machines. There exist three models to represent emotions—discrete, dimensional, and *PAD*.

An appropriate model is selected to represent emotions based on application and modality, the main disparity being in structure and measures that represent emotions. These models are as follows:

5.2.1 Discrete Model

The discrete or basic model is one of the primary models used for describing human emotions for computational purposes. The basic idea is that all emotions are comprised of basic emotions. The emotions are categorized into eight different categories such as anger, fear, sadness, disgust, surprise, curiosity, acceptance, and joy using their developmental properties. Any emotion is described in these predefined terms. It specifies an absolute set for emotion description as shown in Figure 5.1 [4].

In comparison, some emotions have been classified as basic (Ekman's list). This list includes anger, fear, sadness, happiness, disgust, and surprise. Each discrete emotion has its own outline in realizing human physiology and behavior [5]. Once a subject realizes a particular emotion, they will be capable to choose one of the emotions in the discrete model to approximate the subject's feelings. The discrete model acts like a perfect set for the description of emotions.

5.2.2 Dimensional Model

Emotions in the dimensional model are described as continuous manner rather than discrete, based on the intellectual theory of emotions. Here, emotions are represented in two-dimensional space called *valence* and *arousal*. The *arousal* dimension ranges from highly activated to highly deactivated levels, and the *valence* dimension from highly pleasant to highly unpleasant.

The dimensional model is the most used model for the categorization of emotions. Here, all discrete emotions are represented—each discrete emotion corresponds to an

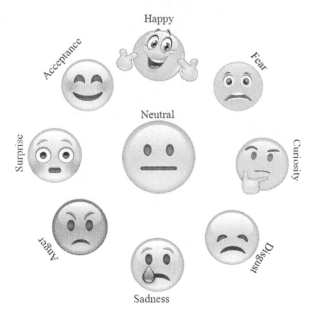

FIGURE 5.1
Discrete model of emotions.

assortment of several dimensions. For example, the happy emotion is represented with positive *valence* and high *arousal*. The emotions are described in *arousal* and *valence* dimension as shown in Figure 5.2.

Dimensional models determine each emotion in a linear series of *arousal* and *valence* dimension; emotions are represented easily using these dimensions rather than discrete structure. Moreover, this model can be used universally, across all cultures, to articulate emotions naturally [6].

5.2.3 Presence Arousal Dominance Model

The addition of a third dimension is used in a Presence Arousal Dominance (PAD) model. The PAD model uses pleasure, arousal, and dominance to represent emotions. This model is based on the idea that the environment influences a person's emotions. Here, pleasure-displeasure measures the degree of pleasant emotion; anger-fear are represented as displeasure; arousal-non-arousal measures emotional intensity; and the dominant-submissive scale measures the dominant nature of the emotion [7]. Anger is a dominant emotion, while fear represents submissive emotion.

5.3 Emotion Recognition Approaches

Understating human emotions frequently consist of human expressions analysis using more than one modality such as texts, audio, image, or video [8]. Various emotions can be identified with the combination of information from facial expressions, body movements,

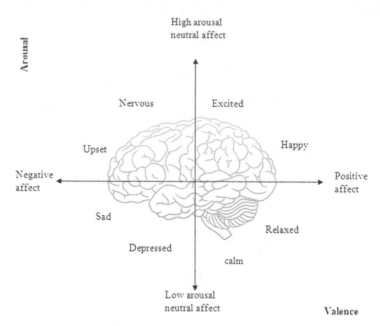

FIGURE 5.2
Two-dimensional model of emotions.

gestures, and speech. To classify emotions, three main categories of emotion recognition approaches are used—knowledge-based, statistical, and hybrid approaches [9].

5.3.1 Knowledge-Based Approaches

Knowledge-based approaches utilize domain knowledge, semantic, and syntactic characteristics of a language to recognize specific emotion. It consists of knowledge-based resources such as WordNet, ConceptNet and EmotiNet etc. during emotion recognition [10]. The economical accessibility of a knowledge-based approach provides great advantage for large resources; however, it is unable to handle complex linguistic rules and concepts. Two types of knowledge-based approaches are *dictionary-based* and *corpus-based*. Dictionary-based approaches find emotional words in a dictionary and search for similar and opposite words to expand the initial list of emotions. On the other hand, corpus-based approaches are initialized with a list of emotion words and expand the database by finding other words with context-specific characteristics in a large corpus [11]. The corpus-based approach is based on context, and its performance varies in different domains (since a word in one domain may have a different meaning in another) [12].

5.3.2 Statistical Approach

Statistical approach uses different supervised machine learning algorithms where a large set of labeled data is fed into the system to learn and predict the appropriate emotions [9]. This approach works on two datasets such as training and testing sets. The training dataset is used for the attributes of the data, whereas testing dataset helps test the performance of the machine learning algorithms [13].

Statistical approach needs a considerable number of training dataset. The most widely used machine learning algorithms includes Support Vector Machine (SVM), linear discriminant analysis, Bayesian networks, etc. Moreover, statistical approach for emotion recognition is also based on unsupervised machine learning algorithms such as deep learning. Some deep learning methods include long-term and short-term memory, convolution neural network, extreme learning machines, etc. [9]

5.3.3 Hybrid Approach

Hybrid approaches for emotion recognition are a combination of knowledge-based and statistical approach, exploiting the complementary characteristics from both techniques [14]. The knowledge-based resources help in the implementation of hybrid approaches for emotion classification process. These approaches tend to have better classification performance than independently applying statistical or knowledge-based approach. However, it suffers from computational complexity during recognition process [15].

5.4 Related Work in Emotion Recognition

The evidence of the importance of emotions in human-to-human interaction provides ways for computers to recognize emotional expressions, achieving the goal of human computer interaction. The classification of emotions into different states shows the way to use pattern recognition approaches for recognizing emotions using different modalities as inputs to the emotion recognition models [16]. Several modalities for recognizing human emotions exist to inculcate the emotional ability in machines. These modalities help computers identify the current emotional state of the user and provide service accordingly. Each modality possesses its own advantage and disadvantage when it comes to specific domain application. The modalities for emotion recognition include face, speech, gesture, physiological signals, and brain signals, and are described as follows:

5.4.1 Facial Expressions

The face is the most capable of expressing human emotion, and it plays a significant role in human emotion reflection and prediction. Facial Action Coding System (FACS) is the most comprehensive and automatic system for measuring the changes in facial expressions during emotions. These changes are tracked through automatic facial actions called as Action Units (AUs). These AUs help identify higher decision-making processes, including recognition of basic emotions [17]. This system has a 3D camera and Kinect device that capture facial images and form feature vectors with special coordinates of the face. Multilayer Perceptron neural network supports this system to recognize six basic emotions, achieving a 96% success rate [1]. The Viola Jones face detection method assists in building efficient emotion recognition system using k-NN classifier, gaining a 97% accuracy. Ada boost algorithm contributes to building an efficient classifier for facial expression to recognize emotion [16].

5.4.2 Speech Signals

Another important manner to recognize human emotions is speech. It conveys information explicitly and implicitly through the way words are pronounced. Although, cognitive scientists are unable to identify the optimal set of vocal cues that reliably distinguish emotional and attitudinal states, listeners are more accurate in decoding basic emotions from rhythm. The best discrimination performance on natural speech using rhythmic features obtains a 70% detection rate [18]. It also helps decode some non-basic affective states such as distress, anxiety, boredom, and sexual interest from nonlinguistic vocalizations like laughter, cries, sighs, and yawns. Basic emotions related to rhythmic features extracted from audio signal include pitch, energy, and speech rate. A comprehensive summary of qualitative acoustic correlations for prototypical emotions has been provided to measure emotions [19]. In real life, however, such data collection might be prohibiting considering the variability of frontal face images or high-quality audio signals under a noisy environment. On the other hand, physiological signals, such as EEG, are captured continuously with nonintrusive means and usually less affected by external noise.

5.4.3 Physiological Signals

Recently, the use of physiological signals has achieved significance in distinguishing different emotional states. The many-to-many mapping that exists between psychological and physiological changes result in emotion detection as a challenging problem.

Physiological signals are divided into two types: one originates from peripheral nervous system and the other from the central nervous system. Physiological signals that originate from the peripheral nervous system include signals captured for heart rate, blood pressure, skin conductance, etc. [20] Despite of physiology, signals captured from the CNS offer instructive characteristics in response to the emotional states. CNS signals are captured from the origin of the emotion, using the brain as a source for signal generation.

Several techniques (EEG, PET, MEG, fMRI, and NIRS) are used to acquire brain signals. EEG technique provides an effortless way to capture brain signals in contrast to frequency Magnetic Resonance Imaging (FMRI), which produces loud scanner noise and have narrow space. Positron Emission Tomography (PET) can measure activity with high spatial resolution. However, it offers a low time resolution and time delay (because of the time it takes for the radioactive material to arrive in the brain). EEG is found to be one of the most suitable modalities. The non-invasive measurement of brain waves with respect to time is provided using continuous brain activity recorded through EEG [21].

5.5 EEG-Based Emotion Recognition

The emerging advancements in processing EEG signals empower it for emotion recognition. Emotion studies inclined towards the development of automated effective emotion recognition systems use EEG. These systems require advanced signal processing techniques to extract hidden information of emotions from EEG. Several techniques have been proposed to recognize human emotion using EEG signals, based on linear and nonlinear features of EEG signals.

5.5.1 EEG-Based Emotion Recognition Using Linear Hjorth Features

The system architecture Hjorth Parameters based Multilayer Perceptron Neural Network (HP-MLP) uses Hjorth features of EEG signals to detect human emotions. The architecture is comprised of four components—raw EEG dataset construction, preprocessing, linear feature extraction, and classification as shown in Figure 5.3. Raw EEG dataset construction component deals with acquiring EEG signals from different subjects for diverse emotions. Three activity subject selection, stimuli selection, and data acquisition are essential for dataset construction. Various stimuli such as audio, video, and images contribute to elicit emotions from the subject.

Preprocessing removes unwanted noise and artifacts present in raw EEG signals during acquisition using filtering methods. The selection of filtering method depends on the kind of artifact present in the captured EEG data and the spatial or temporal features that are to be considered for further analysis. Since there is lack of universally accepted EEG filtering technique for emotion recognition, researchers have the liberty to select and apply any filtering technique to transform raw EEG data.

Linear feature extraction plays a vital role in extracting unseen characteristics (features) from the preprocessed data for accurate classification. Feature extraction component in HP-MLP is based on a set of normalized slope descriptors/features—activity, mobility, and complexity [22]. These features provide representation of statistical properties of EEG signal in time domain and are described by means of first and second order derivatives of EEG signals. The time domain representation of Hjorth features is suitable for ongoing EEG analysis situations. Also, the computation of these features is based on statistical variance, thereby lowering computational cost than other time domain features of EEG signals.

Classification component is concerned with identifying the class to which unknown EEG signal belongs. Here, the EEG signals with emotion labels are classified into different

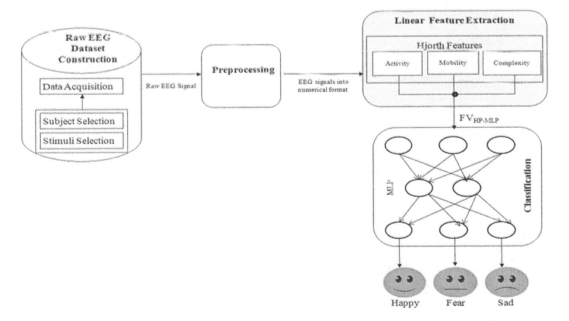

FIGURE 5.3
Components of HP-MLP.

emotional groups. In HP-MLP, the preprocessed EEG signals are classified according to the selected feature vector and the configuration of classifier based on basic model. It uses Multilayer Perceptron (MLP) neural network for emotion classification, utilizing more than one perceptron. MLP consist of one input layer, one or two hidden layers, and one output layer. These layers contain several neurons and different activation functions according to the application domain for making predictions. MLP is configured to classify unknown EEG signals into predefined emotion classes. The HP-MLP system is capable of classifying emotions with computational proficiency. Among three extracted Hjorth features, the mobility feature helps classify emotions with the highest accuracy (94.2% for all 14 individual channels) [23].

5.5.2 Nonlinear Features-Based Emotion Recognition (NFER) Using EEG

The linear feature extraction component of HP-MLP is replaced by nonlinear feature extraction in NFER architecture as shown in Figure 5.4. This architecture is based on self-similarity features of EEG signals, including nonlinear Detrended Fluctuation Analysis (DFA) and Hurst exponents. In NFER architecture, Extract DFA algorithm computes DFA exponent of time series EEG signals. Similarly, Hurst exponent is estimated using its standard mathematical model [24].

Independent nonlinear features are found in classification. DFA and Hurst of EEG signals are the key factors for predicting the suitable emotion class for EEG signals. A trained classifier forms the association between predefined emotion classes and

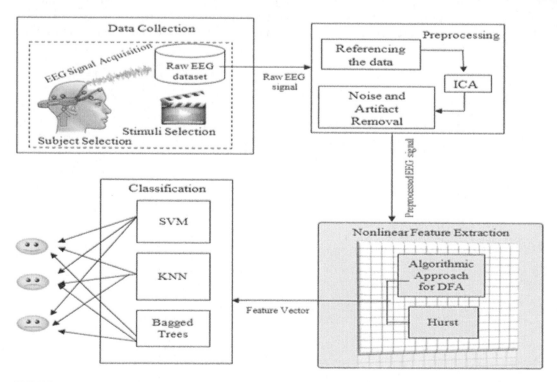

FIGURE 5.4
Nonlinear features-based emotion recognition.

corresponding EEG features. It also categorizes new EEG instances in an unseen testing dataset *NFER* architecture, including three classifiers—Support Vector Machine (SVM), k-Nearest Neighbor (k-NN), and Bagged tree for predicting emotions in the frontal, parietal, temporal, and combined regions of the brain using EEG signals.

The performance of these classifiers is evaluated based on nonlinear features in four different regions of the brain, using performance parameters. The parameters include accuracy, sensitivity, specificity, and precision. SVM classifier performs the best for emotion classification in combined regions for both DFA and Hurst [24]. However, Bagged tree classifier is also useful in discriminating emotions using DFA feature.

5.5.3 Range and Relationship Estimation of EEG Frequency Bands for Emotion Recognition

Relative Power Spectrum based Range Estimation (RPSRE) approach help estimate the range and relationship of EEG frequency bands for emotion recognition. This approach uses Bayesian network to represent the relationships between brain signals and emotions, using absolute and relative powers of EEG signals [25]. Absolute power of a band is integral of all power values within its frequency range and represents the band power of EEG signal in specific emotions.

Relative power is the percentage of power in any band compared with the total power of EEG signal in each emotion. Relative power represents the percentage of signal made up of oscillations in a particular band; it shows the proportion of signal accounted by specific band [26]. RPSRE framework aims to estimate the range of EEG frequency bands based on their relative power values extracted in frequency domain and represent the relationship between frequency bands and each discrete emotion.

Relationships between emotions and frequency bands represented by Bayesian Network, are based on conditional probability values between them. This framework is classified into six distinct phases—input raw EEG signal, preprocessing, power spectrum analysis, relative power prediction, range estimation, and relationship representation. Conditional dependencies between frequency bands and specific emotion exist and is effectively represented using Bayesian Network. The relative power ranges for alpha, beta, gamma, and theta bands are (1–5), (0.5–2), (8–9), and (0.1–1.2) respectively for *Happy* emotion; in the case of *Sad* emotion, ranges are predicted as (3–5), (1–1.5), (0.3–0.8), and (8–10). The ranges also vary for alpha, beta, gamma, and theta bands in *Fear* (2–3.5), (0.6–0.9), (10.0–11.0), and (7–8.9) respectively [25].

5.6 Conclusion

Emotion Recognition has received a great deal of attention in human machine interaction. This study provides a review of available approaches to recognize human emotions, especially focusing on EEG signals. There are several manners to recognize human emotion—facial expressions, speech, gestures, physiological signals, and brain signals. Among those, EEG is proven to be the most effective for emotion recognition. It helps analyze human emotion not only externally but also internally, recognizing the real feeling and not the posed emotions. EEG-based emotion recognition may serve as the best modality for emotion recognition using linear, nonlinear, and frequency domain features of EEG signals.

References

1. Tarnowski P., Kołodziej M., Majkowski A. and Rak R. J., "Emotion recognition using facial expressions", *Elsevier Procedia Computer Science* vol. 108, pp. 1175–1184, 2017.
2. Yuen C. T., San W., Ho J. and Rizon M., "Effectiveness of statistical features for human emotions classification using EEG biosensors", *Research Journal of Applied Sciences, Engineering and Technology*, vol. 5 no. 21, pp. 5083–5089, 2013.
3. Haiyan X., "Towards automated recognition of human emotions using EEG", Ph.D. Thesis, University of Toronto, 2012.
4. Plutchik R., The Emotions: Facts, Theories and a New Model, Random-House, New York, 1962.
5. Ekman P., Basic Emotions Handbook of Cognition and Emotion, John Wiley & Sons Ltd., U.K., 1999, pp. 45–60.
6. Othman M., Wahab A., Karim I., Dzulkifi A. and Alshaikli F., "EEG emotion recognition based on the two dimensional models of emotions", *Procedia Social and Behavioral Sciences*, vol. 97, pp. 30–37, 2013.
7. Gilroy S.W., Cavazza, M., Marcus N., et.al., "Pad-based multimodal affective fusion," *Proceeding of ACII Workshops*, 2009, 1–8.
8. Poria, S., Cambria, E., Bajpai, R., Hussain, A., "A review of affective computing: from unimodal analysis to multimodal fusion", *Information Fusion*, vol. 37, pp. 98–125, 2017. doi:10.1016/j.inffus.2017.02.003.hdl:1893/25490.
9. Cambria, Erik, "Affective computing and sentiment analysis". *IEEE Intelligent Systems*, vol. 31 no. 2, pp. 102–107, 2016. doi:10.1109/MIS.2016.31.
10. https://en.wikipedia.org/wiki/Emotion_recognition.
11. Madhoushi, Z., Hamdan, A. R., Zainudin, S., "Sentiment analysis techniques in recent works", *Science and Information Conference* (SAI), 2015, 288–291. doi:10.1109/SAI.2015.7237157. ISBN 978-1-4799-8547-0.
12. Hemmatian, F., Sohrabi, M. K., "A survey on classification techniques for opinion mining and sentiment analysis", *Artificial Intelligence Review*, vol. 52, no 3, pp. 1495–1545, 2017. doi:10.1007/s10462-017-9599-6.
13. Sharef, N. M., Zin, H. et. al., "Overview and future opportunities of sentiment analysis approaches for big data", *Journal of Computer Science*, vol. 12, no 3, pp. 153–168, 2016. doi:10.3844/jcssp.2016.153.168.
14. Cambria, E., "Affective computing and sentiment analysis". *IEEE Intelligent Systems*, vol. 31, no. 2, pp. 102–107, 2016. doi:10.1109/MIS.2016.31.
15. Medhat, W., Hassan, A. and Korashy, H., "Sentiment analysis algorithms and applications: a survey". *Ain Shams Engineering Journal*, vol. 5, no 4, pp. 1093–1113, 2014. doi:10.1016/j.asej.2014.04.011.
16. Reney D., Tripathi N., "An efficient method for face and emotion detection", *IEEE Fifth International Conference on Communication Systems and Network Technologies*, 2015, pp. 493–497.
17. Ekman P., Friesen W. V. and Hager J. C., "Facial action coding system", Manual and Investigators Guide, Research Nexus, Salt Lake City UT, 2002.
18. Fernandez R., Picard R., "Recognizing affect from speech prosody using hierarchical graphical models", *Elsevier Journal of Speech Communications*, vol. 53, no. 9, pp. 1088–1103, Nov 2011.
19. Cowie R., Cornelius R., "Describing the emotional states that are expressed in speech", *Elsevier Journal of Speech Communication*, vol. 40, no 12, pp. 5–32, 2003.
20. Stephens C., Christie I. and Friedman B., "Autonomic specificity of basic emotions: evidence from pattern classification and cluster analysis", *Biological Psychology*, vol. 4, no 3, pp. 463–473, 2010.
21. Picard R. W., Vyzas E. and Healey J., "Toward machine emotional intelligence: analysis of affective physiological state", *IEEE Transaction on Pattern Analysis and Machine Intelligence*, vol. 23, no 10, pp. 1175–1191, 2001.

22. Hjorth B., "EEG analysis based on time domain properties", *Electroencephalography and Clinical Neurophysiology*, vol. 29, no 3, pp. 306–310, 1970.
23. Bhole L., Ingle M., "System architecture for subject independent emotion recognition based on linear parameters of EEG signals", 4th International Conference on Next Generation Computing Technologies at Dehradun, India, 2018.
24. Bhole L., Ingle M., "EEG based emotion classification using nonlinear features", *International Journal of Advent Technologies*, vol. 7, no 5, pp. 628–635, 2019.
25. Bhole L., Ingle M., "Estimating range and relationship of EEG frequency bands for emotion recognition", *International Journal of Computer Applications*, vol. 78, no 13, pp. 16–21, 2019.
26. Ko K. E., Yang H. C., and Sim K. B., "Emotion recognition using EEG signals with relative power values and Bayesian network", *International Journal of Control, Automation and Systems*, vol. 7, no 5, p. 865, 2009.

6

Text, Visual and Multimedia Sentiment-Analysis, and Sentiment-Prediction

Raj Kamal, Preeti Saxena, and Manojkumar Vilasrao Deshpande

CONTENTS

6.1 Introduction

A definition of Sentiment analysis from Techopedia is "a type of data mining that measures the inclination of people's opinions through natural language processing (NLP), computational linguistics, and text analysis which are used to extract and analyze subjective information from the Web — mostly the social-media and similar sources. The analyzed data quantifies the general public's sentiments or reactions toward certain products, people, or ideas, and reveal the contextual polarity of the information" [1]. Recent research shows the importance of Visual and Multimedia Sentiment-Analyses, giving rise to a new definition of Sentiment analysis — the process of identifying, extracting, studying or mining of information, opinion, or affective states from texts, visuals, multimedia, states, time-series graphs, or charts. Other names of this process are sentiment mining, subjective-analysis, emotion-AI, opinion-extraction, and opinion-mining. [Examples of affecting states are emotion, mood, inter-personal stance (such as supportive), attitudes and personality traits (such as anxious, nervous, confident).]

The rest of the chapter describes the topics as follows: Section 6.2 describes categories, input types, and outputs. Section 6.3 lists sentimental-analysis techniques. Sections 6.3.1 and 6.3.2 describe text sentiment analysis-techniques using lexicon and CNN, respectively. Section 6.4 talks about the various research studies in the field. Section 6.5 lists the challenges in sentiment analysis and prediction. Section 6.6 gives the application areas. Section 6.7 gives the conclusions.

6.2 Sentiments-Analysis Categories, Inputs, and Outputs

The SAs can be classified into three categories: Text, Visual, and Multimedia. The input types for SAs can be files, time-series, real time, and stream [2]. The outputs can be sentiment polarity, text-value (such as opinion and information), behavior, and emotional state. Figure 6.1 shows the sentiment-analysis categories, input-types and the outputs.

6.3 Sentiment-Analysis Techniques

Several techniques are used for sentiment analysis: [3] (i) Lexicon (means words and vocabulary), (ii) semantic (concerning meaning of words, sentences, or description), (iii) dictionary (bag of words relevant to a context), and (iv) AI-based sentiment analysis and prediction models like machine learning (ML), deep learning (DL), neural net (NN), and convolution neural network (CNN) [4]. Figure 6.2 shows the techniques for sentiment analysis.

Sentiment analysis is also performed by the hybrid of techniques mentioned above. For example, the lexicon and the ML created model from training datasets for the TSA [5]. Sentiment analysis is also performed by two or more techniques (e.g., the use of classifiers, which combines classifiers trained with deep and surface features) [6].

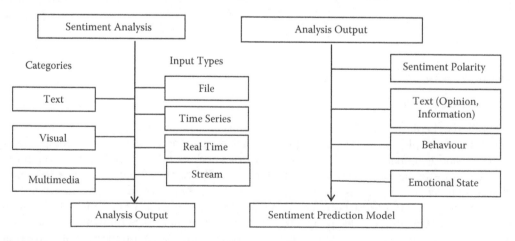

FIGURE 6.1
Sentiment-analysis categories, input-types, and the analysis outputs.

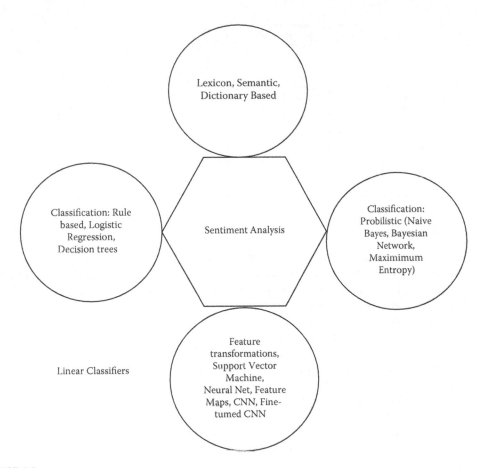

FIGURE 6.2
Sentiment-analysis techniques.

Several techniques have been proposed for the TSA. Two of them are (i) text sentiment-lexicon and (ii) text-sentiment CNN.

6.3.1 Text-Sentiments Analysis (TSA) Using Sentiment-Lexicon

TSA uses text mining, computational-linguistics, and NLP to extract sentiment-classification polarity. Python (using Jupyter Notebook) enables easy development of the codes. Python includes the Keras, Gensim, NumPy, Pandas, Regex(re) and NLTK libraries for ease in development. Figure 6.3 shows that TSA method consists of a *five*-phase processing using Sentiment Lexicon [7].

The five phases of processing for Sentiment Analysis are:

PHASE 1: *Text pre-processing* involves the Syntactic/Semantic text analysis and performs five actions (as shown in the figure). The pre-processing of a document provides a *bag-of-words;* algorithms do not directly apply the bag-of-words.

PHASE 2: *Features Generation* is a process which first defines features (variables and predictors). Techniques for feature generation are *bag-of-words*, stemming, removing stop words, and generating vector-space model.

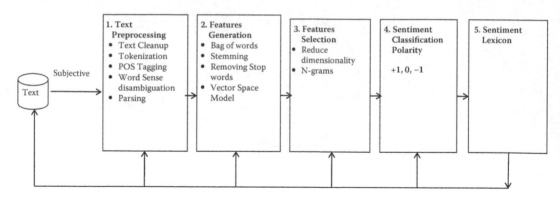

FIGURE 6.3
Five phases in text-sentiment analysis.

PHASE 3: *Features Selection* is the selection of a subset of features by rejecting irrelevant and/or redundant features (variables, predictors, or dimension) according to a defined criterion. Feature-selection process reduces the dimensionality, evaluates N-grams, and detects the noise and outliers.

PHASE 4: *Classification* is a method in which the system is trained using labelled training examples. Each class represents unique features and has a label associated to it. When a word arrives, its features are compared and labelled with a class with maximum matching. Classification also generates sentiment polarity: +1, 0, and −1 (+1 means positive sentiment, 0 means neutral and −1 means negative sentiment).

PHASE 5: *Sentiment Lexicon* is a collection of words each assigned a score indicating the positive, negative, or neutral. Aggregation of scores is calculated for subjective words (i.e. positive, negative, and neutral individually). The highest score gives the overall polarity of the text.

6.3.2 Sentiment CNN Technique for TSA and Sentiment-Prediction

The CNN technique consists of additional phases of processing. Figure 6.4 shows the TSA method using CNN [7].

The first four phases are identical to the ones in Figure 6.3. Sentiment Lexicon splits 75–90% training datasets and 10–25% text datasets for the NN layer. NN data-vectors pass through one to three number CNN filter and maximum pooling layers. The training datasets compute error function with output model (weights) M. The error function propagates to the CNN layers to create new output model (weights) M′. Test datasets finally give decider outputs. Sentiment Analysis results are used to predict future sentiment from time-series analysis or other prediction model developed. The prediction model uses machine-learning logistic-regression tool(s).

6.4 Research Studies on Sentiment-Analysis

Various research studies have been reported using different methods. They have suggested the number of techniques/algorithms, which have been applied to

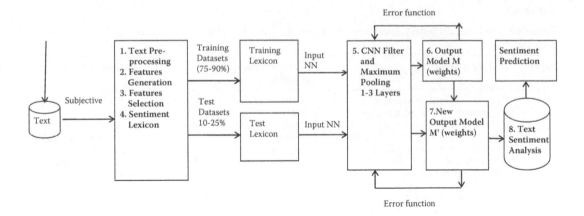

FIGURE 6.4
Text-sentiment analysis and prediction using sentiment CNN.

different Use Cases [5–19]. Table 6.1 gives summaries of methods, techniques, and Use Cases.

6.4.1 Colloborative Filtering for Sentiment-Prediction

A sentiment of a user toward a specific target (or another user) can be predicted based on the sentiments of similar users; a sentiment prediction framework can be designed based on similar users [20]. The authors used collaborative filtering (CF) of messages and message reply-to relations in discussions on Twitter. The framework classifies the context of sentiment. They demonstrated the efficacy of classification using CF. They used datasets for two different Twitter political discussions.

6.4.2 CNN/Fine-Tuned CNNs for Visual Sentiment-Analysis (VSA) and Multimedia Sentiment-Analysis (MMSA)

The automatic detection of sentiments and emotions from the VSA and MMSA images and videos are the challenging tasks. Campos et al. [21] have designed and applied a deep learning NN framework that performs VSA and predicts sentiments using CNNs. The authors also showed that VSA performance enhances by fine-tuning the CNNs. Fine-tuning CNNs are designed by first rigorously analyzing CNNs. They achieved fine-tuning by replacing the last layer with a new one. They also initially used weights in a pre-trained model for the rest of the layers, and data augmentation using flips and crops — ten combinations of flips and crops of the image are used to evaluate the classification scores.

Figure 6.5 shows Visual Sentiment Analysis with fine-tuning the CNN using the approach above. The figure also shows the steps for fine-tuning.

Dotted Layers 7 and 6 becomes Layer 6 with different weights of fully connected neurons. Layers 5, 4, 3, 2 and 1 are the pooling layers. Layer 8 is a convolution layer with fully connected neurons (four or eight times less than the ones in layer 7) and is used until the last (but one) step. Fine tuning steps shown in the figure give 2×2 fully connected neurons at Layer 9 in the last step after fine tuning CNN at Layer 8 (now no more used after that).

TABLE 6.1

Research Studies, Proposed Methods, Analysis Techniques/Algorithms and Used Case-Studies and Datasets

Paper	Proposed Method	Analysis Technique/ Algorithms	Case Study/Datasets
[5]	Proposed technique which first builds a dictionary of words, based on polarity on a small set of positive and negative hashtags related to a given subject. Then, classify posts into several classes, and balance the sentiment weight by using new metrics, such as uppercase words and the repetition of more than two consecutive letter in a word.	Spark on Hadoop managed by YARN and distribute processing across nodes. Spark MLlib's implementation of Naïve Bayes classifier is used.	Case study conducted for the 2016 US presidential election to go through the model step by step to guess which of candidates was the favorite.
[6]	Deep learning-based sentiment classifier using embedding word(s) model and linear machine-learning algorithm. Also proposed two ensemble techniques which aggregate baseline classifier with other surface classifiers widely used in Sentiment Analysis. Proposed two models for combining both surface and deep features to merge information from several sources. Introduced taxonomy for classifying the different models found in the literature.	Ensemble of classifiers which combines classifiers trained with deep and surface features.	Seven public datasets that were extracted from the microblogging and movie reviews domain.
[7]	Text pre-processing, Features generation, Feature selection by reducing dimensionality, evaluating N-grams, and detecting noises and outliers, sentiments polarity, and sentiment lexicon (set of words/ vocabulary to represent the sentiment, and sentiment polarity).	Five Phases Text Processing.	Text documents.
[8]	Neural Network based sequence-model to proposed sentence-level sentiment analysis via sentence type classification:Employs BiLSTM-CRF to extract target expression in opinionated sentences and classifies these sentences into three types according to the number of targets extracted from them. These three types of sentences are then used to train separate 1d-CNNs for sentiment classification	BiLSTM-CRF and CNN.	MPQA opinion corpus v2.0 (MPQA dataset for short) provided by Wiebe, Wilson, and Cardie (2005) a diverse range of 14,492 sentences with opinion target at the phrase level (7,026 targets).
[9]	Hybrid approach that exploits both knowledge-based techniques and statistical methods to perform tasks such as emotion recognition and polarity detection from text or multimodal data.	SVM + Lexicon	Social Media websites
[10]	A lexicon-based approach for sentiment analysis on twitter. Consider the co-occurrence patterns of words in different contexts in tweets to capture their semantics and update their pre-assigned strength and polarity in sentiment lexicons accordingly.	Lexicon based.	Tweets.

(continued)

TABLE 6.1 (*continued*)
Research Studies, Proposed Methods, Analysis Techniques/Algorithms and Used Case-tudies and Datasets

Paper	Proposed Method	Analysis Technique/ Algorithms	Case Study/Datasets
[11]	Brand-Related Twitter Sentiment Analysis Using Feature Engineering and the Dynamic Architecture for Artificial Neural Networks. The feature engineering representation contains only seven dimensions with notable feature density. Demonstrated three-class and five-class tweet sentiment classification.	Dynamic architectural artificial neural networks.	Starbucks twitter dataset.
[12]	Sentiment polarity categorization process using common machine learning algorithms.	Naïve Bayesian, Random Forest, and Support Vector Machine.	Dataset of product reviews collected from Amazon between February and April 2014.
[13]	Employed concept as features and presented a concept extraction algorithm based on semantic parsing to extract features that use semantic relationships in natural language text.	SVM.	Movie, book, product reviews.
[14]	Twitter Sentiment Analysis by combining lexicon-based and learning-based Methods: The method, first adopts a lexicon-based approach to perform entity-level sentiment analysis. This results into high precision, low recall. New tweets that are likely to be opinionated are identified through Chi-square test and are added to improve recall. A classifier is then trained to assign polarities to the entities in the newly identified tweets.	Hybrid (lexicon + learning algorithm).	Tweets.
[15]	Impact of tweets on movie sales using common text mining algorithms.	SVM, Naïve Bayes.	Tweets and movie reviews.
[16–19]	Affective computing for emotion recognition, vision and multimedia Sentiments Analysis, and the sentiment analysis for applications such as affective tutoring and entertainment, troll filtering and spam detection, enhancing the capabilities of customer relationship management and recommendation systems.	Opinion Mining and SentimentAnalysis, Emotion analysis, Concept-LevelSentiment Analysis.	Online social communication.

6.5 Challenges in Sentiment-Analysis and Prediction

Semi-structured and unstructured sentiment text datasets affect the accuracy of analysis and prediction. The outcomes are affected by (i) varying size of dataset, (ii) distinctive features, (iii) rate of data arrival, and (iv) changes in the textual content (e.g., changes in vocabulary and meaning of words). An example is the use of negatives and positives in the same sentence: "I like red, but I hate blue." Such sentence will be classified as neutral sentence if the colors are considered separately.

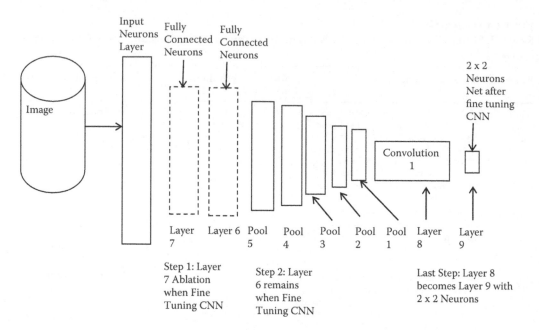

FIGURE 6.5
Visual Sentiment-analyses with fine-tuning the CNN.

Recently, Doaa (2018) has given an exhaustive survey on sentiment analysis challenges, the factors affecting them, and the importance of those factors [22]. The author used 41 research papers to survey the challenges and how they become obstacles. Analysis may not result in providing accurate meaning to sentiments and may not detect the suitable sentiment polarity. The author classified the factors individually or in association with other factor(s). The results showed the following: negation, domain dependence, bi-polar words, entity-features and keywords, huge lexicon, spam, fake, short abbreviations, emotion usage, sarcasm, and ambiguity in usages of nouns, verbs, adjectives, or adverbs.

6.6 Application Areas of Sentiment-Analysis

Use-Cases of Text SA include the monitoring of social media, news, stock market, healthcare, customer-services, brands, and products. Sentiment analysis is significantly useful in social media monitoring. This practice is adopted by several organizations across the world. The following subsections describe select applications:

6.6.1 Social Media Monitoring

Social media — Twitter, LinkedIn, Facebook, blogs, and others — need continuous sentiment analysis; an issue posted by the media can be blown out of proportion and needs timely redress. The methodology is as follows: (i) perform the SA over a period for a particular group of communities using the posts at social media, (ii) execute the SA algorithm over all mentions of the user company of personality, (iii) classify the results according to urgency of actions required, and (iv) activate the response team for redressing.

The importance of urgent action on sentiment-analysis can be understood by the following story: A leader of a party gave a speech under the heavy rain in front of a crowd; he refused to take an umbrella. His brave act spread like wildfire on the social media and his party was favored for 2–3 days.

6.6.2 Brand Monitoring

Many companies build their brand through advertisements, news, blogs, and social media posts. Each company should have high reputation in the communities. The increase in positive sentiments about competing brands creates an alarm and needs timely action. The methodology is as follows: (i) perform SA over a period for a particular group of users of products of the company, and compare the results with the competing brand, (ii) execute the SA algorithms over all mentions of the brand as well as sales in the different target regions of the company, (iii) classify and compare the results with the competing brand, and (iv) activate the response team for redress using new strategies through product advertisement expenditure, packaging, and competition organization such as quizzes for children or any other action required to boost the brand.

6.6.3 Consumer Feedback

Company considers feedback as crucial elements in marketing strategy. Feedback reflects consumer sentiments; it is taken at purchase and after a fixed interval to inquire about the service needs. The methodology is as follows: (i) perform SA over a period for a particular group of users of products of the company, (ii) execute the SA algorithms over all regions and all products of the company, (iii) classify the average period of required service and maintenance for each product, and (iv) activate the response team to redress based on feedback and surveys.

6.6.4 Real-Time Sentiment-Analysis Using Tweets

The real-time data feeds from social media (Twitter) are easy to get for sentiment analysis. The case study provides access to real-time social media information. Tweets received from the stream are pre-processed and analyzed to extract features.

Refer to the steps in the method listed in [23]. First, collect a comprehensive training dataset that consists of potential users of the system. The results give several classifications of tweets and segments them after estimating the influence of each tweet using the predictive analysis library. Sentiment analysis can be carried out through identification of positive or negative statements in the tweets.

6.6.5 Real-Time Sentiment-Analysis and Stock-Market Predictions [23]

The real-time data feeds of stock prices at stock trading exchange are available. These feeds can be used in sentiment analysis and future price predictions. Refer to a practice exercise at [23] as follows: "To analyze 80 exemplary tuples (sale time, ticker symbol, num shares, price per share) every two minutes from 9 AM to 1 PM on the relation-oriented stream tuples model for a chosen stock." Refer online for the solution of this exercise at http://www.mhe.com/kamal/bda. The solution gives the Python code for computing.

The results give the plot for correlation coefficient and stock prices as a function of time from the start of the trade.

6.6.6 Sentiment-Analysis in Transport [24]

Opportunities and advances of usages of data mining and data analytics in railways have been a subject of study [24]. Train users give reviews through forums and blogs, based on the service provided. A novel approach for sentiment classification on train reviews has been proposed in [25]. The authors suggested a classifier based on MapReduce framework.

6.7 Conclusions

Sentiment analysis can be categorized into three categories: *Text, Visual,* and *Multimedia* sentiment analysis. The SA techniques are text processing, AI methods (classifier, collaborative filtering, machine learning, deep learning), and CNNs. The Use Cases of Text SA widely used are social media and healthcare monitoring, news, stock market prediction, customer service support, and brands and products feedback. Recent research includes directions for Affective States computing.

Fine-tuned CNNs are used for VSA and MMSA. *Visual* and *Multimedia* sentiment analyses have emerged as new tools that result in higher prediction accuracies; the use of sentiment along with emotion, mood, interpersonal stance, attitude, and personality trait [21].

An application of VSA is a preliminary robot analyzing the emotion of the viewer's facial expressions in response to an advertisement and responding accordingly [21]. The authors predict that once machines that could analyze human feelings are designed, revolutionary applications in robotics, entertainment, and several areas will be established.

References

1. https://www.techopedia.com/definition/29695/sentiment-analysis (accessed on Oct. 27, 2019).
2. Kamal, R., and Saxena, P., "Machine learning algorithms for big data analytics." In: Big Data Analytics: Hadoop, Spark and Machine Learning. McGraw-Hill Education, New Delhi, 2019, 251–335.
3. Medhat, W., Hassan, A., and Korashy, H., "Sentiment analysis algorithms and applications: a survey," *Ain Shams Engineering Journal*, vol. 5, pp. 1093–1113, 2014.
4. Kaur, H., Mangat, V. and Nidhi, "A survey of sentiment analysis techniques," *International Conference on IoT in Social, Mobile, Analytics and Cloud (I-SMAC)*, 2017, pp. 921–925, IEEE Explore doi: 978-1-5090-3243-3/17/©2017IEEE.
5. Alaoui, I. E., Gahi, Y., Messoussi, R., et al., "A novel adaptable approach for sentiment analysis on big social data," *Journal of Big Data, Springer*, vol. 5, no. 12, pp. 1–18, 2018.
6. Araque, O., Corcuera-Platas, I., Fernando J., et al "Enhancing deep learning sentiment analysis with ensemble techniques in social applications," *Journal on Expert Systems with Applications, Elsevier*, vol. 77, pp. 236–246, 2017.

7. Kamal, R., and Saxena, P., "Text mining." In: Big Data Analytics: Hadoop, Spark and Machine Learning. McGraw-Hill Education, New Delhi, 2019, 410–417.

8. Chen, T., Xu, R., He, Y., et al., "Improving sentiment analysis via sentence type classification using BiLSTM-CRF and CNN," *Journal on Expert Systems with Applications, Elsevier*, vol. 72, pp. 221–230, 2017.

9. Hassan, S., et al., "Contextual semantics for sentiment analysis of Twitter," *Information Processing and Management*, vol. 52, pp. 5–19, 2016.

10. Devika M. D., Sunitha C., and Amal, G., "Sentiment analysis: a comparative study on different approaches." In *Proceedings of the Fourth International Conference on Recent Trends in Computer Science & Engineering*, Chennai, Tamil Nadu, India, Procedia Computer Science vol. 87, pp. 44–49, 2016.

11. Zimbra, D., M. Ghiassi, and S. Lee, "Brand-related Twitter sentiment analysis using feature engineering and the dynamic architecture for artificial neural networks." *49th Hawaii International Conference on System Sciences (HICSS)*, 2016.

12. Fang, Xing, and Zhan, Justin. "Sentiment analysis using product review data," *Journal of Big Data Springer*, vol. 2, no. 5, pp. 1–14, 2015. doi 10.1186/s40537-015-0015-2.

13. Agarwal, B., Poria, S., Mittal, N., et al., "Concept-level sentiment analysis with dependency-based semantic parsing: a novel approach," *Cognitive Computation*, vol. 7, no. 4, pp. 487–499, 2015.

14. Asghar, M. Z, Khan, A., Ahmad, S., Qasim, M., Khan, I, 2017. "Lexicon-enhanced sentiment analysis framework using rule-based classification scheme," vol. 12, no. 2, PLoS ONE, vol. 12, e0171649, 2017. https://doi.org/10.1371/journal.pone.0171649.

15. Huaxia, R., Yizao, L., and Andrew, W. "Whose and what chatter matters? The effect of tweets on movie sales," *Decision Support System*, 2013, vol. 15, no. 4, pp. 863–870.

16. Cambria, E. (Ed.) "Affective computing and sentiment analysis." *IEEE Intelligent Systems*, IEEE Computer Society, pp. 5–19, March/April 2016.

17. Cambria, E. et al., "New avenues in opinion mining and sentiment analysis," *IEEE Intelligent Systems*, vol. 28, no. 2, pp. 15–21, 2013.

18. Cambria, E., Livingstone, A., and Hussain, A. "The hourglass of emotions," *Cognitive Behavioural Systems, LNCS*, vol. 7403, pp. 144–157, 2012.

19. Cambria, E. et al., "The CLSA model: a novel framework for concept-level sentiment analysis," *Computational Linguistics and Intelligent Text Processing, LNCS*, vol. 9042, pp. 3–22, 2015.

20. Kim, J., Yoo, J., Lim, H., Qiu, H., Kozareva, Z., and Galstyan, A., "Sentiment prediction using collaborative filtering." *Association for the Advancement of Artificial Intelligence*, pp. 1–4, 2013. [Download link https://www.isi.edu/~galstyan/papers/icwsm-CF.pdf].

21. Campos, V., Salvador, A., Jou, B., and Giró-i-Nieto, X. "Diving deep into sentiment: understanding fine-tuned CNNs for visual sentiment prediction."Proc. 1st Workshop in Affectand Sentiment in Multimedia (ASM) Brisbane, Australia, DOI:10.1145/2813524.2813530, 2015.

22. Doaa, M. E., "A survey on sentiment analysis challenges." *Journal of King Saud University – Engineering Sciences, Elsevier*, vol. 30, pp. 330–338, 2018.

23. Kamal, R., and Saxena, P., "Real-time analytics platform applications." In: Big Data Analytics: Hadoop, Spark and Machine Learning, McGraw-Hill Education, New Delhi, pp. 368–370, 2019.

24. Thakur, R., and Deshpande, M. V., "Opportunities and advances of data mining and data analytics in railways." *International Journal of Control Theory and Applications*, vol. 9, pp. 213–219, 2016.

25. Thakur, R., and Deshpande, M. V., "A novel approach for sentiment classification on train reviews", *International Journal of Advanced Research in Basic Engineering Sciences and Technology (IJARBEST)*, vol. 3, Special Issue 37, ISSN (Online): pp. 2456–5717, March 2017.

7

Transfer Learning with Convolution Neural Networks Models: An Evolutional Comparison

Aditi Kajala and Vinod Kumar Jain

CONTENTS

7.1 Artificial Intelligence

Artificial Intelligence is the branch of science that enables a man-made device to perform specific tasks in an intelligent manner.

7.1.1 Machine Learning

It is a branch of artificial intelligence consisting of a set of algorithms that use data to train a machine and gain insights about the relationship among features of data. These insights are later used to set parameters required to make the machine intelligent. An intelligent machine can be used to perform various tasks, normally done by humans, with better accuracy and increased computation speed. Machine learning algorithms are now used in all sectors—from healthcare, finance, antifraud companies, and shopping websites. Machine learning algorithms learn from input data and produce the decision that reflects the setting of various parameters used, unlike conventionally where algorithms are used to process input data and produce an output.

7.1.2 Deep Learning

Deep learning is a class of machine learning algorithms that are based on artificial neural networks. Deep learning algorithms achieve great power and flexibility by learning in layers. Deep learning techniques learn things incrementally through its hidden structure — low-level categories (letters) to moderate-level categories (words) to higher-level categories (sentences).

   The structure of the chapter is organized as follows: Section 7.2 is a brief coverage of the convolution neural network. In Section 7.3, the concept of transfer learning as an enhancement of convolutional neural network is discussed. Section 7.4 is a brief explanation of the ImageNet dataset and ImageNet large-scale visual recognition challenge. Section 7.5 presents the results of some CNN architecture for cat and dog image classification. Section 7.6 will discuss the use and limitations of CNN architectures in the domain of image classification.

7.2 Convolutional Neural Networks [10,13]

An experiment by Hubel and Wiesel [1] on cats were made where lines with different slopes (orientation) and width are shown on a screen to a cat, and its reactions were read by connecting electrodes to its brain. The researchers observed that each neuron has a fixed receptive field — in other words, each neuron did not react to every stimulus. This experiment gave the researchers an idea that an image can also be classified in stages using the concept of layered architecture. Before the era of deep learning, people tried to solve complex problems using conventional machine learning algorithms with limited data in substantial amounts of time. They observed that machine learning algorithms using artificial neural networks can improve accuracy by increasing layers in the model; however, the dense connectivity of feedforward causes the number of parameters to increase exponentially with layer. So, feedforward neural networks were not so popular before deep revival in 2006.

7.2.1 Feedforward Neural Network and Convolution Neural Network

The structure of CNN is like that of conventional feedforward. The basic CNN architecture is a stack of layers: convolution, pooling, and fully connected. The convolution operation applies several kernels with specified spaces to the image from the top left corner to the bottom right corner. The input to CNN first layer is image dimension of $W1 \times H1 \times D1$, where W1, H1, and D1 are the width, height, and number of channels, respectively. Each convolution layer applies K kernels (filters) each of $F \times F$ dimensions and produces D2 feature maps as output of each dimension $W2 \times H2$. Here, $W2 = (W1 - F + 2P)/S + 1$, $H2 = (H1 - F + 2P)/S + 1$ and $D2 = K$, with P padding that can be used to maintain the original dimensions of the image and s stride that specifies the gap in number of pixels during convolution operation (Khapra, 2018, slide 22) [2]. The convolution layer is followed by the pooling layer to down sample the result produced by a convolution operation. The combination of convolution and pooling layers is responsible for extracting features from the image. The combination of these layers (or just the convolution layer) can be repeated to extract key features.

- The top layers of CNN are connected with ReLU (to avoid negative values). After a fully connected layer, a layer with softmax or logistic function for multi-class or binary classification, respectively, are used. In the end, there is an output layer that consists of several neurons, each signifying a class. The combination of these top layers is responsible for classifying the image. The basic organization of layers is shown in Figure 7.1.

The advantages of CNN over feedforward neural network can be explained by the following section:

7.2.2 Characteristics of CNN

- **Sparse connection**: In CNN, few neurons from one layer are connected to the next convolution layer, without kernel dimension, based on spatial dimension. This sparse connectivity reduces parameters without losing any information. If two neighboring neurons are connected in one layer they could also be connected

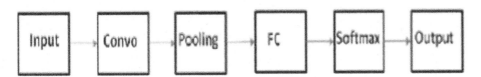

FIGURE 7.1
Organization of layers in CNN.

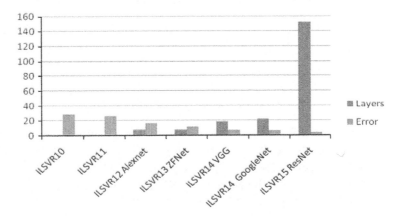

FIGURE 7.2
Comparison of ILSVRC models.

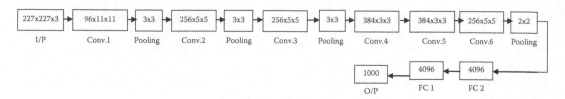

FIGURE 7.3
Architecture of AlexNet.

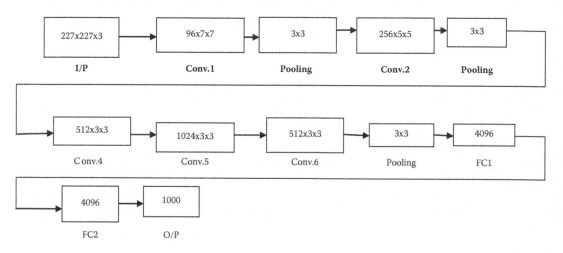

FIGURE 7.4
Architecture of ZFNet.

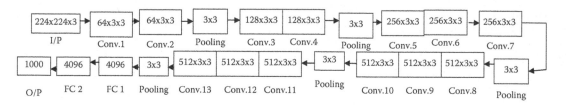

FIGURE 7.5
Architecture of VGGNet.

at a higher layer. It utilizes the structure of an image where two neighboring pixels are interconnected (Khapra, 2018, slide 34) [2].

- **Weight sharing**: Feedforward neural network model requires more weights due to dense connectivity, while the kernel in CNN (used here as weights) are shared and produces one feature map (Khapra, 2018, slide 36) [2].

- **Reduction in number of parameters**: The sharing of kernels in one feature map significantly reduces the number of parameters required for network training.

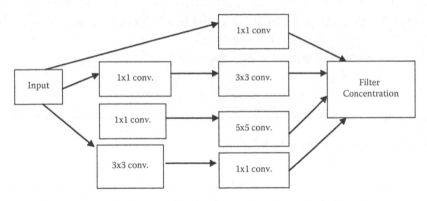

FIGURE 7.6
Architecture of the inception module.

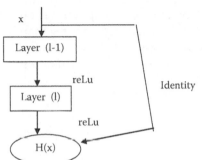

FIGURE 7.7
Architecture of skip connection.

Since the number of layers in an ordinary feedforward neural network model is increased, then the weights will also be increased exponentially. This makes ordinary feedforward neural networks unsuitable for deep learning.

7.3 Transfer Learning

Transfer learning [3] attempts to learn new aspects or concepts from the past; it makes not learning from scratch for a new domain possible. Using the concept of transfer learning Pre-trained CNN models can be used to classify a dog or cat providing the model the images of the same [11,12]. For transfer learning, three questions are required to be answered: what to transfer, when to transfer, and how to transfer.

7.3.1 Basic Steps of Transfer Learning [14,15]

To decrease the time taken for training, and instead of training deep network from scratch for any specific task, the following steps can be followed:

    i.. Select an architecture of a model that has already been trained (pre-trained models) for a particular task on a particular dataset.

ii.. Change the characteristics of some of the top layers of the model according to the requirement of the specific task.

iii.. Adapt the whole model to the specific data.

7.4 ImageNet Dataset and ILVRC

- [4] ImageNet is a dataset of more than 14 million images of over 21,000 objects. It was made to motivate and provide a source for computer vision researchers. This project was developed and maintained by academics at Princeton, Stanford, and other American universities.

- ImageNet Largescale Visual Recognition Challenge (ILVRC) is an annual competition that started in 2010 to promote the development of computer vision techniques and benchmark the state of art. In this challenge, more than one million images (a subset of ImageNet) were given to participants for training. Among the training images, 50,000 are used for validation, and the remaining 150,00 for testing. The participants had to classify the test images into 1,000 classes by their designed algorithm. Two types of error (top-5 and top-1) were recorded:

- **Top-1 Error**: A top-1 error occurs if the class predicted by a model with the highest confidence is **different from** the true class.

- **Top-5 Error**: A top-5 error occurs when the true class is not among the top five classes predicted by a model (sorted in terms of confidence).

- The progress in the first five years of ILSVRC was extremely dramatic; success was achieved by a large CNN. This is explained in Figure 7.2.

- Each model is characterized by the error in the classification of images during competition. Models in the first two years (before the deep learning era) were shallow; in the years that followed, the models were improved by adding layers or modifying the architecture of the existing model. Some of the important models that won the challenge are in the following section.

7.4.1 AlexNet (2012) [4]

Alex Krizhevsky, Ilya Sutskever, and Geoffrey Hinton created a "large, deep convolutional neural network" that won the 2012 ILSVRC. AlexNet consists of eight layers. It is shown in Figure 7.3 (Khapra, 2018, slide 49) [2].

7.4.2 ZF Net (2013) [5]

Matthew Zeiler and Rob Fergus from NYU used a CNN model and won the challenge in 2013. The researchers used the architecture of AlexNet by increasing the number of small-sized kernels in the last three convolutional layers to fine-tune the model and improve the classification error by 11.2%. Its architecture is shown in Figure 7.4 (Khapra, 2018, slide 52) [2].

7.4.3 VGG Net (2014) [6]

Karen Simonyan and Andrew Zisserman of the University of Oxford generated 16–19 layers CNN architecture (Figure 7.5) which used 3 × 3 kernels with a stride and padding of 1 in each convolutional layer, and 2 × 2 kernels in each max pooling layer with a stride of 2. It was the runner-up of the challenge in 2014. Its architecture is shown in Figure 7.5 (Khapra, 2018, slide 54) [2].

7.4.4 GoogLeNet (2014) [7]

Christian Szegedy, et al. introduced a concept called inception module, in which kernels of multiple granularities are applied in parallel (Figure 7.6). They also introduced the use of 1 × 1 kernel to reduce computation before applying the convolution operation. The architecture consists of 22 layers (Khapra, 2018, slide 60) [2] and was the winner of the challenge in 2014.

7.4.5 Residual Network (ResNet2015) [8,9]

Kaiming He, et al. introduced a concept of skip connection in the network to resolve the vanishing and exploding of gradients for deeper networks. The skip connection is shown in Figure 7.7 (Khapra, 2018, slide 66) [2]; the identity label ensures that the performance of a deeper network will either be better or equal to a shallow network. In such a network,

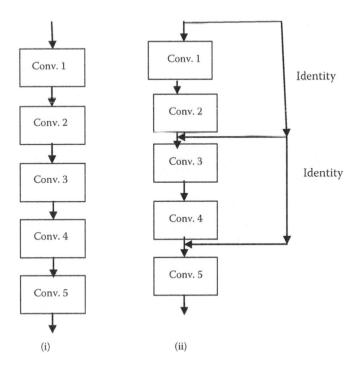

FIGURE 7.8
VGG net (i) and VGG net (ii) with skip connection (ResNet).

gradient may flow using skip connection. Kaiming He, et al. created a CNN architecture with 152 layers and skip connections after some intervals of feature extraction layers. The hyperparameters include kernel size, stride, and padding were similar to the VGGNet — an extension of VGGNet with more skip layers. (Figure 7.8).

7.4.6 Summary of ILSVRC Winner Models

The performance of ILSVRC models can be compared in Table 7.1 (Khapra, 2018, slide 47) [2].

7.4.7 Recently Used Pre-Trained Models Summary

Other pre-trained CNN models that can be used for transfer learning are specified in Table 7.2 [10–21].

TABLE 7.1

Table of ILSVRC Models

Year	Model Description Name	No. of Layers	Top-5 Error
2010	Shallow		28.2
2011	Shallow		25.8
2012	AlexNet	8	16.4
2013	ZFNet	8	11.7
2014	VGG16	19	7.3
2014	GoogLeNet	22	6.7
2015	ResNet	152	3.57

TABLE 7.2

Description of Pre-Trained CNN Models

S.No.	Model	Image Size	Weight Size	Top-1 Accuracy	Top-5 Accuracy	Parameters	Depth
1.	Xception	299 × 299	88 MB	0.79	0.945	22,910,480	126
2.	VGG16	224 × 224	528 MB	0.715	0.901	138,357,544	23
3.	VGG19	224 × 224	549 MB	0.727	0.91	143,667,240	26
4.	ResNet50	224 × 224	99 MB	0.759	0.929	25,636,712	168
5.	InceptionV3	299 × 299	92 MB	0.788	0.944	23,851,784	159
6.	Inception ResNetV2	299 × 299	215 MB	0.804	0.953	55,873,736	572
7.	MobileNet	224 × 224	17 MB	0.665	0.871	4,253,864	88

(a)

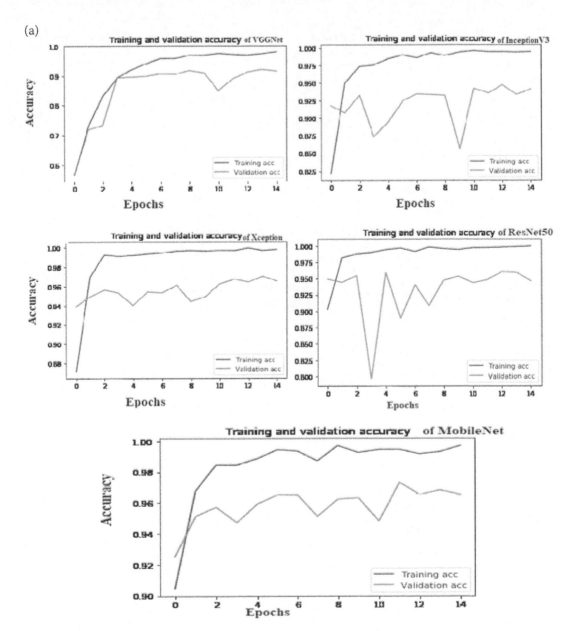

FIGURE 7.9A
Classification accuracy of pre-trained models.

7.5 Results

We have used some pre-trained CNN models to classify the image of dogs and cats. For this implementation, the "Dogs vs Cats" dataset publicly available on Kaggle is used. We have each pre-trained model used as a base model while the top layers are modified. We

(b)

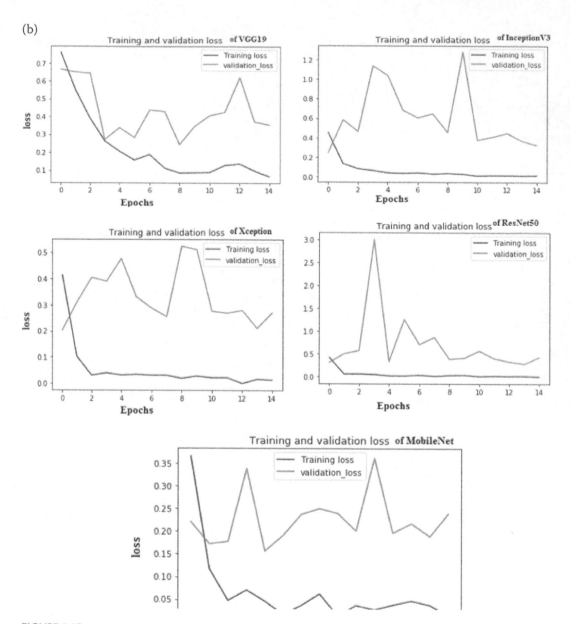

FIGURE 7.9B

Classification of binary cross-entropy loss of pre-trained models.

used two fully connected layers. The sigmoid activation function is used on the output layer to get the value between 0 and 1. We performed 15 epochs; for each epoch, 2000 images — sizes of 150 × 150 are used for training and 1000 images are used for validation. The performance of each model is measured in terms of accuracy Figure 7.9 (a) and loss Figure 7.9 (b). We computed binary cross-entropy loss and RMSprop optimizer with a learning rate of 0.001.

7.6 Conclusion

The increase of data does not improve the performance of a conventional machine learning model, but the performance of deep learning neural network models increases with data. Deep learning models can be used to achieve better accuracy in results; however, training of deep learning models is a time-consuming task, and requires high computation speed. The training time of such models can be reduced through transfer learning. In transfer learning, some pre-trained models can be used for feature extraction, by freezing some of the layers and changing the top layers (i.e. classification layers according to the requirement of a specific task or feature learning), and prediction. These models can also be used for images apart from the ImageNet dataset (large dataset on which they are trained) but hyperparameters like the number of hidden layers, number of kernels and kernel size, stride, padding, etc. must be set before training. Their performance critically depends on the expertise of hyperparameter tuning.

References

1. Hubel, D.H. and Wiesel, T.N., "Receptive fields of single neurones in the cat's striate cortex," *The Journal of Physiology*, vol. 148, pp. 574–591, 1959.
2. Khapra, M. CS7015: Deep Learning, week 10[lecture notes]. 2018. Retrieved from https://swayam.gov.in/nd1_noc19_cs85/preview.
3. Dipanjan, S. (2018, Nov 15). A comprehensive hands-on guide to transfer learning with real-world applications in deep learning. Retrieved from https://towardsdatascience.com/a-comprehensive-hands-on-guide-to-transfer-learning-with-real-world-applications-in-deep-learning-212bf3b2f27a.
4. Devopedia. "ImageNet." Version 15, October 25. Accessed 2020-01-03. Retrieved from http://devopedia.org/imagenet 2019.
5. Krizhevsky, A., Sutskever, I. and Hinton, G. "ImageNet classification with deep convolutional neural networks," *Neural Information Processing Systems*. 2012. 25.10.1145/3065386.
6. Zeiler M.D., Fergus R., "Visualizing and understanding convolutional networks," In: Fleet D., Pajdla T., Schiele B., Tuytelaars T. (eds) Computer Vision – ECCV 2014. ECCV 2014. Lecture Notes in Computer Science, vol 8689, Springer, Cham, 2014.
7. Imonyan, Karen & Zisserman, Andrew, "Very deep convolutional networks for large-scale image recognition," *arXiv* vol. 1409.1556, 2014.
8. Szegedy, C. et al., "Going deeper with convolutions," *IEEE Conference on Computer Vision and Pattern Recognition (CVPR)*, Boston, MA, pp. 1–9. doi: 10.1109/CVPR.2015.7298594, 2015.
9. Kaiming H. et al., "Deep residual learning for image recognition", *IEEE Conference on Computer Vision and Pattern Recognition (CVPR)*, arXiv1512.03385v1, 2015.
10. Zeiler M.D., Fergus R. Visualizing and understanding convolutional networks. In: Fleet D., Pajdla T., Schiele B., Tuytelaars T. (eds) Computer Vision – ECCV 2014. ECCV 2014. Lecture Notes in Computer Science, vol. 8689. Springer, Cham, 2014.
11. Surma, G. (Nov 19, 2018). Image Classifier – Cat Vs Dogs Leveraging Convolutional Neural Networks (CNNs) and Google Colab's Free GPU. Retrieved from https://towardsdatascience.com/image-classifier-cats-vs-dogs-with-convolutional-neural-networks-cnns-and-google-colabs-4e9af21ae7a8.
12. Jain, A. (2018, May 26) Creating a Simple Dog vs Cat Image Classifier Using Keras. Retrieved from https://medium.com/data-science-101/creating-a-simple-dog-cat-image-classifier-using-keras-7dffdeea0f66.

13. Thomas, C. (2019, May 27). An Introduction to Convolutional Neural Network. Retrieved from https://towardsdatascience.com/an-introduction-to-convolutional-neural-networks-eb0b60b58fd7.
14. Marcelino, P. (2018, Oct 23) Transfer Learning from pre-Trained Models. Retrieved from https://towardsdatascience.com/transfer-learning-from-pre-trained-models-f2393f124751.
15. Avinash (2019, Jun 14) Pretrained Machine Learning Models Vs Models Trained from Scratch. Retrieved from https://heartbeat.fritz.ai/pre-trained-machine-learning-models-vs-models-trained-from-scratch-63e079ed648f.
17. Simonyan, K. and Zisserman, A. Very deep convolutional networks for large-scale image recognition. *arXiv: Computer Vision and Pattern Recognition*, abs/1409.1556, 2014.
18. He, K., Zhang, X., Ren, S., and Sun, J. "Deep residual learning for image recognition." In *Proceedings of the IEEE Computer Vision and Pattern Recognition*, 2016, 770–778.
19. Huang, G., Liu, Z., Van Der Maaten, L., & Weinberger, K. Q. (2017). "Densely connected convolutional networks." In *Proceedings of the IEEE Conference on Computer Vision and Pattern Recognition* (pp. 4700–4708).
20. LeCun, Y., Bengio, Y., & Hinton, G. "Deep Learning." *Nature*, vol. 521, no. 7553, p. 436, 2015.
21. Talo, M., Baloglu, U. B., Yıldırım, Ö., & Acharya, U. R. "Application of deep transfer learning for automated brain abnormality classification using MR images." *Cognitive Systems Research*, vol. 54, pp. 176–188, 2019.

8

Multicriteria Decision-Making Using Interval Valued Neutrosophic Soft Set

D. P. Acharjya and Dhruv Arya

CONTENTS

8.1 Introduction

With the rapid increase in population and prevalent consumerism, the number of super-markets has continuously been rising in urban areas. This creates the need for accurate choice mechanisms in supermarkets that will help consumers make better shopping decisions, and managers evaluate their standing. A supermarket can be the best choice for customers based on multiple criteria; rating a supermarket can be done using multi-criteria decision analysis (MCDA) [1]. This type of analysis is useful in scenarios where several conflicting criteria are involved. Multi-criteria decision making (MCDM) can be described as selecting the most suitable alternative for a given set of criteria. Several techniques have been developed for MCDM. This also helps a supermarket be the best choice for customers. In the weighted sum approach [2], customer choice is obtained by assigning weights to each criterion and then taking the sum of the product of the values of the criterion with their respective weights (like in an approach where a product of the weighted criteria has also been used). Both these approaches involve manually assigning weights to each criterion. A criterion having a higher weight is given more importance [3].

Bernard Roy divided the MCDM problem into four categories: alpha, beta, gamma, and delta [4]. In the gamma approach, we are required to rank alternatives; therefore, this problem would fall under this approach. The ELECTRE family of decision-making methods was also introduced [5], which involves creating outranking relations which can be used to assign ranks to the alternatives from best to worst. Brans developed a simpler ranking methodology called the Preference Ranking Organization Method for Enrichment Evaluations (PROMETHEE) [6].

PROMETHEE and ELECTRE methods both rely on creating outranking relations amongst alternatives, but PROMETHEE reduces the need for a person to manually set parameters to generate ranks. It works by generating preference values on each criterion for an alternative using a preference function. These values are used to compute differences between alternatives and that criterion. The weighted aggregates of these differences give us a numerical value that can be used to compare alternatives. Brans introduced six preference functions, each to be used with a different type of constraint. Extensive research and several variations have been developed in this direction [7–10]. Zhaoxu and Min have developed an approach that infers aggregation parameters in PROMETHEE from the labeled samples [7].

Information system contains uncertainties due to several factors. To process them, Zadeh introduced the concept of partial belongingness of an element to a set called fuzzy sets [11]. This methodology has been extensively worked upon as it manages to capture real-world uncertainty quite accurately. Intuitionistic fuzzy sets by Atanassov added the concept of non-belongingness of an element to a set [12]. It has proved its usefulness in cases of imperfect information available (such as handwriting recognition), but the major limitation of such method is the design of the membership function. A rough set — that has several variations in obtaining decisions — was introduced in obtaining decisions from an information system [13] [14–17]. Many hybrid models also have been developed for multi-criteria decision-making [18–21]. There are situations where humans do not have extreme feelings of like or dislike towards something, and it is difficult to model such situations using only two parameters of the intuitionistic fuzzy set so Smarandache introduced the concept of neutral thought. This concept can be used to model the human decision-making process very well; the intuitionistic fuzzy set has been extended to another parameter of neutrality [22].

In statistics, prediction is a part of statistical inference but, it can be undertaken with other statistical approaches such as regression analysis, time series analysis, and various subcategories like logistic regression, regressive models, etc. However, statistical techniques have their own limitations and cannot produce better predictions when the data contains uncertainties. Also, such methods fail to consider hesitation and indeterminacy. To address these, an intuitionistic fuzzy rough set on two universal set for multi-criteria decision making was first introduced [20], then an additional decision-making method using a soft set and rough set on fuzzy approximation spaces, [18], and finally, a method using radial basis neural network and rough set on two universal sets for decision making was also proposed [23] but all these methods failed to consider indeterminacy. Additionally, these methods normalized the raw data collected from the user using the aggregation method so that the concerned technique can be applied but such process may lead to loss of information. This motivates the authors to consider both indeterminacy and hesitation while analyzing raw data without any manipulation.

In this approach, values lying in the non-standard unit interval are assigned to the truth, falsity, and indeterminacy parameters. The use of the standard unit interval, which limits the value of the parameters to the interval [0, 1], was introduced by Wang, et al. [24]. This interval enables more practical applications of neutrosophic soft sets in engineering. A more generalized approach is to specify a range of values for each parameter instead of one value. Humans are more comfortable specifying a range of values for a parameter rather than a single value, so this approach enables us to gather data without loss of valuable information and leads to interval valued neutrosophic soft sets (IVNSS) [25].

In this article, we have presented our work on a survey conducted in Bangalore, India. Data is collected through the opinions of 921 people in various supermarkets in Bangalore. The data undergoes data cleaning procedures, then IVNSS is used to analyze. The prime objective of this article is to use IVNSS in multi-criteria decision making, and an empirical study on the ranking of supermarkets in a particular city is used for analysis. We will discuss multi-criteria decision making from an empirical study using IVNSS later; the rest of the article is organized as follows: neutrosophic set and neutrosophic soft set is briefly discussed in Section 8.2. It is further extended to interval valued neutrosophic soft set in Section 8.3. The proposed research design is presented in Section 8.4, followed by the results and discussion in Section 8.5. The article is concluded in Section 8.6.

8.2 Neutrosophic Set

In this section, we briefly discuss neutrosophic set. A neutrosophic set is defined by three parameters: belongingness, indeterminacy, and non-belongingness. The indeterminacy parameter describes belongingness or non-belongingness. For example, a customer might rate a given supermarket as (0.7, 0.6, 0.4) for its ambiance. Thus, the said supermarket has a probability of 70% good ambiance, and 40% probability of bad ambiance. The indeterminacy regarding the belongingness or non-belongingness is considered as 60%.

A neutrophic set is defined formally as: let Q be the universe of discourse. A neutrosophic set B in Q is characterized with three parameters such as truth membership (t_B), indeterminacy membership (i_B), and falsity membership (f_B) where t_B, i_B, f_B: $Q \rightarrow [0, 1]$ are functions and for all $q \in Q$, $q = q(t_B, i_B, f_B) \in B$ is a single-valued element of B. A single-valued neutrosophic set B (NS) over a finite universe $Q = \{q_1, q_2, \cdots, q_n\}$ is represented as in Equation (8.1). More detail on neutrosophic set can be found in [26].

$$B = \sum_{i=1}^{n} \frac{q_i}{<t_{B_i}, i_{B_i}, f_{B_i}>} \tag{8.1}$$

8.2.1 Neutrosophic Soft Set

Data analysis is of prime importance today and dealing with uncertainties is a challenge. Research growth in this direction deals with fuzzy set [11], intuitionistic fuzzy set [12], rough computing [13], etc. but all these theories have their own limitations. To overcome these limitations, the concept of soft set was introduced by Molodtsov [27].

Let Q be the universe and E be the set of parameters. Let $P(Q)$ denote the powerset of Q and $A \subseteq E$. A pair (F, A) is known as a soft set over Q, where $F: A \rightarrow P(Q)$ is a mapping. In other words, for $e \in A$, $F(e)$ may be considered as the set of e- approximate elements of the soft set (F, A). In general, a soft set describes a given element with respect to several parameters $E = \{e_1, e_2, \cdots, e_n\}$ [28]. This is extremely useful when we want to establish the ranking of supermarkets based on various criteria E; the set of all supermarkets under consideration would be Q.

Let $Q = \{q_1, q_2, q_3, q_4, q_5, q_6\}$ be a set of supermarkets and $E = \{$Ambience, Customer service, Offers, Locality$\}$ be the set of parameters. Let us assume $F($Ambience$) = \{q_1, q_4, q_6\}$; $F($customer service$) = \{q_2, q_5, q_6\}$; $F($offers$) = \{q_3, q_4, q_5\}$; $F($locality$) = \{q_1, q_2\}$. This can be represented in the form of an information system. The soft set representation of the information system is presented in Table 8.1.

In real-life applications, belongingness and non-belongingness never work, so the concept of neutrosophic set was introduced. Partial belongingness of objects using fuzzy proximity relation is also introduced in soft set and the concept of hybridization of soft set with rough set on fuzzy approximation space is defined [18]. Further, Maji applied the concept of neutrosophic to soft sets to introduce the concept of neutrosophic soft sets (NSS) [29]. The entity would have belongingness, non-belongingness, and indeterminacy for each parameter.

Let Q be the set of supermarkets surveyed such that $Q = \{q_1, q_2, q_3, q_4, q_5, q_6\}$. Let E be the set of criteria in the questionnaire such that $E = \{$ambience, customer service, offers, locality$\}$. Therefore F will be mapping from E to $P(Q)$ such as $F($Ambience$) = \{q_1(0.7, 0.6, 0.2)$, $q_2(0.0, 0.5, 0.2), q_3(0.2, 0.0, 0.2), q_4(0.3, 0.3, 0.5), q_5(0.5, 0.5, 0.5), q_6(0.2, 0.4, 0.0)\}$ $F($Customer service$) = \{q_1(0.8, 0.2, 0.0), q_2(0.5, 0.4, 0.4), q_3(0.3, 0.6, 0.4), q_4(0.1, 0.5, 0.2), q_5(0.9, 0.7, 0.7), q_6(0.4, 1.0, 0.4)\}$ $F($Offers$) = \{q_1(0.8,0.7,0.3), q_2(0.0,0.9,0.2), q_3(0.1,0.6,0.1), q_4(0.3,0.2,0.3), q_5(0.6,0.8,0.4), q_6(1.0,0.2,0.3)\}$, and $F($locality$) = \{q_1(0.3, 0.9,0.6), q_2(0.1,0.1,0.2), q_3(0.3,0.3,0.3), q_4(0.5,0.7,0.2), q_5(0.4,0.4,0.2), q_6(0.7,0.5,0.6)\}$. For example, the supermarket q_1 has a belongingness of 0.7, indeterminacy of 0.6, and non-belongingness of 0.2 for the parameter ambience. This can be viewed as an information system presented in Table 8.2.

TABLE 8.1

Soft Set Representation of Information System

Q	Ambiance	Customer Service	Offers	Locality
q_1	1	0	0	1
q_2	0	1	0	1
q_3	0	0	1	0
q_4	1	0	1	0
q_5	0	1	1	0
q_6	1	1	0	0

TABLE 8.2

Neutrosophic Soft Set Representation of Information System

Q	Ambiance	Customer Service	Offers	Locality
q_1	[0.7, 0.6, 0.2]	[0.8, 0.2, 0.0]	[0.8, 0.7, 0.3]	[0.3, 0.9, 0.6]
q_2	[0.0, 0.5, 0.2]	[0.5, 0.4, 0.4]	[0.0, 0.9, 0.2]	[0.1, 0.1, 0.2]
q_3	[0.2, 0.0, 0.2]	[0.3, 0.6, 0.4]	[0.1, 0.6, 0.1]	[0.3, 0.3, 0.3]
q_4	[0.3, 0.3, 0.5]	[0.1, 0.5, 0.2]	[0.3, 0.2, 0.3]	[0.5, 0.7, 0.2]
q_5	[0.5, 0.5, 0.5]	[0.9, 0.7, 0.7]	[0.6, 0.8, 0.4]	[0.4, 0.4, 0.2]
q_6	[0.2, 0.4, 0.0]	[0.4, 1.0, 0.4]	[1.0, 0.2, 0.3]	[0.7, 0.5, 0.6]

8.3 Interval Neutrosophic Soft Set

In the previous section, we discussed neutrosophic set B defined over universe Q with the help of belongingness (t_B), indeterminacy (i_B), and non-belongingness (f_B), where t_B, i_B, $f_B \in [0,1]$ for each $q \in Q$. However, in many real-life problems, it is observed that t_B, i_B, and f_B are defined in terms of an interval. To handle such cases, the concept of neutrosophic set has been extended to interval valued neutrosophic set [23]. Further, a soft set that provides parameterization is hybridized with an interval-valued neutrosophic set, and the concept of interval-valued neutrosophic soft set has been developed [24]. For wholeness of the paper, we briefly recall the notions and concepts of interval-valued neutrosophic soft set in this section.

Let Q be universal set and $q \in Q$. An interval neutrosophic set B in Q is characterized with belongingness t_B, indeterminacy i_B, and non-belongingness f_B and $\forall q \in Q, q \equiv q$ ($t_B(q)$, $i_B(q)$, $f_B(q)$) and $t_B(q)$, $i_B(q)$, $f_B(q)$ are closed subintervals of $[0,1]$. Let Q be the universe and E be a set of parameters. Let $IN(Q)$ denote the set of all interval valued neutrosophic sets on Q. A pair (G, B) is called an interval-valued neutrosophic set (IVNSS) over Q if G is a mapping given by $G: B \rightarrow IN(Q)$, where $B \in E$. Thus, for all $e \in B$, $G(e) = \{q, t_e^G(q), i_e^G(q), f_e^G(q)\} \in IN(Q)$.

An interval-valued neutrosophic soft set (G, B) is said to be null or empty if and only if it satisfies the following conditions for all $q \in Q$ and for all $e \in B$. It is denoted as $\tilde{\phi}_N$.

1. $\inf t_e^G(q) = \sup t_e^G(q) = 0$
2. $\inf i_e^G(q) = \sup i_e^G(q) = 1$
3. $\inf f_e^G(q) = \sup f_e^G(q) = 1$

An interval-valued neutrosophic soft set (G, B) is said to be absolute if and only if it satisfies the following conditions for all $q \in Q$ and for all $e \in B$. It is denoted as $\tilde{B}_N$.

1. $\inf t_e^G(q) = \sup t_e^G(q) = 1$
2. $\inf i_e^G(q) = \sup i_e^G(q) = 0$
3. $\inf f_e^G(q) = \sup f_e^G(q) = 0$

8.3.1 A Numerical Illustration

Let $Q = \{q_1, q_2, q_3\}$ the universal set containing supermarkets that are tested on some parameters $E = \{e_1, e_2\}$, where e_1 is good locality and e_2 is good service. Values for the set Q are obtained from a survey of customers who assign values to each parameter of a supermarket based on the degree of belongingness, indeterminacy, and non-belongingness to that parameter set. Then G is an interval-valued neutrosophic soft set of Q defined as $G = \{G(e_1), G(e_2)\}$, where

$$G(e_1) = \frac{\{[0.5,0.7],[0.2,0.7],[0.4,0.8]\}}{q_1} + \frac{\{[0.1,0.5],[0.3,0.6],[0.7,0.9]\}}{q_2}$$
$$+ \frac{\{[0.2,0.6],[0.4,0.9],[0.3,0.5]\}}{q_3}$$

$$G(e_2) = \frac{\{[0.3, 0.8], [0.3, 0.6], [0.6, 0.7]\}}{q_1} + \frac{\{[0.3, 0.5], [0.6, 0.7], [0.2, 0.5]\}}{q_2}$$
$$+ \frac{\{[0.4, 0.7], [0.3, 0.8], [0.7, 0.9]\}}{q_3}$$

The interval-valued neutrosophic soft set G can be represented in the form of a matrix as $G = \{G_1, G_2\}$, where each row of G_1 and G_2 describes a supermarket.

$$G_1 = \begin{pmatrix} \{[0.5, 0.7], [0.2, 0.7], [0.4, 0.8]\} \\ \{[0.1, 0.5], [0.3, 0.6], [0.7, 0.9]\} \\ \{[0.2, 0.6], [0.4, 0.9], [0.3, 0.5]\} \end{pmatrix} \quad G_2 = \begin{pmatrix} \{[0.3, 0.8], [0.3, 0.6], [0.6, 0.7]\} \\ \{[0.3, 0.5], [0.6, 0.7], [0.2, 0.5]\} \\ \{[0.4, 0.7], [0.3, 0.8], [0.7, 0.9]\} \end{pmatrix}$$

8.4 Research Methodology

Present research work has used the classification technique of data mining to categorize supermarkets of a particular city through the customer's survey. We use an interval valued neutrosophic soft set to rank the supermarkets in Bangalore, India. Prior to the present study, factor analysis is being conducted to determine the dimensions of these stores and their relationships with the overall service quality. For the factor analysis, a questionnaire survey was conducted with a sample selected from multiple apparel stores located in different regions of the city. Simple random sampling is used to select a sample of ten supermarkets. 24 parameters, aside from demographic parameters, are considered for the study. The questionnaire uses a ten-point rating scale, where a customer can rate a supermarket from a range ($[a, b]; 1 \leq a, b \leq 10$) for belongingness, indeterminacy, and disagreement with a particular risk source. The parameters considered for the analysis are presented in Table 8.3. In addition, all the parameters have equal weights. However, different weights for the criteria may also be considered for the analysis. An abstract view of the proposed model is depicted in Figure 8.1.

TABLE 8.3

Parameter Description

Serial No.	Notation	Parameters
1	e_1	Product quality that deals with freshness and durability
2	e_2	Location
3	e_3	Interim adornment that deals with exhibits, music, interiors
4	e_4	Process that deals with queues, number of check-out counters, opening hours
5	..	Additional amenities (membership cards, baby area, goods delivery)
6	e_6	Personnel related (availability and knowledge of staff, individual attention)
7	e_7	Reliability (accuracy of bill, correct information on discounts)
8	e_8	Facilities (clean environment, number of trolleys, free good delivery)
9	e_9	Product variety (availability of goods of various brands, expiry date)
10	e_{10}	Staff friendliness and availability

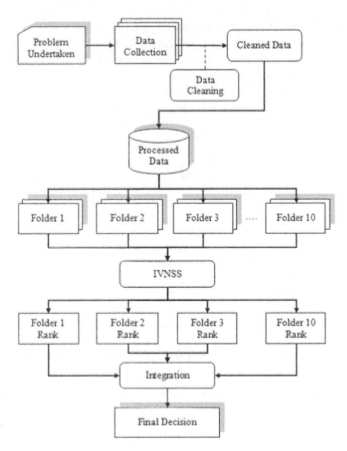

FIGURE 8.1
An abstract view of proposed IVNSS design.

The raw data obtained does not give any information in the form it appears in [30]. The raw data stored could contain errors like missing data, inconsistencies that arise due to merging data, incorrect data entry, and so on. Deriving meaningful information from the raw data requires pre-processing that converts real-life data into a computer-readable format. The pre-processing stage involves attribute selection, data cleaning, and data transformation [31]. This process starts off with data collection, and then the required features or attributes are selected for analysis. Then, data cleaning is performed by eliminating errors and missing values, with the correction of syntaxes. Finally, the data is prepared and transformed into a suitable and readable format for data mining using an interval valued neutrosophic soft set. The dataset for the model is divided into ten folders. Each folder is used to obtain the rank of supermarkets. Considering the rank of each folder, the final rank of a supermarket is obtained.

Now, to decide which supermarket is best for each folder, one must compute the "parametric score" and "total score" of a supermarket using IVNSS. The parametric score and total score of an object are as follows: $S_e(q)$ indicates the parametric score and $S_t(q)$ denotes the total score.

Let $q \in Q$ be an element of an interval valued neutrosophic soft set A such that $B = \{B(e), e \in E\}$. Now for $q \in B(e)$, $q \equiv q(t_B(q), i_B(q), f_B(q)) \in B$ and $t_B(q), i_B(q), f_B(q) \subseteq [0,1]$. The parametric score, $S_e(q)$, of an element $q \in B$ is defined in Equation (8.2) whereas total score, $S_t(q)$, is defined in Equation (8.3),

where $\quad t_B^+(q) = \sup t_e^B(q); \quad t_B^-(q) = \inf t_e^B(q); \quad i_B^+(q) = \sup i_e^B(q);$
$\qquad\qquad i_B^-(q) = \inf i_e^B(q); f_B^+(q) = \sup f_e^B(q); \quad f_B^-(q) = \inf f_e^B(q)$

$$S_e(q) = \frac{\left[\left(t_B^+(q) - f_B^+(q)\right) + \left(t_B^-(q) - f_B^-(q)\right)\right]}{2} \times \left(1 - \frac{i_B^+(q) + i_B^-(q)}{2}\right) \qquad (8.2)$$

$$S_t(q) = \sum_{e \in E} S_e(q) \qquad (8.3)$$

8.5 Empirical Study on Customer Choice towards Supermarket

This section analyzes the proposed design by considering a case study between customers and supermarkets. To examine our methodology, we have used the data collected from various supermarkets in Bangalore, India. The attributes of each supermarket are described by the set $E = \{e_1, e_2, e_3, e_4, e_5, e_6, e_7, e_8, e_9, e_{10}\}$ as reported in Table 8.3. Each element of this set is further affected by many factors, making it an aggregate of these factors. For instance, product quality for vegetables are based on freshness, while products such as blenders are rated based on their durability. The location also affects accessibility and familiarity of the market. Thus, these factors affect how customers rates the place. The interim decoration attribute of a supermarket is affected by how the products are displayed, other decorations, interior music, and whether there is an area for kids to play. The process attribute consists of three key elements: queue waiting time, number of checkouts, and opening hour; market membership, presence of a baby area, and delivery of goods affect the amenities attribute; personnel-related features consist of staff availability and individual attention to loyal customers; reliability lies in the accuracy of the bill and correct price and discount information; facilities include clean and spacious atmosphere, availability of trolleys, and free door-to-door delivery; product variety pertains to availability of various branded products; and the staff dimension refers to subject knowledge and quick response.

The survey was conducted offline at different supermarkets over a period. The survey questionnaire is distributed to willing customers at random. The questionnaire was narrative, and respondents were given three options for every attribute of each market: "Good," "Bad," and 'Hesitate to Mention'. Each respondent was further asked how confident they were about that option. For example, if a respondent is 70% to 80% sure that a particular supermarket belongs to the set of supermarkets with good amenities, they would select the option for "good" for amenities within the range [7,8]. The respondents were asked only to fill in values for supermarkets they have visited.

The supermarkets considered in this survey are Reliance Fresh, More, Namdhari's Fresh, Big Bazaar, Food World, Star Bazaar, Spar Hypermarket, Metro Cash & Carry, Nilgiris, and D Mart. Data cleaning was performed before analysis. Out of 921 respondents, only 37 entries were found for Food World, Namdhari's Fresh, and Star Bazaar and we have excluded these for further analysis as it may lead to erroneous decisions. The rest of the supermarkets have 121-128 entries. The data is categorized according to supermarkets; for each supermarket-attribute combination, we established the average of lower and upper bound of the intervals for each option. The average of lower bounds and upper bounds of the intervals of each attribute formed our interval for belongingness, non-belongingness, and indeterminacy. We have captured this information in the form of interval-valued neutrosophic soft sets.

8.5.1 Results and Discussions

For easy analysis, Reliance Fresh, More, Big Bazaar, Spar Hypermarket, Metro Cash & Carry, Nilgiris, and D Mart are denoted as q_1, q_2, q_3, q_4, q_5, q_6, and q_7, respectively. It indicates that $Q = \{q_1, q_2, q_3, q_4, q_5, q_6, q_7\}$. The interval-valued neutrosophic soft set G of Q is defined as $G = \{G_i: i = 1, 2, \ldots, 10\}$ where $G_i = G(e_i)$.

Experimental analysis has been carried out to reconnoiter the enactment and characteristic of the proposed model. The experiments were conducted with the help of laptops with the following configuration: Intel Pentium Processor, 8GB RAM, Windows 8 operating system, and MATLAB R2015a. We considered 884 respondents' data after the exclusion of the 37 respondents (due to low entries for the supermarkets Food World, Namdhari's Fresh, and Star Bazaar). We have considered a ten-fold analysis to rank the supermarkets according to customer's choice. Random partition of data into folders are done; each fold contains 89 respondents' data (except the tenth fold, which contains 83 respondents' data). The interval valued neutrosophic soft set G for all ten folds are obtained. We present the interval valued neutrosophic soft set G obtained for the first folder below:

$$G_1 = G(e_1) = \begin{pmatrix} \{[0.6, 0.9], [0.2, 0.8], [0.4, 0.6]\} \\ \{[0.6, 0.9], [0.7, 1.0], [0.4, 0.5]\} \\ \{[0.7, 0.9], [0.8, 1.0], [0.6, 0.9]\} \\ \{[0.9, 1.0], [0.3, 0.5], [0.6, 0.7]\} \\ \{[0.6, 0.9], [0.2, 0.7], [0.4, 0.5]\} \\ \{[0.5, 0.9], [0.4, 0.6], [0.1, 0.8]\} \\ \{[0.5, 0.9], [0.3, 0.5], [0.4, 0.5]\} \end{pmatrix} G_2 = G(e_2) = \begin{pmatrix} \{[0.8, 0.9], [0.3, 0.7], [0.6, 0.9]\} \\ \{[0.7, 0.9], [0.5, 0.9], [0.3, 0.6]\} \\ \{[0.8, 0.9], [0.0, 0.7], [0.5, 0.9]\} \\ \{[0.9, 1.0], [0.4, 0.7], [0.7, 0.8]\} \\ \{[0.5, 0.9], [0.4, 0.7], [0.2, 0.5]\} \\ \{[0.6, 0.8], [0.5, 0.6], [0.5, 0.6]\} \\ \{[0.6, 0.9], [0.3, 0.5], [0.8, 1.0]\} \end{pmatrix}$$

$$G_3 = G(e_3) = \begin{pmatrix} \{[0.5, 0.9], [0.3, 0.8], [0.7, 0.9]\} \\ \{[0.6, 0.9], [0.5, 0.8], [0.5, 0.9]\} \\ \{[0.6, 0.9], [0.3, 0.8], [0.6, 0.9]\} \\ \{[0.6, 0.7], [0.3, 0.5], [0.5, 0.8]\} \\ \{[0.6, 0.8], [0.5, 0.8], [0.3, 0.9]\} \\ \{[0.6, 0.8], [0.5, 0.6], [0.5, 0.8]\} \\ \{[0.7, 0.8], [0.5, 0.8], [0.8, 0.9]\} \end{pmatrix} G_4 = G(e_4) = \begin{pmatrix} \{[0.6, 0.9], [0.1, 0.5], [0.6, 0.9]\} \\ \{[0.6, 0.9], [0.1, 0.5], [0.5, 0.8]\} \\ \{[0.6, 0.9], [0.2, 0.7], [0.6, 0.9]\} \\ \{[0.6, 0.8], [0.3, 0.6], [0.7, 1.0]\} \\ \{[0.7, 0.8], [0.4, 0.7], [0.2, 0.8]\} \\ \{[0.4, 0.8], [0.5, 0.7], [0.3, 0.5]\} \\ \{[0.6, 0.9], [0.1, 0.4], [0.5, 0.6]\} \end{pmatrix}$$

$$G_5 = G(e_5) = \begin{pmatrix} \{[0.6, 0.9], [0.5, 0.8], [0.7, 0.8]\} \\ \{[0.6, 0.9], [0.3, 0.7], [0.6, 0.8]\} \\ \{[0.6, 0.9], [0.3, 0.7], [0.5, 0.8]\} \\ \{[0.6, 0.8], [0.4, 0.6], [0.2, 0.6]\} \\ \{[0.8, 0.9], [0.4, 0.7], [0.3, 0.5]\} \\ \{[0.5, 0.6], [0.5, 0.6], [0.1, 0.6]\} \\ \{[0.6, 0.8], [0.2, 0.7], [0.5, 0.7]\} \end{pmatrix} \quad G_6 = G(e_6) = \begin{pmatrix} \{[0.6, 0.9], [0.1, 0.5], [0.6, 0.7]\} \\ \{[0.6, 0.9], [0.2, 0.6], [0.2, 0.5]\} \\ \{[0.6, 0.9], [0.5, 0.7], [0.6, 0.9]\} \\ \{[0.5, 0.9], [0.3, 0.5], [0.4, 0.6]\} \\ \{[0.7, 0.8], [0.5, 0.7], [0.4, 0.5]\} \\ \{[0.5, 0.9], [0.5, 0.6], [0.6, 0.9]\} \\ \{[0.4, 0.8], [0.1, 0.6], [0.6, 1.0]\} \end{pmatrix}$$

$$G_7 = G(e_7) = \begin{pmatrix} \{[0.7, 1.0], [0.5, 0.7], [0.2, 0.5]\} \\ \{[0.6, 0.9], [0.4, 0.5], [0.5, 0.7]\} \\ \{[0.7, 1.0], [0.6, 0.7], [0.3, 0.6]\} \\ \{[0.6, 0.9], [0.3, 0.9], [0.4, 0.7]\} \\ \{[0.6, 0.9], [0.5, 0.7], [0.4, 0.5]\} \\ \{[0.8, 1.0], [0.2, 0.6], [0.2, 0.6]\} \\ \{[0.6, 0.9], [0.4, 0.7], [0.3, 0.6]\} \end{pmatrix} \quad G_8 = G(e_8) = \begin{pmatrix} \{[0.6, 0.9], [0.5, 0.8], [0.6, 0.8]\} \\ \{[0.6, 0.9], [0.3, 0.6], [0.4, 0.6]\} \\ \{[0.8, 0.9], [0.3, 0.5], [0.5, 0.7]\} \\ \{[0.9, 1.0], [0.4, 0.5], [0.4, 0.5]\} \\ \{[0.9, 1.0], [0.3, 0.5], [0.4, 0.5]\} \\ \{[0.5, 0.7], [0.4, 0.7], [0.3, 0.6]\} \\ \{[0.8, 0.9], [0.4, 0.6], [0.6, 0.9]\} \end{pmatrix}$$

$$G_9 = G(e_9) = \begin{pmatrix} \{[0.7, 0.9], [0.5, 0.8], [0.5, 0.8]\} \\ \{[0.6, 0.9], [0.3, 0.5], [0.5, 0.6]\} \\ \{[0.8, 0.9], [0.2, 0.7], [0.3, 0.6]\} \\ \{[0.5, 0.9], [0.3, 0.6], [0.3, 0.5]\} \\ \{[0.9, 1.0], [0.1, 0.7], [0.3, 0.6]\} \\ \{[0.6, 0.7], [0.5, 0.6], [0.5, 0.7]\} \\ \{[0.7, 0.9], [0.5, 0.7], [0.4, 0.6]\} \end{pmatrix} \quad G_{10} = G(e_{10}) = \begin{pmatrix} \{[0.6, 0.9], [0.5, 0.6], [0.6, 0.7]\} \\ \{[0.6, 0.9], [0.2, 0.7], [0.3, 0.5]\} \\ \{[0.6, 0.9], [0.4, 0.7], [0.6, 0.9]\} \\ \{[0.6, 0.9], [0.4, 0.6], [0.2, 0.6]\} \\ \{[0.5, 0.9], [0.5, 0.7], [0.3, 0.4]\} \\ \{[0.7, 0.9], [0.3, 0.6], [0.6, 0.8]\} \\ \{[0.6, 0.8], [0.4, 0.7], [0.6, 1.0]\} \end{pmatrix}$$

Afterwards, we compute the parametric score of the parameters ei; $1 \leq i \leq 10$ using Equation (8.2). For instance, the parametric scope of the parameters e_1 and e_2 about Reliance Fresh (q_1) is given as $S_{e1}(q_1)$ and $S_{e2}(q_1)$ respectively, where

$$S_{e_1}(q_1) = \left(\frac{(0.9 - 0.6) + (0.6 - 0.4)}{2} \right) \left(1 - \frac{0.2 + 0.8}{2} \right) = 0.125$$

$$S_{e_2}(q_1) = \left(\frac{(0.9 - 0.9) + (0.8 - 0.6)}{2} \right) \left(1 - \frac{0.7 + 0.3}{2} \right) = 0.05$$

Similar computation has been carried out for each parameter and supermarket. The computational steps are omitted for concision. The parametric score of the supermarkets across all parameters is presented in Table 8.4. The total score, $S_t(q)$, of each supermarket is computed using Equation (8.3) presented in Table 8.5. For better visualization, the results obtained for folder one is depicted in Figure 8.2.

From Figure 8.2 in folder one, Metro Cash & Carry is the first choice of customers and Spar Hypermarket is the second. More Supermarket comes in third choice, Nilgiris in fourth, Big Bazar is the fifth, and Reliance Fresh is the sixth choice. The last choice of customers is D Mart. A similar analysis is being carried out for the rest of the folders, and the total score obtained for all the folders is presented in Table 8.6. A graphical view of the total score for all supermarkets across all the folders is depicted in Figure 8.3.

TABLE 8.4

Parameter Score of All Supermarkets

Supermarkets	e_1	e_2	e_3	e_4	e_5	e_6	e_7	e_8	e_9	e_{10}
q_1	0.125	0.05	−0.045	0.0	0.0	0.07	0.2	0.0175	0.0525	0.045
q_2	0.045	0.105	0.017	0.07	0.025	0.24	0.0825	0.1375	0.12	0.1925
q_3	0.005	0.0975	0.0	0.0	0.05	0.0	0.14	0.15	0.165	0.0
q_4	0.18	0.09	−0.0	−0.0825	0.15	0.12	0.08	0.275	0.165	0.175
q_5	0.165	0.1575	0.035	0.1125	0.2025	0.12	0.12	0.3	0.3	0.14
q_6	0.125	0.0675	0.0225	0.08	0.09	−0.0225	0.3	0.0675	0.0225	0.055
q_7	0.15	−0.09	−0.035	0.15	0.055	−0.13	0.135	0.05	0.12	−0.045

TABLE 8.5

Total Score of Supermarkets in Folder 1 Using IVNSS

Supermarkets	e_1	e_2	e_3	e_4	e_5	e_6	e_7	e_8	e_9	e_{10}	$S_t(q)$
q_1	0.125	0.05	−0.045	0.0	0.0	0.07	0.2	0.0175	0.0525	0.045	0.515
q_2	0.045	0.105	0.017	0.07	0.025	0.24	0.0825	0.1375	0.12	0.1925	1.035
q_3	0.005	0.0975	0.0	0.0	0.05	0.0	0.14	0.15	0.165	0.0	0.6075
q_4	0.18	0.09	−0.0	−0.0825	0.15	0.12	0.08	0.275	0.165	0.175	1.1525
q_5	0.165	0.1575	0.035	0.1125	0.2025	0.12	0.12	0.3	0.3	0.14	1.6525
q_6	0.125	0.0675	0.0225	0.08	0.09	−0.0225	0.3	0.0675	0.0225	0.055	0.8075
q_7	0.15	−0.09	−0.035	0.15	0.055	−0.13	0.135	0.05	0.12	−0.045	0.36

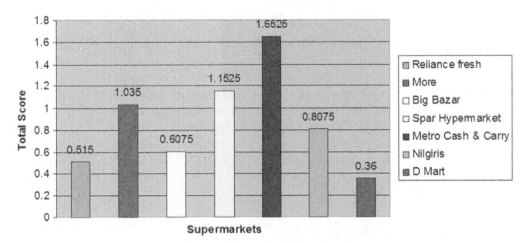

FIGURE 8.2
Graphical view of total score of Supermarket for Folder 1.

90   *Artificial Intelligence and Global Society*

TABLE 8.6

Total Score of Supermarkets for All Folders

Total score (Supermarket)	Folder 1	Folder 2	Folder 3	Folder 4	Folder 5	Folder 6	Folder 7	Folder 8	Folder 9	Folder 10
q_1	0.515	0.625	0.515	0.625	0.515	0.625	0.515	0.625	0.625	0.625
..	1.035	1.2515	1.1525	1.1525	1.1525	1.1525	1.035	1.1525	1.035	1.1525
q_3	0.6075	0.7025	0.6075	0.6075	0.7025	0.515	0.6075	0.7025	0.575	0.6075
..	1.1525	1.3515	1.035	1.035	1.3515	1.3515	1.3515	1.035	1.3515	1.035
q_5	1.6525	1.4575	1.6525	1.6075	1.6525	1.6525	1.6075	1.6075	1.6075	1.6075
..	0.8075	0.6515	0.8075	0.9015	0.7075	0.8075	0.9015	0.8075	0.8075	0.9015
q_7	0.36	0.296	0.36	0.375	0.2950	0.36	0.425	0.295	0.36	0.296

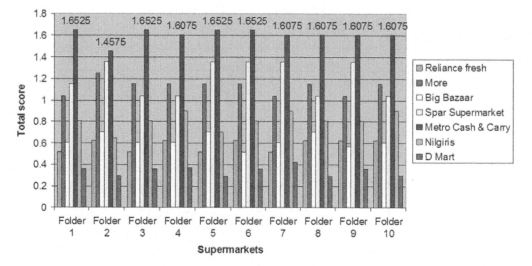

FIGURE 8.3

Graphical view of total score of Supermarket for all Folders.

From Figure 8.3, Metro Cash & Carry is the first choice of customers in all folders. Spar Hypermarket is the second choice in six folders, with More Supermarket in four folders. It means that Spar Hypermarket and More Supermarket are the second and third choices of customers. Nilgiris remains as the fourth choice in all folders. Big Bazaar is the fifth choice in six folders and the sixth in four folders; Reliance Fresh is the fifth choice in four folders and the sixth in six folders. This indicates that Big Bazaar and Reliance Fresh hold the fifth and sixth ranks. Consistently, D Mart remains in seventh place for all folders.

8.5.2 Experimental Comparative Analysis

An experimental comparative study has been carried out to explore the characteristics and performance of the proposed model. The experiments were conducted with the aid of a laptop with the following configurations: Intel Pentium processor, 8GB RAM, Windows 8 operating system, and MATLAB R2015a. We considered 884 respondents' data after the exclusion of 37 responses (due to low entries for Food World, Namdhari's Fresh, and Star Bazaar) for experimental comparative study. We have considered a ten-fold analysis to rank the supermarkets according to customer's choice. Random partition of data into folders have been done. Each fold contains 89 respondents' data (except for the tenth fold, which contains 83 respondents' data). The proposed IVNSS model is compared with four different models of the same kind. The first model for comparison is a Bayesian classification. The second model is a rough association rule-based class prediction (RARCP) attributed to Rao and Mitra [32]. The third model is a fuzzy rough set on two universal set with dynamic clustering due to the radial basis function neural network (FRSTUDA) [23]. The fourth model for the comparative study is the hybrid of soft set and rough set on fuzzy approximation space (SSRSFAS) [18]. The experimental comparative study is carried out by using all the models for every object in every folder. The results for folder one are presented in Table 8.7; the graphical view is depicted in Figure 8.4. A similar analysis is carried out for all the folders using all models and the results are presented in Table 8.8.

The analysis presented in Table 8.8 shows that the model IVNSS gives better results in all folders compared to other models. The results from Bayesian classification are poor compared to RARCP. Also, the model SSRSFAS provides better results than FRSTUDA, and FRSTUDA provides better results than RARCP. The supermarket Metro Cash & Carry (q_5) occupies the first choice in majority of the folders across all models. Again, in the maximum number of folders, the supermarket Nilgiris (q_6) attained fourth place. Similarly, Reliance Fresh (q_1) and Big Bazaar (q_3) remained as the fifth and sixth choice for customers. This is clearly seen from Table 8.8. D Mart (q_7) consistently remained as the last choice (seventh) for customers, but it is difficult to draw a conclusion for the second and third choices. It is observed that the variation of choice is remarkably high in all models except in IVNSS. Spar Hypermarket (q_4) and More (q_2) remained in either second or third choice of customers in all models aside from IVNSS.

8.5.3 Managerial Implications

Business failure and expansion is a worldwide problem. To enhance growth in business throughout the country, some mechanism should be available to study the customer's behavior and their choice in selecting a supermarket. Reports on the Indian retail industry reveals that an expanding middle class, higher income and spending capacity, a growing youth population, rapid urbanization, and several other factors have shaped India's consumption pattern. Due to heightened expectations, escalated competition, and rapid ingress

TABLE 8.7

Total Score of Supermarkets in Folder 1 Using Various Techniques

Supermarkets	IVNSS	Bayesian	RARCP	FRSTUDA	SSRSFAS
q_1	0.515	0.765	0.925	0.825	0.515
q_2	1.035	1.302	1.315	1.425	1.3215
q_3	0.6075	0.525	0.735	0.535	0.945
q_4	1.1525	1.4215	1.125	1.0635	1.5325
q_5	1.6525	1.025	1.525	1.5075	1.6275
q_6	0.8075	0.975	0.905	0.765	0.745
q_7	0.36	0.415	0.55	0.47	0.365

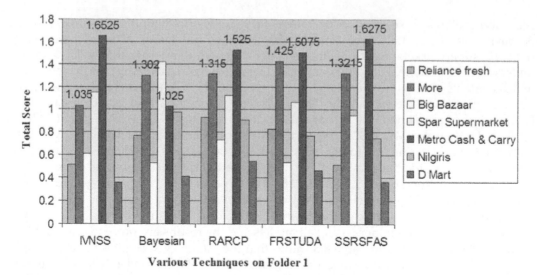

FIGURE 8.4

Graphical view of total score of Supermarket by various techniques in Folder 1.

TABLE 8.8

Choice of Supermarkets across All Folders Using Various Techniques

Supermarkets	IVNSS	Bayesian	RARCP	FRSTUDA	SSRSFAS
q_1	5th (4)6th (6)	5th (3)6th (7)	5th (2)6th (8)	4th (1) 5th (5) 6th (4)	5th (8)6th (2)
q_2	2nd (4) 3rd (6)	2nd (2)3rd (8)	2nd (3) 3rd (6) 4th (1)	3rd (7)4th (3)	3rd (8)4th (2)
q_3	5th (6)6th (4)	4th (4)–5th (5) 6th (1)	5th (8)6th (2)	5th (4)6th (6)	5th (2)6th (8)
q_4	2nd (6) 3rd (4)	1st (3)–2nd (6) 3rd (1)	1st (4) 2nd (5) 3rd (1)	1st (2)2nd (8)	1st (3)2nd (7)
q_5	1st (10)	1st (7) 2nd (2) 3rd (1)	1st (6) 2nd (2) 3rd (2)	1st (8)2nd (2)	1st (7)2nd (3)
q_6	4th (10)	4th (6) 5th (2) 6th (2)	3rd (1)4th (9)	3rd (3)4th (6) 5th (1)	3rd (2)4th (8)
q_7	7th (10)	7th (10)	7th (10)	7th (10)	7th (10)

of new business concepts and formats, supermarkets are finding it difficult to keep their customers and remain profitable. The costs associated with this problem have led to special disclosure responsibilities for both management and auditors. Ranking of supermarkets based on customer's choice is a problematic issue since the development of a cause-and-effect relationship between many attributes based on several factors. Many approaches have been proposed for dealing with this type of problem; however, these approaches have limitations, and the interval valued neutrosophic soft set is believed to provide better managerial implications.

8.6 Conclusion

Customer satisfaction has a significant impact on supermarket sales. Thus, it is important to study how satisfied the customers are. It must be noted, however, that satisfaction is a subjective parameter that involves uncertainty and neutral thought. Furthermore, customer satisfaction is affected by location, staff, quality of goods, etc. This paper presents the application of interval valued neutrosophic soft sets to this multi-criteria decision analysis problem. The interval valued neutrosophic soft set incorporates factors specific to this problem (neutral thought and uncertainty) and multiple attributes associated with the supermarket into one framework. We have carried out an empirical study on supermarkets in Bangalore, India and the analysis shows that Metro cash & Carry is the first choice of customers, while Spar Hypermarket and More Supermarket remain in the second and third positions. D Mart was consistently the last choice. The application of interval valued neutrosophic soft set to this problem results in stability across all folds of cross-validation. Therefore, this framework is suitable for customer choice prediction in supermarkets. The main objective of this paper is to provide the concept application of interval-valued neutrosophic soft set to a larger crowd. Further research is planned to identify the chief factors affecting customer's choice.

References

1. Greco, S., Matarazzo, B., & Slowinski, R., "Rough sets theory for multi-criteria decision analysis," *European Journal of Operational Research*, vol. 129, no. 1, pp. 1–47, 2001.
2. Marler, R. T., & Arora, J. S., "The weighted sum method for multi-objective optimization: new insights," *Structural and Multidisciplinary Optimization*, vol. 41, no. 6, pp. 853–862, 2010.
3. Marler, R. T., & Arora, J. S., "Survey of multi-objective optimization methods for engineering," *Structural and Multidisciplinary Optimization*, vol. 26, no. 6, pp. 369–395, 2004.
4. Roy, B. "Decision-aid and decision-making," *European Journal of Operational Research*, vol. 45, no. 2-3, pp. 324–331, 1990.
5. Govindan, K., & Jepsen, M. B., "ELECTRE: A comprehensive literature review on methodologies and applications," *European Journal of Operational Research*, vol. 250, no. 1, pp. 1–29, 2016.
6. Behzadian, M., Kazemzadeh, R. B., Albadvi, A., & Aghdasi, M., "PROMETHEE: A comprehensive literature review on methodologies and applications," *European Journal of Operational Research*, vol. 200, no. 1, pp. 198–215, 2010.
7. Zhaoxu, S., & Min, H., "Multi-criteria decision making based on PROMETHEE method," *International Conference on Computing, Control and Industrial Engineering*, IEEE, Vol. 1, pp. 416–418, 2010.
8. Brans, J. P., "The space of freedom of the decision-maker modeling the human brain. European Journal of Operational Research, vol. 92, no. 3, pp. 593–602, 1996.
9. Brans, J. P., & Mareschal, B., The PROMETHEE VI procedure: how to differentiate hard from soft multi-criteria problems," *Journal of Decision Systems*, vol. 4, no. 3, pp. 213–223, 1995.
10. Brans, J. P., & Vincke, P., "A preference ranking organization method: (The PROMETHEE method for multiple criteria decision making)," *Management Science*, vol. 31, no. 6, p. 647656, 1985.
11. Zadeh, L. A., "Information and control," *Fuzzy Sets*, vol. 8, no. 3, pp. 338–353, 1965.

12. Atanassov, K. T., "Intuitionistic fuzzy sets," *Fuzzy Sets and Systems*, vol. 20, no. 1, pp. 87–96, 1986.
13. Pawlak, Z., "Rough sets," *International Journal of Parallel Programming*, vol. 11, no. 5, pp. 341–356, 1982.
14. Acharjya, D. P., & Tripathy, B. K., "Rough sets on fuzzy approximation spaces and applications to distributed knowledge systems," *International Journal of Artificial Intelligence and Soft Computing*, vol. 1, no. 1, pp. 1–14, 2008.
15. Acharjya, D. P., & Tripathy, B. K., "Rough sets on intuitionistic fuzzy approximation spaces and knowledge representation," *International Journal of Artificial Intelligence and Computational Research*, vol. 1, no. 1, pp. 29–36, 2009.
16. Dubois, D., & Prade, H., "Rough fuzzy sets and fuzzy rough sets," *International Journal of General System*, vol. 17, no. 23, pp. 191–209, 1990.
17. Liu, G., "Rough set theory based on two universal sets and its applications," *Knowledge Based Systems*, vol. 23, no. 2, pp. 110–115, 2010.
18. Das, T. K., & Acharjya, D. P., "A decision making model using soft set and rough set on fuzzy approximation spaces," *International Journal of Intelligent Systems Technologies and Applications*, vol. 13, no. 3, pp. 170–186, 2014.
19. Acharjya, D., & Anitha, A., "A comparative study of statistical and rough computing models in predictive data analysis," *International Journal of Ambient Computing and Intelligence*, vol. 8, no. 2, pp. 32–51, 2017.
20. Das, T. K., Acharjya, D. P., & Patra, M. R., "Multi criterion decision making using intuitionistic fuzzy rough set on two universal sets," *International Journal of Intelligent Systems and Applications*, vol. 7, no. 4, pp. 26–33, 2015.
21. Acharjya, D. P., "Rough set on two universal sets and knowledge representation." In: B. Issac & N. Israr (eds) Case Studies in Intelligent Computing: Achievements and Trends, CRC Press, USA, pp. 79–107, 2014.
22. Smarandache, F., "Neutrosophic set-a generalization of the intuitionistic fuzzy set," *International Journal of Pure and Applied Mathematics*, vol. 24, no. 3, pp. 287–297, 2005.
23. Anitha, A., & Acharjya, D. P., "Customer choice of supermarkets using fuzzy rough set on two universal sets and radial basis function neural network," *International Journal of Intelligent Information Technologies*, vol. 12, no. 3, pp. 20–37, 2016.
24. H. Wang, F. Smarandache, R. Sunderraman, and Y. Q. Zhang, Interval Neutrosophic Sets and Logic: Theory and Applications in Computing, Hexis, Arizona, pp. 21–38, 2005.
25. Mukherjee A., "Interval-valued neutrosophic soft sets." In: Generalized Rough Sets. Studies in Fuzziness and Soft Computing, Springer, New Delhi, Vol 324, pp. 89–109, 2015.
26. Wang, H., Smarandache, F., Zhang, Y., & Sunderraman, R., "Single valued neutrosophic sets," *Review of the Air Force Academy*, vol. 1, pp. 10–14, 2010.
27. Molodtsov, D., "Soft set theory first results," *Computers & Mathematics with Applications*, vol. 37, no. 4-5, pp. 19–31, 1999.
28. Maji, P. K., Roy, A. R., & Biswas, R., "An application of soft sets in a decision making problem," *Computers & Mathematics with Applications*, vol. 44, no. 8-9, pp. 1077–1083, 2002.
29. Maji, P. K., "Neutrosophic soft set," *Annals of Fuzzy Mathematics and Informatics*, vol. 5, no. 1, pp. 157–168, 2013.
30. Gupta, A., Mohammad, A., Syed, A., & Halgamuge, M. N., "A comparative study of classification algorithms using data mining: Crime and accidents in Denver city the USA," *International Journal of Advanced Computer Science and Applications*, vol. 7, no. 7, pp. 374–381, 2016.
31. Deb, R., & Liew, A. W. C., "Incorrect attribute value detection for traffic accident data." In *Proceedings of IEEE International Joint Conference on Neural Networks*, pp. 1–7, 2015.
32. Rao, D. J., & Mitra, P., "A rough association rule based approach for class prediction with missing attribute values." In *Proceedings of 2nd Indian International Conference on Artificial Intelligence*, Pune, India, pp. 2420–2431, 2005.

9

Artificial Intelligence in Healthcare

Ajay Kumar Yadav and Rajesh Mamilla

CONTENTS

9.1 Introduction

Artificial intelligence is making knowledgeable machines by collecting data from several sources, learning from them, and creating intuitive decision-making capacities. Through the AI paradigm, we are outsourcing human-based capabilities to machines. In Industry 4.0, we have seen digitization, automation, and robotic process in healthcare. With the use of Internet of Things (IOT) devices, healthcare professionals could get patient information and use these data to make decisions specific to the patient. IOT is any electronic device that transmits data to the internet without human interventions—they are generally goal-oriented task devices that collect information and transmit these to the server to extract business processing information.

For example, smartwatches can collect data regarding pulse rate, blood pressure, heart rate, and step counts of a person. These data can be used by healthcare professionals to analyze the patient's problem (psychological disorder, sleep, or stress problems). By using machine learning algorithms, we are training the machines with several data sets, analyzing the patterns of data, and giving suggestions. With the data collected from different patients, machine learning could help find patterns in the patient's disease—its root cause and the impact of its symptoms. In Industry 5.0, the collaborative effort of man and machines, with the use of artificial intelligence technologies, would help give suitable solutions for specific patients. Humans are creative people, so the focus of future human labor would be on the creative side, while repetitive tasks will be given to a robot. Doctors are expected to exercise their analytical skills rather than prescribing drugs on patient symptoms. Healthcare professionals would benefit from AI machine learning technology as they make better decisions with several options. These machines can also suggest proper precautions the patients can take in the future. Moreover, error on machine learning tools are less than human professionals. The future of healthcare and insurance is an AI-based customizable solution for patients. Medical professionals can use the AIML to know the pattern of a child psychological disorder, people's writing patterns (left- or right-handedness), patient's dietary solution, therapy, and medications. For example, the sleeping habit of a person can be analyzed through mobile phones, giving access to the timing and trends of that person's sleeping pattern.

The healthcare insurance industry will have major changes in their premium and policy plans with the customized solutions. Currently, basic healthcare insurance policies rely on the average age group and package premiums are quoted through the analysis of risks based on the history of groups of people. For example, health insurance policies consider age as a major criteria for the premium (younger people pay less premium than older ones). With the use of customer-specific biodata, insurance companies can come up with a proper risk assessment with their customer's daily habits—AI and machine learning could suggest risk predictions of customers. The future of the Insurance industry in healthcare would consist of less customer interactions and more technology-oriented decisive solutions. There would be more personalized and customized insurance plans available to the public. The risk assessment quantifiable would be automated by analyzing the customer data collected through several IOT devices and mobile app interactions with the big data analytics system of the insurance company. The data collected by Growth Enabler in Figure 9.1 under market overview (Gartner/World bank) shows that IOT devices have already surpassed human population in 2017, and by 2020, there will be more than 20 billion IOT devices.

Some of the reasons for the rapid growth of IOT devices are:

- Fast computing power;
- Small size of IOT devices;
- IOT devices are made with user suggestive assistance that gives fast feedback to

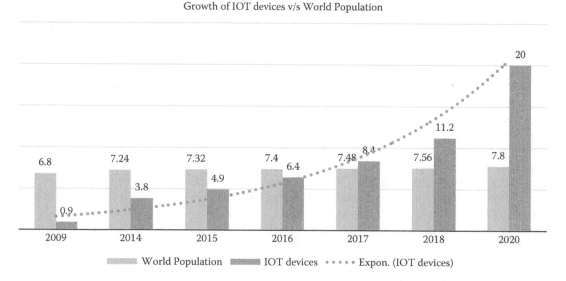

Growth of IOT devices v/s World Population

■■■ World Population   ■■■ IOT devices   •••• Expon. (IOT devices)

FIGURE 9.1
Market overview (number in billion).

humans (calories burned through step count), health monitor (blood pressure, heart rate);

- Efficient patient care management through real-time data tracking; and
- Reduced human errors (IOT devices are automated with input and output functions, so no human interventions are needed, and patient reports error-free which provides precise decisions for doctors).

Moore's Law states that the number of transistors on integrated circuits doubles approximately every two years. Thus, the technological progress has been growing exponentially rather than linearly (Figure 9.2).

9.2 Technological Changes that Impact Human Lifestyle Changes

Until recently, we have viewed the impact of technological changes as linear, as they produce more efficient outputs and never really replace humans. However, with the advance in AI and machine learning algorithms, there can be a crucial shift in the type of jobs humans and machines are assumed to take. In terms of error, for several job categories, machine and automated work has done better (healthcare). For example, machines taking a blood sample of patients, putting the patient code, and then automating the process of

FIGURE 9.2
Moore's Law: Technological progress in integrated circuits with transistor count.

blood test would show better precision, whereas human errors like incorrectly encoding the patient name or code can happen. More powerful computers at a lower price create more impact on human lifestyle changes. The following graph shows the amount of power consumers could purchase for a price of $1,000. It is especially insightful if one wants to understand how technological progress matters as a driver of social change (Figure 9.3).

With the increase of processing power, the price for electronic items has dropped; other consumption needs such as college tuition fees and healthcare have increased over time. The graph shows the changes in the prices of computers relative to other consumer goods (Figure 9.4).

People who use the internet are expected to triple from 2015 to 2022, hitting 6 billion. 90% of the human population, ages six and above, will be online by 2030 as shown in Table 9.1.

9.3 Data Generation Trends

In over five years, around 95% of data has been created in the world, and an enormous amount of data is currently generated due to the rise of several IOT devices and machine learning (Figures 9.5 and 9.6).

9.4 Data Generation by AI in Healthcare

The machine learning algorithm uses a lot of data to train machines to think. These are comprised of several types of data and come from various sources (human-generated data and from IOT devices). Business analytics and ML algorithm are used in the

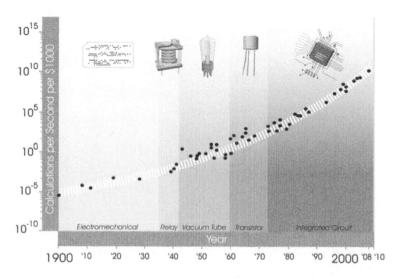

FIGURE 9.3
Exponential growth of computing in 110 years.

Price changes in consumer goods and services in the USA

Price change in consumer goods and services in the USA, measured as the percentage change since 1997. Data is measured based on the reported consumer price index (CPI) for national average urban consumer prices.

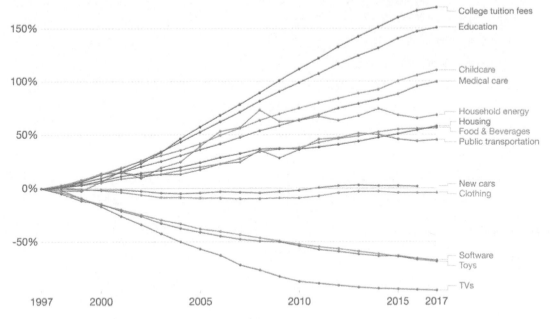

FIGURE 9.4
Price changes in consumer goods and services in the USA.

TABLE 9.1

Approximate Percentage of People Connected to the Internet

Country	Population (Billion)	Percentage of People Connected
China	1.4	63%
India	1.3	54%
United States	0.32	90%
Indonesia	0.27	64%
Brazil	0.211	67%
Pakistan	0.216	36%
Nigeria	0.2	66%
Bangladesh	0.16	62%
Russia	0.14	79%
Mexico	0.12	76%

background of data processing to find hidden patterns from data that will add value to organizations. AI can be used to identify medical fraud (whether the patient is really sick or not). Since we get the data from several IOT sources and customer habits, prediction of sickness can be estimated by AI tools. 5G technology would transfer data 100 times faster compared to current cellular network speed. The rapid data transmission from client to

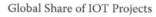

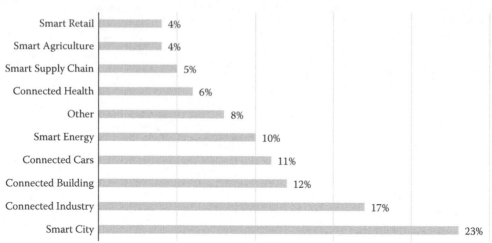

FIGURE 9.5
Large-scale use of Internet of Things (IoT).

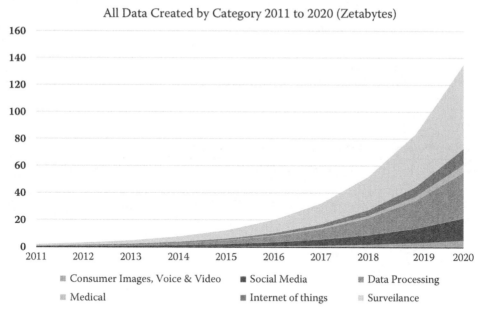

FIGURE 9.6
Data created from 2011–2020.

server would help AI to process the task quicker. 5G would help take more real-time decisions as the algorithm can be optimized with more real-time data to give instantaneous suggestions to the user. With an increase in the number of sensors that collects data from human, the business healthcare sector can segregate people by health risk and formulate common policy.

9.5 Conclusion

The responsible use of artificial intelligence technology in the healthcare industry would be beneficial to both hospitals and patients. Doctors can get help to give optimal solutions with several options suggested by AI. The drug success rate on patients can be predicted by AI solutions. The insurance company can get a prediction of health risks on patients and inform them beforehand to do a health checkup and take required medications to prevent diseases. The dark side of AI technology would be the possibility of fake data created by users shared with different third-party consumers (hospital or insurance companies) that could impact their business, so a more effective policy and data usage by the AI and machine learning technologies [1–9] are suggested.

Suggested Reading

Online Documents

1. "AI and robotics are transforming healthcare," *PWC*, accessed December 23, 2019, https://www.pwc.com/gx/en/industries/healthcare/publications/ai-robotics-new-health/transforming-healthcare.html.
2. Martin, R., "10 ways artificial intelligence is transforming healthcare," *Healthcare*, accessed December 22, 2019. https://igniteoutsourcing.com/healthcare/artificial-intelligence-in-healthcare.
3. Svetlana, Yurkevich, "How IoT is changing health insurance," eliNext, accessed December 22, 2019, https://www.elinext.com/industries/healthcare/trends/how-iot-disrupts-health-insurance.
4. Best, J., "VR, AR, and the NHS: how virtual and augmented reality will change healthcare," *Can Technology Save the NHS*, accessed December 20, 2019, https://www.zdnet.com/article/vr-ar-and-the-nhs-how-virtual-and-augmented-reality-will-change-healthcare.
5. Roser, M. and Ritchie, H., "Technological progress," OurWorldInData.org, accessed December 15, 2019, https://ourworldindata.org/technological-progress.
6. Morgan, S., "Humans on the internet will triple from 2015 to 2022 and hit 6 billion," *Cybercrime Magazine*, accessed December 10, 2019, https://cybersecurityventures.com/how-many-internet-users-will-the-world-have-in-2022-and-in-2030.
7. "The IoT data explosion: how big is the IoT data market," *Priceonomics*, accessed December 10, 2019, https://priceonomics.com/the-iot-data-explosion-how-big-is-the-iot-data.
8. Floyer, D., "The vital role of edge computing in the internet of things," *Wikibon*, accessed December 10, 2019, https://wikibon.com/the-vital-role-of-edge-computing-in-the-internet-of-things.
9. Marr, B., "How much data do we create every day? The mind-blowing stats everyone should read," *Forbes*, accessed December 10, 2019, https://www.forbes.com/sites/bernardmarr/2018/05/21/how-much-data-do-we-create-every-day-the-mind-blowing-stats-everyone-should-read.

10

Computer-Aided Cataract Detection Using MLP and SVM

Simran Agarwal, Manish Kumar, Sunil Kumar Jangir, and
Chandraprakash Sharma

CONTENTS

10.1 Introduction

The eye is a significant organ in the human body. It includes interconnected subsystems like the lens, iris, retina, cornea, and optic nerve. There are many ocular disorders associated with different parts of the eye such as glaucoma, macular degeneration due to trachoma and aging, hereditary myopia, retinitis pigmentosa, and diabetic retinopathy but patients are not usually conscious of their progress. An ophthalmologist or optometrist detects eye disease through slit-lamp (retinal examination) or visual acuity checks after inspecting the pupil. Visual acuity tests are done using a chart or display device, interpreting a series of progressively smaller letters. Using an intense light line, an ophthalmologist can examine the eye under magnification. During retinal evaluation, the pupil is dilated with drops enlarging the lens to test eye motions and pupil response. These methods of screening require costly medical equipment that only an experienced ophthalmologist can use. Manual methods are also time-consuming and subjective to the experience of the ophthalmologist. In the past few years, the researcher has made so many attempts to detect eye disorders automatically. According to a WHO survey, the world's estimated number of visually impaired people is 285 million — 39 million are blind and 246 million have damaged vision; 33% of visual impairment cases and 51% of blindness cases are caused by cataracts (Shaheen & Tariq, 2019).

For low- and middle-income countries, the incidence of cataracts is higher due to decreased spending on health. Age is the biggest risk factor for cataract development. In developing countries, more than 90% of these blind people live. A cataract is characterized as an intraocular clouding of the lens that causes vision impairment; it is the most common cause of blindness. The longer the cataract of a patient is left untreated, the more severe the vision impairment becomes. This happens when the protein within the lens clumps together with age. The protein builds up when the older cells compact into the center of the lens, causing a blurred retina image. It has three main forms that depend on the position and shape of the cataract: nuclear cataract, cortical cataract, and posterior subcapsular cataract. Due to aging, the most commonly occurring type of cataract is Nuclear Cataract (NC). It is caused by the hardening and yellowing of the middle portion of the lens nucleus. In the lens cortex, Cortical Cataract (CC) appear in the form of white wedged-shaped and radially oriented opacities that function from the lens' outer edge towards the middle in a spoken-like manner. Posterior Subcapsular Cataract (PSC) occurs under the capsule of the lens like small crumbs of bread or sand grains. This usually happens in patients with diabetes or are taking steroids (Michael & Bron, 2011).

Digital Image Processing (DIP) techniques are the promising solution, processing an image according to the user's software. Generating outputs using image processing techniques enables one to perform image enhancement, segmentation, evaluation, and diagnosis, etc. (Gautam, Jangir, Kumar, & Sharma, n.d.; Kumar & Mishra, 2017). Modern DIP techniques have enabled automated diagnosis and assisted in eye-related diagnostic process through machine learning, extraction, and identification of crucial features from an eye image (Cao, Li, Zhang, Zhang, & Xu, 2020) (e.g., cataract detection can be accomplished by identifying clouding in eye lens protein structure by examining various image mapping parameters). Image processing and heuristic tools like neural networks and deep learning are implemented not only for classification or prediction but also for diagnostic purposes (Kumar et al., 2020). In addition, implementing an automatic identification system can help a physician identify or narrow down the diagnosis and medication accordingly. Not only will it improve the accuracy of the diagnosis, but also save patients time and money. Automatic cataract detection and diagnosis alleviates the stress for doctors and ophthalmologists. It also provides an objective way of measuring cataract incidence and helps reduce vision loss through prompt and reliable diagnosis.

The contribution of this chapter can be summarized as follows: a learning-based approach for cataract classification is implemented through two basic learning models — MLP and SVM — that are investigated for basic classification building. Empirical studies on real-world data sets are presented, showing that the best performance of an ensemble classifier can achieve significant accuracy in cataract detection classification levels (binary classification). The experiments also show that the group learning method is superior to single learning model. We conclude that based on fundus image analysis, our experimental study will serve as an important guide for the diagnosis of cataract

The layout of this chapter is as follows: related work is discussed in Section 10.2. Section 10.3 describes the details of the implemented fundus image classification learning approach. Section 10.4 reports the experiment and evaluation results. The chapter is concluded in Section 10.5.

10.2 Literature Review

Cataracts are usually diagnosed by ophthalmologists by directly using a slit-lamp microscope or clinicians by measuring the presence and extent of the cataract, contrasting its appearance in slit-lamp photos to a collection of standard reference photographs. These photographs come with cataract grading protocols such as the Lens Opacities Classification System III (LOCS III) and the cataract grading system in Wisconsin. The work done in the past by many authors in the field to detect cataract apply modern ML and deep learning methodologies. They have given better results compared to traditional methods being used. The machine learning techniques such as random forest, naïve Bayes, and feature selection are applied as data mining for the prediction of cataract in the patient (Zhang et al., 2019). Similarly, improved Haar wavelets are introduced to classify cataracts and improve cataract identification accuracy up to 95% (Cao et al., 2020). Currently, various heuristic techniques are available that can be applied for various engineering or medical purposes (Kumar & Mishra, 2020). Various intelligent techniques are available today, which can be applied for cataract detection, and a few of them are listed in Table 10.1. It also presents a comparative study of the work done by different authors in different domains to obtain better results.

Analyzing various results from different systems already designed provides an effective result with an accuracy of 90-96%.

10.3 Background

Manual detection and treatment can prevent cataract complications. Sometimes, the doctor's anxiety and workload also affect disease identification. Doctors nowadays cannot carry out a full analysis of a patient as various diseases are so widespread. Manual methods are time-taking and subjective, grounded on the ophthalmologist's experience. People living in rural areas face a lot of problems due to doctor and equipment availability. The diagnosis of requires highly skilled technicians. However, available automated machines are expensive, difficult to install, and ultimately affects the treatment of poor people.

Available conventional methodologies fail because they require heavy training, are tedious, and need highly skilled professionals to diagnose. The use of these techniques requires economic effort exceedingly difficult to maintain. Fortunately, rapid automated diagnostic tests for cataract is available through image processing and ML. These techniques are comparatively easy to implement, tests take less time compared to conventional techniques, and can assist physicians in detecting or verifying the stages or severity of the cataract. In fact, such algorithms can even be developed as mobile or computer application.

10.4 Requirement Analysis

The problem with the existing system for detecting cataract (manual diagnosis) needs to be addressed through an automated system. There was a greater need to design a system

TABLE 10.1

Study of Different Methodologies Used for the Detection of Cataracts

S. No	Author and Year	Methodologies Implemented	Results and Discussions
1	(Dixit, Pathak, Raj, Naveen, & Satpute, 2018)	Gaussian filtering, Fuzzy Logic, Circular Hough Transform	Results came out with 96.44% accuracy.
2	(Yang et al., 2016)	Ensemble learning, SVM, Neural network	Automated way turns out to be cheap, simple, and reliable.
3	(Shaheen & Tariq, 2019)	Slit-lamp, Retro-illumination, Retinal, Digital, and Ultrasonic Nakagami images	Automated way of cataract detection turns out to be cheap, simple, and reliable.
4	(Ran, Niu, He, Zhang, & Song, 2018)	Deep Convolutional Neural Network (DCNN), Random Forests (RF)	Results came out with 90.69% average detection accuracy.Features of the datasets were extracted automatically
5	(Rana & Galib, 2018)	Android Studio, SDK, NDK, and OpenCV	Provides self-screening cataract mobile application.Enables early cataract detection using a smartphone with a camera and a flash
6	(Li et al., 2018)	Deep-learning	Results came out with 94.91% for detecting and grading cataracts.
7	(Agarwal, Gupta, Vashisht, Sharma, & Sharma, 2019)	Machine Learning, Image Processing, SVM, KNN	Helps detecting cataract by user interactive method
8	(Zhang & He, 2019)	SVM, Fully Connected Neural Network (FCNN), Residual Network (ResNet18), GLCM	Results came out with 92.66% accuracy of six-level grading on average age and 94.75% accuracy on four-level grading of cataract.
9	(Pratap & Kokil, 2019)	CNN, SVM	The classification accuracy obtained was 92.91%.
10	(Zhang et al., 2019)	Random Forest (RF), Naïve Bayesian (NB), SMOTE (synthetic minority oversampling technique)	The accuracy obtained was over 65%.A webserver was developed to assist doctors.
11	(Cao et al., 2020)	Haar wavelet, Discrete cosine transformation (DCT)	Results came out with 94.83% and 85.98% accuracy for two-class classification and four-class classification, respectively.
12	(Xiong, He, Niu, Zhang, & Song, 2018)	GLCM, ResNet, SVM	Results came out with 91.5% average detection accuracy.
14	(Rayan, Alfonse, & Salem, 2018)	ANN, SVM, CNN	Shows an overview of the challenges and techniques involved in smart health.

that are cost-effective and could generate results with higher accuracies. The automation system for detecting cataract became a major requirement for resource-scarce areas. Designing of the automation system does not require manual labor, is not time-consuming as well, and enables a machine to work with greater efficiency to generate results with higher accuracy.

10.5 Solutions and Recommendations

Considering the failures in the results obtained from the existing system, designing a system that operates on modern methodologies to find better results becomes a requirement. The automated system should be designed accurately to study the image given as input and generate corresponding results. The working of the automated systems should take place systematically.

In designing various automated systems to detect cataracts in the eye, several machine learning algorithms have been tested based on the accuracy of their prediction. Computer-Aided Diagnosis, SVM, and MLP algorithms have been designed to get results with higher accuracy. ML algorithms generated effective results and worked very efficiently with the datasets containing many training images.

10.6 Methodologies

In this work, an MLP and SVM Model-based algorithm is used to detect cataracts from the American origin dataset taken as input. The cataract identification block diagram is shown in Figure 10.1. It contains three parts: pre-processing, extraction of features, and classification. During the acquisition of a digital cataract image, noise can be

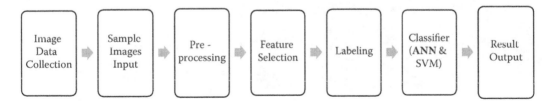

FIGURE 10.1
Block diagram of cataract detection.

TABLE 10.2

Parameters of Implemented Classifier

Sl No.	Methodology	Parameters
1	MLP (Multilayer Perceptron)	Iterations = 1,000
		Training Algorithm = Levenberg-Marquardt
		Performance: Mean squared error
		Number of inputs = 7
		Number of hidden layers = 10
		Number of output layer = 1
		Number of outputs = 1
2	SVM (Support Vector Machine)	Kernel function
		Radial basis function

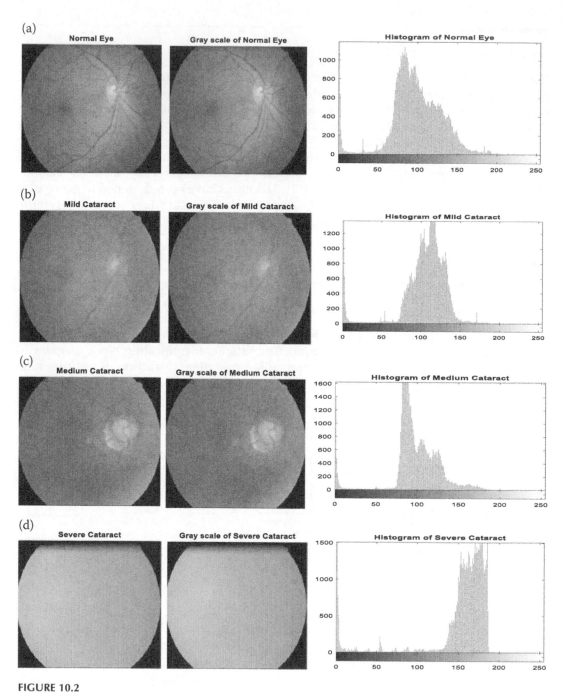

FIGURE 10.2

The fundus images with and without different levels of cataract and their histogram. (a) normal, (b) mild, (c) medium, and (d) severe.

TABLE 10.3

Extracted Features for Classification of Cataracts

Image	Mean (F1)	Standard Deviation (F2)	Contrast (F3)	Energy (F4)	Homogeneity (F5)	Entropy (F6)	Variance (F7)	Labeled Data
1.	47.9946	50.5466	0.2348	0.3046	0.9530	4.4588	0.2240	0
2.	58.4756	61.2941	0.3815	0.3700	0.9585	3.8474	0.2500	1
3.	46.4854	47.8612	0.2646	0.3164	0.9447	4.2940	0.2298	0
4.	69.1099	68.9725	0.5913	0.3522	0.9396	4.4074	0.1109	0
5.	77.0293	76.8491	0.6022	0.3376	0.9506	4.5267	0.0804	0
6.	53.3877	55.6906	0.2686	0.4495	0.9743	3.6290	0.2500	1
7.	52.5288	55.9217	0.2953	0.3279	0.9567	4.1057	0.2500	1
8.	66.2808	69.6939	0.4938	0.3271	0.9495	4.0990	0.2500	0
9.	36.9358	39.4212	0.1698	0.3991	0.9770	3.8379	0.2500	1
10.	48.9561	52.7651	0.2862	0.3286	0.9649	4.2052	0.2499	1
11.	29.7461	33.1445	0.1492	0.3517	0.9675	4.4080	0.2154	0
12.	58.9331	59.7155	0.4192	0.3325	0.9524	4.2422	0.2262	0
13.	51.6323	53.2643	0.4135	0.2983	0.9386	4.4240	0.1911	0
14.	46.7285	50.7876	0.2162	0.3340	0.9635	4.1984	0.2499	1
15.	51.8279	57.6985	0.5639	0.3081	0.9565	4.3947	0.2498	1
16.	51.5552	56.1945	0.4873	0.3144	0.9580	4.3411	0.2500	1
17.	46.1948	53.7191	0.4933	0.2933	0.9516	4.4934	0.2499	1
18.	30.7446	33.2586	0.1658	0.3527	0.9753	3.8640	0.2500	1
19.	51.4194	54.2422	0.3873	0.3008	0.9480	4.6186	0.1828	0
20.	59.0613	62.6429	0.4026	0.3434	0.9530	4.0810	0.2499	0
21.	63.2292	66.9519	0.4732	0.3199	0.9449	4.1140	0.2500	0
22.	48.8735	52.8796	0.2807	0.3164	0.9477	4.1463	0.2499	0
23.	48.5955	52.1298	0.3159	0.3204	0.9456	4.0918	0.2500	0
24.	39.1533	44.6495	0.3109	0.3144	0.9662	4.3002	0.2499	1
25.	24.1890	28.9054	0.1895	0.4625	0.9729	4.3957	0.2394	1
26.	48.5029	52.5265	0.2711	0.3217	0.9552	4.1409	0.2499	0
27.	79.1040	81.9029	0.8022	0.3620	0.9554	3.5374	0.2498	1
28.	49.7546	51.9362	0.3119	0.3126	0.9628	4.4290	0.2193	1
29.	48.0291	48.3915	0.2862	0.3373	0.9675	4.1448	0.1802	1
30.	47.1941	51.0052	0.2429	0.3275	0.9571	4.1603	0.2499	0
31.	42.9854	44.7263	0.2406	0.3184	0.9537	4.3509	0.2265	0
32.	74.3198	74.0852	0.6515	0.4208	0.9648	3.7692	0.2023	1
33.	59.1909	62.1393	0.3512	0.3478	0.9626	3.9581	0.2500	1
34.	57.9490	60.9588	0.4696	0.3498	0.9561	4.0288	0.2500	0
35.	51.8713	54.5469	0.4011	0.2931	0.9387	4.5963	0.2083	0
36.	68.4751	68.6762	0.4757	0.3230	0.9554	4.5405	0.1935	1
37.	49.6135	52.5776	0.3915	0.2930	0.9524	4.6452	0.2003	1
38.	70.6248	74.0008	0.5225	0.3300	0.9480	4.0869	0.2500	0
39.	61.9792	65.5886	0.4792	0.3135	0.9402	4.1618	0.2500	0
40.	58.0586	58.2014	0.3585	0.4162	0.9664	3.9572	0.2049	1

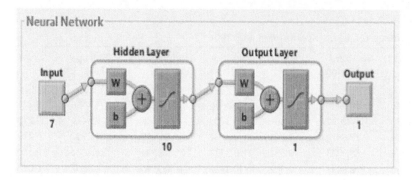

FIGURE 10.3
Implemented MLP network for cataract detection.

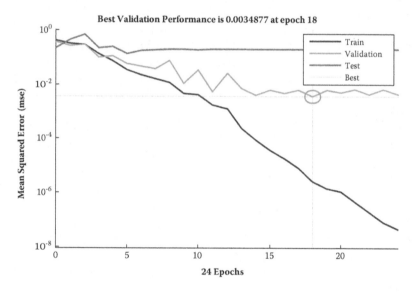

FIGURE 10.4
Performance plot of implemented feedforward neural network.

systematically introduced into images to improve features such as image enhancement and noise reduction. After pre-processing, the size of each image is reduced to 64 × 64 and changed into greyscale to reduce computational time.

Sample images are taken in two categories (i.e. normal eye and cataract eye) that are considered as inputs. After the pre-processing, image features such as mean, standard deviation, contrast, entropy, homogeneity, energy, and variance are extracted and further applied as a classifier input. Target data is labeled as '0' for normal eye and '1' for cataract eye. In this chapter, these image features are given as inputs to the MLP and SVM classifiers.

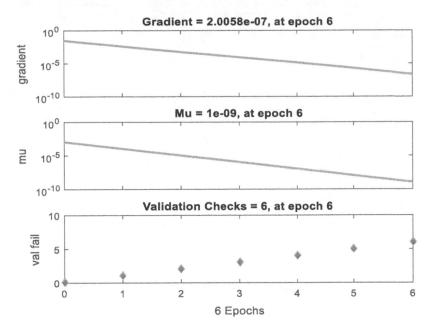

FIGURE 10.5
Training state plot of implemented feedforward neural network.

10.7 Results and Discussion

The MATLAB software environment and a computer with specification of Intel ® Pentium (R) CPU 3825U @1.90 GHz, 4 GB installed Random Access Memory (RAM) is used to perform all the experimental task. In classifying data using MLP classifier, 80% is taken for training and 20% is taken for testing. The parameters considered for the classification of data using MLP and SVM classifier is shown in Table 10.2:

Figure 10.2 shows cataract and non-cataract images in RGB and grayscale. This figure highlights the histogram of grayscale image and demonstrates the different stages of cataracts (i.e. mild, medium, and severe). Data samples were considered for extraction of features and the samples were taken from a website called 'Kaggle' ("Cataract Image Dataset," 2019). The output is labeled, where 0 is for normal eye and 1 is for the cataract eye.

The histograms present a significant difference between cataract and non-cataract graphs; images and other similar features are also to be derived. These features are depicted in Table 10.3.

Table 10.3 presents the extracted features for the classification of cataracts; the data and other features (mean, standard deviation, contrast, entropy, homogeneity, energy, and variance of 40 images) are shown. Figure 10.3 shows the graph of the implemented feedforward neural network with seven input features, ten hidden layers, and one output layer were considered for simulation. Figure 10.4 demonstrates the performance plot; Figure 10.5 shows the training state plot; and Figure 10.6 presents the regression plot of the implemented feedforward neural network.

The implemented feedforward neural network classifier achieved a performance of 94%. In the case of SVM classifiers, the accuracy achieved is at 75% — lesser than the

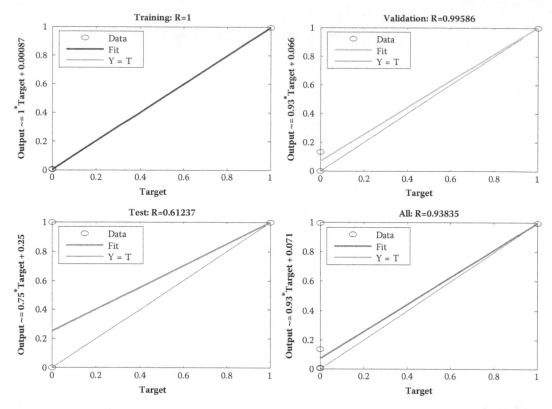

FIGURE 10.6
Regression plot of implemented feedforward neural network.

feedforward neural network. These results can be improved by considering distinctive features of cataract images as well as applying recent ML techniques. However, apart from the conventional procedures, ML can be a potential medium for early detection of eye cataract.

10.8 Conclusion

In this chapter, eye cataract is successfully detected through SVM and feedforward MLP networks. From these methods, we achieve an accuracy of 75% and 94%, respectively. This work also exhibits the significance of machine learning techniques in the diagnosis of cataracts and similar diseases. ML and fundus image-based cataract detection approach can be applied in early cataract screening and diagnosis. The significance of this chapter is the automated identification of cataracts that can be beneficial for patients and doctors in terms of cost and time.

In the future, this implemented work can be extended to develop a smartphone or software program that will help any person easily detect cataract. Also, it can help in the remote diagnosis of patients in rural areas. It is also possible to implement feature reduction techniques to reduce programming and time complexity and improve classification accuracy. Automation and adaptability can also be enhanced through recent state-of-the-art classification techniques such as Deep Learning, Decision Tree, Ada-Boost.

References

Agarwal, V., Gupta, V., Vashisht, V. M., Sharma, K., & Sharma, N., "Mobile application based cataract detection system," Proceedings of the *International Conference on Trends in Electronics and Informatics, ICOEI 2019*, 2019, pp. 780–787. https://doi.org/10.1109/ICOEI.2019.8862774.

Cao, L., Li, H., Zhang, Y., Zhang, L., & Xu, L., "Hierarchical method for cataract grading based on retinal images using improved Haar wavelet," *Information Fusion*, vol. 53(June 2019), 2020, pp. 196–208. https://doi.org/10.1016/j.inffus.2019.06.022.

Cataract Image Dataset, 2019. Retrieved from https://www.kaggle.com/jr2ngb/cataractdataset/version/2.

Dixit, A., Pathak, S., Raj, R., Naveen, C., & Satpute, V. R., "An efficient fuzzy based edge estimation for iris localization and pupil detection in human eye for automated cataract detection system," *2018 9th International Conference on Computing, Communication and Networking Technologies, ICCCNT 2018*, 2018, pp. 1–6. https://doi.org/10.1109/ICCCNT.2018.8493740.

Gautam, K., Jangir, S. K., Kumar, M., & Sharma, J. S. (2020), "Malaria detection system using convolutional neural network algorithm," In *Machine Learning and Deep Learning in Real-Time Applications*. https://doi.org/10.4018/978-1-7998-3095-5.

Kumar, M., & Mishra, S. K., 2017. "Teaching learning based optimization-functional link artificial neural network filter for mixed noise reduction from magnetic resonance image,"*Bio-Medical Materials and Engineering*, vol. 28, no. 6, pp. 643–654.

Kumar, M., & Mishra, S. K., "A comprehensive review on nature inspired neural network based adaptive filter for eliminating noise in medical images," *Current Medical Imaging*, vol. 16, no. 4, pp. 278–287, 2020. https://doi.org/10.2174/1573405614666180801113345.

Kumar, M., Mishra, S. K., Choubey, S. K., Tripathy, S. S., Choubey, D. K., & Das, D., "Cat swarm optimization based functional link multilayer perceptron for suppression of Gaussian and impulse noise from computed tomography images," *Current Medical Imaging*, vol. 16, no. 4, pp. 329–339, 2020. https://doi.org/10.2174/1573405614666180903115336.

Li, J., Hu, Q., Imran, A., Zhang, L., Yang, J. J., & Wang, Q., "Vessel recognition of retinal fundus images based on fully convolutional network," *Proceedings – International Computer Software and Applications Conference*, vol. 2, 2018, pp. 413–418. https://doi.org/10.1109/COMPSAC.2018.10268.

Michael, R., & Bron, A. J., "The ageing lens and cataract: a model of normal and pathological ageing," *Philosophical Transactions of the Royal Society B: Biological Sciences*, vol. 366, no. 1568, pp. 1278–1292, 2011. https://doi.org/10.1098/rstb.2010.0300.

Pratap, T., & Kokil, P., "Computer-aided diagnosis of cataract using deep transfer learning," *Biomedical Signal Processing and Control*, vol. 53, p. 101533, 2019. https://doi.org/10.1016/j.bspc.2019.04.010.

Ran, J., Niu, K., He, Z., Zhang, H., & Song, H., "Cataract detection and grading based on combination of deep convolutional neural network and random forests," Proceedings of *2018 6th IEEE International Conference on Network Infrastructure and Digital Content, IC-NIDC 2018*, vol. 7, 2018, pp. 155–159. https://doi.org/10.1109/ICNIDC.2018.8525852.

Rana, J., & Galib, S. M., "Cataract detection using smartphone," *3rd International Conference on Electrical Information and Communication Technology, EICT 2017*, 2018-Janua(December), 2018, pp. 1–4. https://doi.org/10.1109/EICT.2017.8275136.

Rayan, Z., Alfonse, M., & Salem, A. B. M., "Machine learning approaches in smart health," *Procedia Computer Science*, vol. 154, no. 1985, pp. 361–368, 2018. https://doi.org/10.1016/j.procs.2019.06.052.

Shaheen, I., & Tariq, A., 2019. *Survey Analysis of Automatic Detection and Grading of Cataract Using Different Imaging Modalities*, pp. 35–45. https://doi.org/10.1007/978-3-319–96139-2_4.

Xiong, Y., He, Z., Niu, K., Zhang, H., & Song, H., "Automatic cataract classification based on multi-feature fusion and SVM," *2018 IEEE 4th International Conference on Computer and Communications, ICCC 2018*, 2018, pp. 1557–1561. https://doi.org/10.1109/CompComm.2018.8780617.

Yang, J. J., Li, J., Shen, R., Zeng, Y., He, J., Bi, J., ... Wang, Q., "Exploiting ensemble learning for automatic cataract detection and grading," *Computer Methods and Programs in Biomedicine*, vol. 124, pp. 45–57, 2016. https://doi.org/10.1016/j.cmpb.2015.10.007.

Zhang, H., & He, Z., "Automatic cataract grading methods based on deep learning," *Computer Methods and Programs in Biomedicine*, vol. 182, p. 104978, 2019. https://doi.org/10.1016/j.cmpb.2019.07.006.

Zhang, K., Liu, X., Jiang, J., Li, W., Wang, S., Liu, L., ... Wang, L., "Prediction of postoperative complications of pediatric cataract patients using data mining," *Journal of Translational Medicine*, vol. 17, no. 1, pp. 1–10, 2019. https://doi.org/10.1186/s12967-018-1758-2.

11

Artificial Intelligence Wave: Reshaping Indian Healthcare Sector

Dharminder Kumar, Babita G Kataria, and Sangeeta Gupta

CONTENTS

11.1 Introduction

In modern healthcare sector, the Artificial intelligence (AI) technique is used as the latest and effective technology. In various clinical environment, it is used to analyze medical data and develop patterns that support diagnosis and treatment. AI is also used in various healthcare-related researches—control, detection, delivery, and management of diseases, and discovery of new drugs. Medical data is accessible and there is advancement in diagnostic methods through the latest technology with AI use. It is further helpful in decision-making and getting medical support on time and during early stages. With the use of AI, the health sector is getting digitalize; pen and paper processes are transformed into computer-based applications. The use of AI applications shows improvements in healthcare.

Analysis of data can help identify different patterns of diseases (kept in knowledge banks for future use and study), discover drugs, help people evaluate their own symptoms, and provide timely health care support through machine learning electrophysical data, imaging data, and genetic data analysis. The tools developed using artificial intelligence are highly supportive of the independence and quality of life of the disabled—chronically, mentally, etc.

Neural network is introduced as a subfield of artificial intelligence, and innovative work is in process. It is interesting to know that several private domains of healthcare, along with public areas, are working together to get better results in medical care. Healthcare-based apps that can be used through smartphones are being developed.

Any innovative technology introduced in healthcare faces various challenges in implementation—genetics, disease pattern identification, new drug recognition, lack of data availability, adaptation issues by healthcare workers, and other stakeholders. Employing artificial intelligence is good but it has overbearing limitations in terms of data availability, quality, confidentiality, and relevance; application acceptance, ethical issues, etc. of data, The problems in AI research consist of data collection, quality, reasoning, analysis, knowledge presentation, planning, learning, natural language processing, and application implementation. Inconsistencies and the quality of data are directly proportional to the proper use of artificial intelligence as it relies on the digital data available for its full potential. Any industry (especially healthcare) needs a real transformation to face the global challenges. Machine learning (ML) and artificial intelligence (AI) are making the inoperable feasible.

The chapter will discuss Artificial Intelligence (AI)—its application in global and Indian healthcare, its challenges, and future in the healthcare system.

11.2 Artificial Intelligence

Nowadays, most of the cognitive abilities of the human mind (problem-solving, decision making, and learning) are also available in computers or computerized machinery. This feature is known as artificial intelligence. Artificial intelligence (AI) means that the mental or cognitive abilities of human beings are associated with machines and imitates human beings (Russell Stuart and Norvig, 2009).

In computer science, machine intelligence or machine learning is synonymous with artificial intelligence (AI). Artificial intelligence, different to natural intelligence within living beings, are shown in computers or machines (Wikipedia, 2020).

11.3 Application of AI in the Service Sector

In this era of digitization, machines perform various domestic jobs, like household work. Several machines are industrialized to perform specific tasks and are widely used in different fields. Intelligent machines and systems support the service sector—education, research, healthcare, agriculture, finance, transportation, aviation, defense, remote sensing, robot controls, and many more. Figure 11.1 shows a view of AI applications in different service sectors.

FIGURE 11.1
Artificial Intelligence (AI) applications.

11.3.1 Agriculture

Supports the research of fertility of seeds, crop growth, yield gain, crop health, and farming efficiency through harvest time prediction. Some progress include agricultural robots, predictive analytics, and crop and soil monitoring. Greenhouse automation, modeling, simulation, and optimization techniques are examples of AI use for farming.

11.3.2 Aviation

The AI is used by the Air Operation Division (AOD) (Jones et al., 1999) as expert systems for strategic decision making, management, and training simulators. Data collected through simulated flights and warfare are posted and processed into symbolic summaries for expert decisions. The conceptual designs of aircraft or AIDA are created with the help of AI in airplanes. In the future, air traffic controller will be trained by computer-simulated pilots. The Interactive Fault Diagnosis and Isolation System, or IFDIS, is an expert system used to measure AOD performance. AI is also used in speech recognition software by AOD; from time to time, improvement in software is required. Software communication needs to be accurate because air traffic controllers use extremely specific language and dialog. A software was created for damaged aircraft based on neural network. The software needed to compensate components of damaged aircraft and support it until it lands in a safe zone. It was developed in 2003 by various companies and NASA's Dryden Flight Research Centre (Tomayko, 2003).

11.3.3 Computer Science

The most difficult problems of computer science are solved by AI researchers. The developed tools of AI are accepted, and it became part of computer science. No one can recognize these built-in tools in computer as AI-developed tools. AI laboratories are called to be an origin of automatic storage management, graphical user interface, computer mouse, interpreters, object-oriented programming, dynamic programming, and many more. AI is used in many advance and complex processes of computer science (e.g., Google AutoML created NASNet to optimize ImageNet, an AI-designed for objects detection) (Sulleyman, 2017).

11.3.4 Education

Specific needs of students are undertaken (computer-based lessons, online tutorials, games, and other education-related problems) and customized. The ambient informatics idea adjusts information through technology that can support classroom teaching in the future, and AI tutors can provide individual knowledge. Every phenomenon has two faces: using AI can create a massive drawback in a student's focus, reducing their solving power and concentration, and lack of interest in self-learning that can lead to slow growth.

11.3.5 Data Analytics

For financial practices and investment decisions, AI engines (like BlackRock's AI engine, Aladdin) are used for both the clients and the internal working of companies. The AI engines have a feature of natural languages that help read text in social media, reports, broker's news, and general news. There are several platforms that does market analysis not only through natural language processing, but also statistical computing of big data. An AI engine known as Sqreem (Sequential Quantum Reduction and Extraction Model) is used by banks like UBS and Deutsche (Crosman, 2017) to mine data of consumers and map their profiles (fondness with wealth management products). Kensho, a market analytics platform, is used by Goldman Sachs for statistical computing (including natural language processing and big data) (Antoine, 2017).

11.3.6 Heavy Industry

In heavy industries, robots are commonly used to replace humans in dangerous labor. Robots are found highly effective in repetitive jobs, while humans tend to lose concentration due to fatigue. Other heavy machines can also be developed with high-end technology.

11.3.7 Recruitment

AI is used by talent acquisition and human resource professionals to identify and map the best resource. The résumés are screened; candidates are ranked per qualification and experience. Candidate success can be predicted according to matched roles through job portals. All these typically require human intervention but can be replaced with AI search engines.

11.3.8 Media

Audiovisual content like TV programs, advertisements, movies, etc. are analyzed and edited by some AI applications. The analysis of videos or images using face recognition or object recognition techniques for relevant scenes is also done through AI applications. The analysis depends on AI companies that provide REST API services. These services enable automatic access to technology that does further machine reading work and analysis of content. Some companies like Amazon, IBM, and Microsoft use RESTful APIs for media recognition data.

11.3.9 Music Industry

Artificial Intelligence with scientific advances enables human-like music composition. Advanced technology helps create algorithmic computer music. David Cope created Emily Howell, a well-known AI in the field of algorithmic computer music (Cope, 2010). Computerized music albums are also produced. Artificial Intelligence Virtual Artist (AIVA) is an intelligent system that composes symphonic music (classical music) recognized by a musical professional association, becoming the first virtual composer in the world (Sacem, 2020). AI can also produce music through Melomics's effort for medical treatment like pain and stress relief (Requena et al., 2014). Through optimizing techniques and analysis of unique combinations, music can be composed in any style.

11.3.10 News Publishing

Computer-generated reports and news are commercially available through a company called Narrative Science. It creates news related to sport events, real estate, and financial reports (Narrative Science, 2020). Twitter, Facebook, and other social media platforms are managed by the Echobox Software Company (Williams, 2019), intelligently posting articles to increase traffic. It identifies the trends from past and current data, and posts accordingly. The articles are designed according to the interest of the readers by another AI application as Boomtrain. Creative work like storytelling can be done through computers, and AI has been an active field of research in this sector. (Wolk, 2018). James Meehan developed TaleSpin and made stories like the Fables of Aesop. Researchers have a great and innovative interest in this field, gaining lots of curiosity in research work.

11.3.11 Defense

Firearms and other equipment developed through AI are majorly used for target acquisition, enemy position marking, threat detection, etc. The machine learning coordination of effectors and sensors, interoperability, command, integration, control, marking positions of enemy, and target acquisition are managed by AI tools. Some examples of AI tools implemented in military equipment are lethal autonomous weapons, unmanned combat aerial vehicles, and artificial intelligence arms race.

11.3.12 Power Electronics

Researchers use AI to create and develop automated design with precise parameters for reliable power electronics converters. Renewable energy or energy storage power electronic converters are prone to failure; lifetime converters are needed to ensure critical process to continue.

11.3.13 Transportation

Automatic gearboxes in cars are developed using fuzzy logic-based controllers. These days, cars have various AI-based driven features in controls like self-parking assistance and other advanced features. Traffic management applications are also developed to reduce waiting time and manage the use of the full energy system. Autonomous cars (driverless cars, self-driving cars, robocars, or robotic cars) are a work in progress. Traffic management applications are improved by utilizing AI. The transportation provided by AI is anticipated to deliver reliable, safe, efficient, controlled, and managed transportation with minor impact on the community.

11.3.14 Medical

Clinical decision support system such as concept processing technology in EMR software is based on an artificial neural network used in medical diagnosis. There are several tasks in the medical sector that can be accomplished through artificial intelligence, like analysis of medical records in identifying patterns, region, or demographic features of diseases; examination of heart sound (Reed et al., 2004), scanning of digital images, and computer-aided interpretation of medical images for detection of tumors; designing treatments and knowledge enhancement in mining clinical medical records; and in-demand computerized reports. In caring for the elderly, companion robots (Yorita and Kubota, 2011) are being developed. Repetitive jobs can be performed by machines and robots; clinical trainings can be done on avatars instead of patients (Luxton, 2014). Telemedicine, remote training, bone age from any x-ray, and consultation can be provided using AI applications. The first self-sufficient AI-based diagnostic structure authorized for commercialization by the FDA is IDx-DR (IDx, 2020).

11.4 Healthcare Sector in India

In India, healthcare is provided by two major players: the private and public sector. The private sector is completely driven by self-practitioners, clinics, nursing homes, not-profitable dispensaries, charitable hospitals, and profit-earning hospitals (Nair, 2020). The public sector has government hospitals, dispensaries, special hospitals for children, women, mentally challenged, mobile health clinics running in the country through the directorate of health. There are several functioning bodies in Delhi; however, the national capital is lagging, not able to map patients with healthcare services. If technology like artificial intelligence applications can be applied with the present system, it will meet the requirement and manage healthcare service demands better and patients can be served timely. Table 11.1 depicts health outlets in the capital of the nation in the year 2018-2019 (Kumar, 2020).

11.5 Data Flow in Healthcare System

The data flow in the Indian healthcare information system begins in villages to the state and central departments (i.e. Department of Health and Central Bureau of Health). The complete data travels through several channel sub-centers to PHC or a hospital (where the data is compiled in monthly reports sent to districts). These reports are further processed by the district statistical officer. The officer sends these reports with analysis to the joint director or state level deputy director. From the state, the reports are forwarded to the Department of Health and Central Bureau of Health. Table 11.2 shows the flow and compilation of data for a given period (Ranganayakulu, 2020). Data collected from a multi-layered procedure result in substantial amounts of data; this data needs proper handling and management to mine meaningful information. Data compilation on different analysis may support timely decision making and treatment of the patient. (Kataria and Saini, 2020). The data, if automated using the latest AI technology, can be utilized for quality healthcare services. The Indian sector is lacking in research and development because of unmanageable and unstructured data. AI applications can overcome this limitation and support the health department in providing excellent healthcare services.

11.6 Transformation of Global and Indian Healthcare by Implementing Artificial Intelligence

The last few years have seen the development of different sectors through artificial intelligence (AI). There are several AI applications introduced and installed in countries under the high-income groups. According to an analysis, the use of AI applications could save healthcare costs of up to $150 billion in the USA by 2026. In case of limited resources (where management is difficult), AI applications have shown promising

TABLE 11.1

Number of Health Outlets under GNCT of Delhi in 2018–2019

S. No.	Year Health Outlets	2007–08	2008–09	2009–10	2010–11	2011–12	2012–13	2013–14	2014–15	2015–16	2016–17	2017–18	2018–19
1	Allopathic Dispensaries	188	214	220	234	247	256	260	260	242	245	242	241
2	Mohalla Clinics	–	–	–	–	–	–	–	–	107	162	166	189
3	Polyclinics	–	–	–	–	–	–	–	–	23	24	24	24
4	Hospitals	34	35	38	38	38	39	39	39	38	38	38	38
5	Mobile Health Clinics	68	72	90	90	90	90	90	43	43	24	24	24
6	School Health Clinics/ Referral Centers	28	28	32	34	93	100	100	68	70	59	55	58
	Ayush												
I	Homeopathy Dispensaries	78	80	87	92	92	95	100	101	101	103	104	105
II	Ayurvedic Dispensaries	25	26	27	32	32	33	35	36	39	40	44	44
III	Unani Dispensaries	10	10	11	15	15	16	17	18	19	20	21	22
	Total	**431**	**465**	**505**	**535**	**607**	**629**	**641**	**565**	**682**	**715**	**718**	**745**

TABLE 11.2

Data Flow in Healthcare Information System

Location	Health Care Worker	Data Flow	Periodicity
Sub-Center	ANM	Sub-Center to PHC	Monthly
PHC/Hospital	Computer statistical assistant, Pharmacist	PHC/District Hospital	Monthly
District	Statistical officer – health, family welfare, TB, Leprosy, Malaria officer (district)	District to (HQ) State	Monthly
State	Dy/Joint director – Vital Statistics Surveillance Unit Sample Registration System and Statistics Family Welfare	State HQ to Center	Monthly
Central Government	Department of Health Sample Registration System (headquartered), Central Bureau of Health Intelligence Statistics Division and Department of Family Welfare CGHS	Center for Govt.	Monthly Compiled Annual

results. Implementation of innovative ideas, modern technology, and new systems always has tremendous challenges and difficulties in limited resource sectors, but it is possible. The deprived healthcare sector can be overwhelmed with the use of AI and other emerging technologies, but the advancement of AI tools can accelerate and improve the conditions in the global health sector (Wahl et al., 2018).

People are open to the adoption of artificial intelligence In Indian healthcare. The population in India is huge and managing with limited resources can be tough and rigorous. To handle this pressure, the government, healthcare institutions, and medical professionals are looking towards emerging trends and innovation in the medical field. Doctors, with the help of deep learning algorithms, can provide better prognosis of patients and give timely treatment. AI has the potential to capture a good amount of data from numerous patients and analyze them to reach a diagnosis and treatment plan for the patient. It gives great support to budding doctors who have less experience in reaching the right diagnosis or line of treatment. The doctors can request for video conferencing or online discussions, proactively working with senior doctors at different locations.

The risk of heart patients can be identified, and their treatment can be classified according to the intensity, through AI applications; AI can be an immense help in prevention and diagnosis. As a nation with a shortage in nurses and doctors, authorities must work on innovation, technology, and skill development to deliver quality and timely healthcare services. The country is focused on providing better health services, but limited infrastructure, insufficient health care workers, and facilities also need to be considered. To provide healthcare in an effective manner India needs to address cost, technology, infrastructure, and quality issues. With the development in technology, healthcare can be provided at a lower cost, with an increase in efficiency, by removing limitations. The aim is to adopt scaled digital health data and AI technology to work towards developing countries. Doctors can save time, cost, and effort, and provide quality diagnosis and the best treatment through AI-enabled healthcare. The artificial intelligence applications, if accepted, will provide improved patient healthcare in a cost-effective manner (Mabiyan, 2018).

11.7 Challenges

India is a developing country in all aspects—technology, healthcare, infrastructure, and scalable living. It has a great area of innovation in healthcare sectors to improve the standard of medical services and lives. There is a vast difference in healthcare distribution (lack of healthcare workers, infrastructure, technology, equipment, medicine, and low spending of funds from the government). The public and private sectors are trying to handhold, but none can scale the problems and challenges of the healthcare sector. With the use of smartphones and the internet, people are connected through technology; however, digital technology has not impacted significantly on healthcare. The nation needs to adapt but there are various challenges in the healthcare sector (especially in cost)—to change a country, one must spend on technology. If proven useful and cost-effective, the next challenge lies in distributing, sustaining, and scaling technology. Implementation and the use of AI can bring a change and support distribution of scarce knowledge to the masses by training algorithms on machines. The system must further be made robust to allocate knowledge to beneficiaries. There are various gaps (i.e. geographical, urban-rural, skill, adaptation, infrastructure, and cost) that must be filled with the advent of AI. Using AI means digitalization, but hospital medical records are still penned down on medical cards, radiology images still use films, various villages and districts are not connected, and infrastructure is limited. There is no computerization in hospitals (and if there was, the staff do not know how to use them). Changes are slow and needs speedy work to transition from paper & pen to digitalization; other industries are faster compared to healthcare. The private sector is providing paid service; other countries are funding public health programs, while the government lacks funding in innovation and medical projects—this means that the technology is imported rather than innovated from our own. In comparison, the private sector is working at a good pace. In India, medical education does not give much weight to research and developing technology. Clinicians are practicing but are working much on adopting technology and innovating. The digital innovation in telemedicine, e-training, e-learning, and e-consultation demonstrated success, but the implementation is either slow or incomplete to limitations (acceptability, lack of training, deficiency of resources, technology, and infrastructure) (Rao, 2018).

11.8 Future

The country is working on technology and the onset of the internet and smartphones, digital solutions can be provided in every sector. The government is also on the same track and enthusiastic to adopt technology on the central and state levels. The public and private sectors, together, are planning to work on modern technology to resolve old problems. The innovation in the field of health can resolve and benefit various hitches. Some of the major diseases like tuberculosis, diabetes, and many more can be treated and managed through the implementation of artificial intelligence (Tirunagarie, 2019).

The nation is working on innovation and accepting the latest technology. Artificial intelligence is the latest technology, trending worldwide with several areas open for research and development. People are expecting transformation—less cost and better quality of

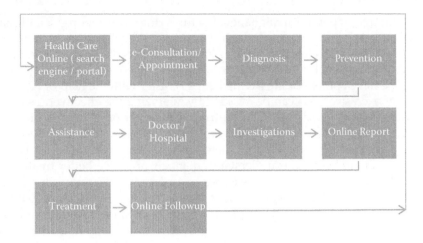

FIGURE 11.2
Future of artificial intelligence in healthcare.

healthcare services. The primary and secondary medical data is utilized to give effective, quick, and error-free treatment. AI is helping in various fields to give better, quality, and fast service to patients. The patients can get immediate support in insurance verification as insurance coverage can be confirmed digitally, without wasting time. With the help of live and automated chatbots, patients' queries can be attended to, saving time and money from traveling. The doctor's time is also saved by providing online solutions to patients. In cases where patient confidentiality must be maintained, a password-protected AI will save the digital data. In admission, documenting a patient's record is the most critical; this can also be done by using AI applications. AI can help treat chronic patients by keeping track of pre- and post-treatment diagnosis. Robots can be used to explain lab reports in a continuously changing environment. Perhaps, using AI in hospital administration, patient care, problem solving, and holding documents, will enhance one's quality of life and improve healthcare services. Any deficiency is an opportunity for AI; healthcare sector in India can be a premier area for the advancement of technology (Insight success, 2020). Figure 11.2 tries to depict a futuristic view of AI in the healthcare sector.

11.9 Conclusion

AI can make healthcare cost-effective, affordable, and streamlined; it can help provide controlled quality and cost-effective healthcare in several ways (choice of treatment, diagnosis, drug development and clinical trials, and patient empowerment). In healthcare, standardized formats are getting introduced to get patient data, then it is utilized and analyzed for disease patterns that will help in decision making and treatment. Moreover, post and pre-follow-ups can be defined according to the patients. The treatments are customized, creating the right intervention for individual patients. The effective and accurate treatment will save costs related to complications post-treatment. Diagnosis can be made more efficiently with the use of technology. Complicated CT scans for diseases like bleeding in the brain, mammography for malignancy, fractures due to osteoporosis, and many more remain unidentified, which lead to delay in treatment. With the introduction of artificial intelligence applications, doctors can analyze and review reports much faster, timelier, and more accurately. It will enable early detection, efficient diagnosis, and timely treatment of the patients. The development of life-saving drugs is faster with the help of AI applications; physical tests of excessive costs can be avoided by analyzing the effectiveness of medicines through simulators and algorithms. Clinical trials can be performed using biomarker platforms that monitor gene-level identification of various diseases. AI is empowering patients to make better decisions for their health. There are several mobile apps that provide basic information to users to help them understand, manage, and take better treatment of their diseases. It will lead to reduced cost, healthier manpower, and a more developed nation who live better lives. AI can bring significant transformation; India, along with other developing countries, may soon understand the benefits of this technology in healthcare. Development means bridging resources with innovative technology in the health sector; AI applications in India are starting to be deployed in different fields of healthcare, and will soon scale the challenges and bring digital transformation in the medical sector.

References

Antoine, G., "Kensho's AI for investors just got valued at over $500 million in funding round from Wall Street," *Forbes*. March 01, 2017. Accessed August 01, 2020. https://www.forbes.com/sites/antoinegara/2017/02/28/kensho-sp-500-million-valuation-jpmorgan-morgan-stanley/#53e2a7645cbf.

Collier, M. D., R. N. Fu, and L. Yin, Artificial Intelligence: Healthcare's New Nervous System. Accenture. 2020.

Cope, D. H., "Recombinant music composition algorithm and method of using the same," U.S. Patent 7696426, issued April 13, 2010. https://patents.google.com/patent/US7696426.

Crosman, P., "Beyond robo-advisers; how AI could rewire wealth management," *American Banker*, vol. 182, no. 4, p. 1, 2017.

IDx, "Press Release: FDA permits marketing of IDx-DR for automated detection of diabetic retinopathy in primary care," Accessed August 01, 2020. https://www.eyediagnosis.co/press-releases/press-release-fda-permits-marketing-of-idx-dr-for-automated-detection-of-diabetic-retinopathy-in-primary-care.

2020. "Indian Healthcare System: A.I," Insights Success. April 03, 2020. Accessed July 21, 2020. https://www.insightssuccess.in/future-aspects-of-indian-healthcare-system-with-a-i/.

Jones, R. M., John E. L., P. E. Nielsen, K. J. Coulter, P. Kenny, and F. V. Koss, "Automated intelligent pilots for combat flight simulation," *AI Magazine*, vol. 20, no. 1, 27-27, 1999.

Kataria B. G., Saini A. K., "Recent trends in health care sector: a study of Indian perspective," *International Journal of Latest Trends in Engineering and Technology*, vol. 9, no. 3, pp. 268–272, 2020.

Kumar A., "Annual Report of Directorate General of Health Services," Accessed July 22, 2020. http://health.delhigovt.nic.in/wps/wcm/connect/.../ Annual +Report.PDF.

Luxton, D. D., "Artificial intelligence in psychological practice: current and future applications and implications," *Professional Psychology: Research and Practice*, vol. 45, no. 5, p. 332, 2014.

Mabiyan, R., "How artificial intelligence can help transform Indian healthcare," *ET Health World*, May 23, 2018. Accessed July 22, 2020. https://health.economictimes.indiatimes.com/news/health-it/how-artificial-intelligence-can-help-transform-indian-healthcare/64285489.

Nair C. R. K., "Rural Health Statistics," Accessed July 24, 2020. https://wcd.nic.in/sites/default/files/RHS_1.pdf.

Narrative Science. "Bring Your Data to Life," Accessed July 25, 2020. https://web.archive.org/web/20111103192105/http://www.narrativescience.com/solutions.html.

Norvig P., "Artificial Intelligence: A Modern Approach," Accessed July 25, 2020. https://www.javatpoint.com/application-of-ai.

Ranganayakulu B., "Evaluation of health management information system in India: need for computerized in HMIS," Accessed July 25, 2020. https://cdn1.sph.harvard.edu/wp-content/uploads/sites/114/2012/10/rp176.pdf.

Rao, P., "AI and healthcare technology in India: Opportunities, challenges, and emerging trends," *Health Management Journal*, vol. 18, no. 3, pp. 236–238, 2018.

Reed, T. R., Nancy E. R., and P. Fritzson, "Heart sound analysis for symptom detection and computer-aided diagnosis," *Simulation Modelling Practice and Theory*, vol. 12, no. 2, pp. 129–146, 2004.

Requena, G., C. Sánchez, J. L. Corzo-Higueras, S. Reyes-Alvarado, F. Rivas-Ruiz, F. Vico, and A. Raglio, "Melomics music medicine (M3) to lessen pain perception during pediatric prick test procedure," *Pediatric Allergy and Immunology*, vol. 25, no. 7, pp. 721–724, 2014.

Sacem, "Symphonic Overture in a Minor OP 23 AIVA," Accessed July 25, 2020. https://repertoire.sacem.fr/resultats?filters=parties&query=aiva&nbWorks=20.

Russell Stuart, J., and P. Norvig, Artificial Intelligence: A Modern Approach, Prentice-Hall, 2009.

Sulleyman, A., "Google AI creates its own 'child' AI that's more advanced than systems built by humans," 2017. https://www.independent.co.uk/life-style/gadgets-and-tech/news/google-child-ai-bot-nasnet-automl-machine-learning-artificial-intelligence-a8093201.html.

Tirunagarie S., "Some challenges and opportunities for AI in healthcare: Part-1," April 3, 2019. Accessed July 26, 2020. https://santosh-tirunagari.com/2019/04/03/some-challenges-and-oppurtunities-for-ai-in-healthcare-part-1/.

Tomayko, J. E., The Story of Self-repairing Flight Control Systems, Edwards: NASA Dryden Flight Research Center, 2003.

Wahl, B., A. Cossy-Gantner, S. Germann, and N. R. Schwalbe, "Artificial intelligence (AI) and global health: how can AI contribute to health in resource-poor settings?" *BMJ Global Health*, vol. 33, no. 4, p. e000798, 2018.

Wikipedia, Accessed July 23, 2020. https://en.wikipedia.org/w/index.php?title=Artificial_intelligence&oldid=954843041.

Williams H., "AI online publishing service Echobox closes $3.4m in funding," *Startups*, January 23, 2019. Accessed July 21, 2020. https://startups.co.uk/ai-publishing-service-echobox-closes-3-4m-in-funding/.

Wolk A., "User data is so 2018. Here comes content data," *Forbes* September 12, 2018. Accessed June 20, 2020. https://www.forbes.com/sites/alanwolk/2018/09/12/user-data-is-so-2018-here-comes-content-data/#5233eeab2116.

Yorita, A., and N. Kubota, "Cognitive development in partner robots for information support to elderly people," *IEEE Transactions on Autonomous Mental Development*, vol. 3, no. 1, pp. 64–73, 2011.

12

Adoption of Artificial Intelligence in Industrial Sectors and Its Impact

Somil Jain and Puneet Kumar

CONTENTS

12.1 Introduction

Artificial intelligence is used in fields with an intent to automate the process—in other words, to make machines capable to work like a human being. This technology was introduced over six decades ago [1]. AI has recorded its strong presence in areas like computer, mathematics, industry, psychology, etc. [2]. The concept of AI was generated from Turing machines by Alan Turing in 1912–1954, with the tagline: "thinking machines"—machines that think like humans [3]. As the entire world moves toward digital technological advancements rapidly, there is a need for intelligent technologies that provide innovation, competitiveness, and ability to handle complex data to keep up [4]. Here, AI will act as a helping hand through automation of various tasks that result in an efficient and faster outcome. This technology can be used in various sectors like education, transportation, telecommunication, healthcare, R&D, etc. [5]. If we take the example of industries associated with power and energy, this technology can be used to predict optimal energy utilization by developing various energy computing models [6]. On the other hand, if the transportation sector considers AI, then it can help create voice-automated vehicles and built-in GPS that generate real-time traffic information, reducing the number of road accidents and improving the flow of traffic [7]. Citizens' safety can be advanced through high-tech surveillance cameras with GPS at public places (malls, roads, etc.) to reduce crime rate and identify criminals by live tracking [8].

12.2 Application of Artificial Intelligence in Various Domains

12.2.1 Public Healthcare

Artificial intelligence has the potential to transform healthcare by assisting medical practitioners in making real-time treatment decisions. It is also helpful in maintaining health records and managing the entire health system electronically [9]. The data generated from this sector—whether structured or unstructured—is analyzed through its sub-branch (i.e. machine learning). Various methods of ML are quite helpful in predictive analysis, which is beneficial in controlling mortality rate due to chronic diseases like cancer, heart failure, kidney failure, and neurological disorder. Control over the mortality rate can be achieved through early detection, timely diagnosis, and better predictive capability [10,11]. The use of this technology in medical devices is also beneficial, especially in monitoring patients' blood pressure, heartbeat, oxygen level, etc. regularly [12,13].

12.2.2 Transportation

Technological advancements are facing various obstacles in the transportation industry— traffic prediction, human errors, accidents, etc. [14]. Nowadays, the transportation industry is relying on artificial intelligence for better prediction and decision-making. It is adopted by various forest departments; upgrading vehicles with this technology to conserve animals by monitoring their real-time movement in the forest. This can also be beneficial in providing better medical assistance at the time of accident by generating geographical location [9,15]. AI is also helpful in freight transportation, where companies can predict the volume of goods to be transported, which can be a productive investment as it helps utilize resources and avoid wastage [16]. Many nations are facing traffic problems. In such scenarios, traffic lights can be made smarter using AI to manage traffic in an efficient and effective manner, forming a traffic pattern [17]. Other uses of this technology can be seen in self-driven cars and trucks that reduce human impact and make machines smarter [14].

12.2.3 Finance and Economy

Economic and financial organizations like insurance, banks, share markets, etc. are using AI to achieve better growth and returns from the market through a smarter strategy. Out of all these organizations, banks were the first to adopt by providing "Smart Banking" to customers through chatbots and robots, resulting in reduced fraud and higher level of security [18–20]. Various stock traders also use different robots to assist customers in trading and managing their portfolio [21]. Financial regulatory bodies of governments are also applying the concept of machine learning for their project supervision [22]. Other important aspect of AI is assessing the political risk of different political parties, predicting the mood of citizens about them and eventually assist in the economic growth of a nation [23,24]. Most developing nations are facing the crisis of unemployment which is somehow affecting their growth. In such conditions, various AI algorithms can help in getting a deeper insight into the root cause and taking the necessary action accordingly [25]. The darker side is that if we regularly opt for automation, then this will lead to loss of jobs, which will impact several households.

12.2.4 Environment

Nowadays, agriculture is the area most prominent in utilizing artificial intelligence. For example, beehive management is using a fully integrated approach — custom sensors help beekeepers monitor beehives through their cell phones [26]. Energy sector firms are also using various AI technologies to form smarter and intelligent grids for utilizing energy and power per usage, restricting the wastage of energy, and forecasting about a range of factors that can hamper environmental balance [27,28].

The adaptability rate ofaArtificial intelligence in various domains is shown in Figure 12.1.

12.3 Challenges and Advantages of AI

Every technology has some challenges and advantages and the same is true with AI, and these are discussed in Sections 12.3.1 and 12.3.2.

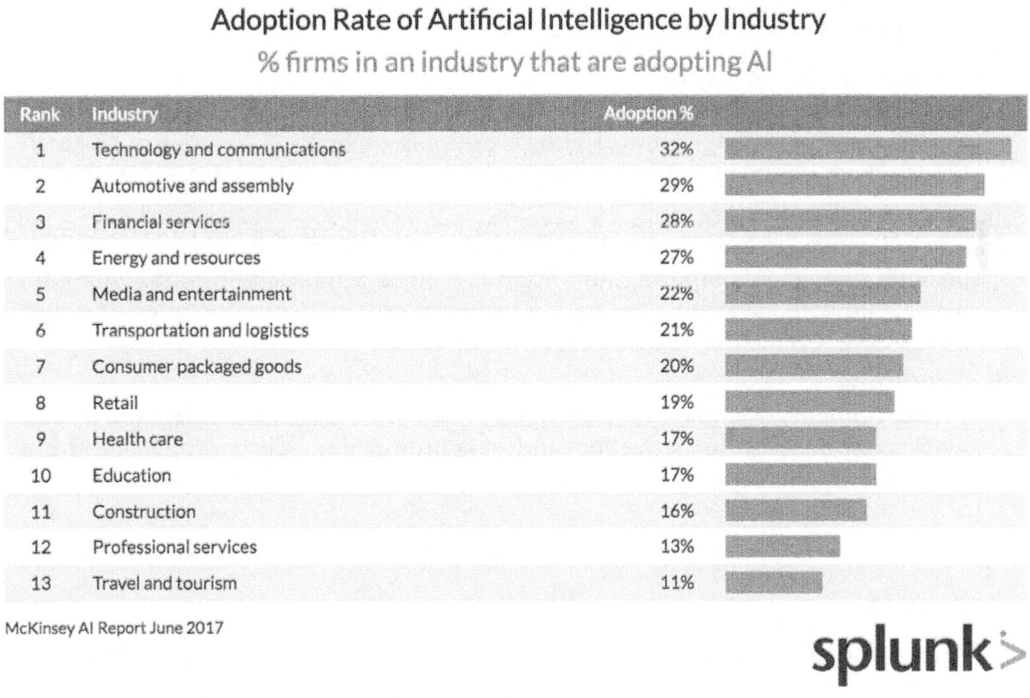

Adoption Rate of Artificial Intelligence by Industry
% firms in an industry that are adopting AI

Rank	Industry	Adoption %	
1	Technology and communications	32%	
2	Automotive and assembly	29%	
3	Financial services	28%	
4	Energy and resources	27%	
5	Media and entertainment	22%	
6	Transportation and logistics	21%	
7	Consumer packaged goods	20%	
8	Retail	19%	
9	Health care	17%	
10	Education	17%	
11	Construction	16%	
12	Professional services	13%	
13	Travel and tourism	11%	

McKinsey AI Report June 2017

splunk>

FIGURE 12.1
Adoption rate of AI by different industries [29].

12.3.1 Challenges [30]

i. **Trustworthiness**
As the technology responsible for automation, it is impossible for everyone to be fully aware of it. The trust rate of the technology also depends on the literacy rate of any nation.

ii. **Lack of Manpower**
AI is a technology facing scarcity of trained professionals in various subfields like data analytics, data science, etc. Most business owners adopting this technology are training their employees or hiring new ones based on their skills in the field.

iii. **Huge Investment**
AI is an expensive technology and if one wants to adopt it, a huge investment is to be made to create infrastructures like high computing devices, GPUs, FPGA, etc. Apart from this, firms who have adopted this have to be patient in their return of investment.

iv. **Data Security**
Vulnerability is a major issue with any technology as AI deals with a huge volume of data which can often be sensitive in nature, so any leak in sensitive information may lead to a disastrous situation for various stakeholders.

12.3.2 Benefits of Artificial Intelligence [31,32]

i. **Decrease in Manual Error**
As most of the work done by AI is considered smart and intelligent, there are very few chances of having errors. The best example of this can be seen in research fields where various machines help researchers get accurate and precise results.

ii. **Wide Application Area**
Nowadays each sector is heading towards artificial intelligence due to its enormous power of computing and accuracy. AI is applicable in various sectors like healthcare, aviation, energy, transportation, etc. and includes weather forecasting, prediction of diseases, navigation, etc.

iii. **Continuity**
Unlike humans, machines do not require breaks for tea or snacks etc., so they can work continuously to perfection and synchronization, decreasing computing time and enhancing productivity.

12.4 Conclusion

In this chapter, we have emphasized the impact of AI in various industries. Through various literature, it is evident that this technology can create a massive impact on the economic growth of any nation. Due to its advanced subdomains (machine learning, deep learning, etc.), it is becoming a prominent area for researchers in generating new insights for enhanced productivity and performance.

References

1. Mohasses, M. "How AI-Chatbots can make Dubai smarter?" in *Proceedings of the Amity International Conference on Artificial Intelligence (AICAI)*, 2019, pp. 439–446.

2. Darlington, K. The emergence of the age of AI, open mind, 2017, https://www. bbvaopenmind.com/en/technology/artificial-intelligence/the-emergence-of-the- age-of-ai/.

3. Russell, S. and Norvig, P. Artificial Intelligence: A Modern Approach, Prentice-Hall Englewood Cliffs, NJ, 1995.

4. Kankanhalli, A., Charalabidis, Y. and Mellouli, S. "IoT and AI for smart Government: a research agenda", in *Government Information Quarterly*, Vol. 36, no. 2, pp. 304–309, April 2019. DOI: 10.1016/j.giq.2019.02.003.

5. Marda, V. "Artificial intelligence policy in India: A framework for engaging the limits of data-driven decision-making", *Philosophical Transactions of The Royal Society A Mathematical Physical and Engineering Sciences*, Vol. 376, no. 2133:20180087, pp.1–19, Nov. 2018.

6. Ozoegwu, C. G. "The solar energy assessment methods for Nigeria: the current status, the future directions and a neural time series method", *Renewable and Sustainable Energy Reviews*, Vol. 92, pp. 146–159, 2018.

7. Casares, A. P. "The brain of the future and the viability of democratic governance: the role of artificial intelligence, cognitive machines, and viable systems", *Futures*, Vol. 103, pp. 5–16, 2018.

8. Gasser, U. and Almeida, V. A. F. "A layered model for AI governance", *IEEE Internet Computing*, Vol. 21, no. 6, pp. 58–62, Nov. 2017. DOI:10.1109/mic.2017.4180835.

9. Hengstler, M., Enkel, E. and Duelli, S. "Applied artificial intelligence and trust-The case of autonomous vehicles and medical assistance devices", *Technol. Forecast. Soc. Change*, Vol. 105, pp. 105–120, Apr. 2016.

10. Jiang, F. et. al. "Artificial intelligence in healthcare: past, present, and future", *Stroke Vasc. Neurol*, Vol. 2, no. 4, pp. 230–243, June 2017. DOI: 10.1136/svn-2017-000101.

11. Ho, C. W. L., Soon, D., Caals, K. and Kapur, J. "Governance of automated image analysis and artificial intelligence analytics in healthcare", *Clinical Radiology*, Vol. 74, no. 5, pp. 329–337, 2019.

12. Yaeger, K. A., Martini, M., Yaniv, G., Oermann, E. K., and Costa, A. B. "United states regulatory approval of medical devices and software applications enhanced by artificial intelligence," *Health Policy Technology*, Vol. 8. no. 2, pp. 192–197, 2019.

13. Long, J. M. "Computer-based medical systems", *Advanced Computing*, Vol. 38, pp. 145–195, 1994.

14. Antony, A. "How will AI impact the transportation industry? [Cited 2020 April 25]. Available: https://www.prescouter.com/2017/12/ai-impact-transportation-industry/.

15. Gonzalez, L. F., Montes, G. A., Puig, E., Johnson, S., Mengersen, K. and Gaston, K. J. "Unmanned aerial vehicles (UAVs) and artificial intelligence revolutionizing wildlife monitoring and conservation", *Sensors*, vol. 16, no. 1, p. 97, 2016. https://doi.org/10.3390/ s16010097.

16. Mrowczynska, B., Ciesla, M., Krol, A. and Sladkowski, A. "Application of artificial intelligence in prediction of road freight transportation", *Promet - Traffic & Transportation*, Vol. 29, no. 4, pp. 363–370, Aug. 2017.

17. Vidoni, R., F., García-Sánchez, Gasparetto, A. and Martínez-Béjar, R. "An intelligent framework to manage robotic autonomous agents", *Expert System Application*, Vol. 38, no. 6, pp. 7430–7439, 2011.

18. Fethi, M. D. and Pasiouras, F. "Assessing bank efficiency and performance with operational research and artificial intelligence techniques: a survey", *European Journal of Operational Research*, Vol. 204, no. 2, pp. 189–198, 2010.

19. Hinge, D. "Artificial intelligence in powered banking sector", *The Management Accountant Journal*, Vol. 54, no. 3, pp. 55–57, 2019.

20. Caron, M. S. The transformative effect of ai on the banking industry, *Banking & Finance Law Review*, Vol. 34, no. 2, pp. 169–214, 2019.
21. Zavadskaya, A. "Artificial intelligence in finance: forecasting stock market returns using artificial neural networks", Hanken School of Economics, Department of Finance and Statistics, Finance, 2017.
22. Wall, L. D. "Some financial regulatory implications of artificial intelligence", *Journal of Economics and Business*, Vol. 100, pp. 55–63, 2018. DOI: 10.1016/j.jeconbus.2018.05.003.
23. Kang, C.-M., Lin, S.-J. and Lin, L. "The hybrid artificial intelligence model for analyzing the default risk of non-profit financial intermediation", *Journal of Testing and Evaluation*, Vol. 44, no. 5, pp. 2045–2058, Sep. 2016. DOI: 10.1520/JTE20140203.
24. Herrero, Á., Corchado, E. and Jiménez, A. "Unsupervised neural models for country and political risk analysis", *Expert System and Application*, Vol. 38, no. 11, pp. 13641–13661, 2011.
25. Keilis-Borok, V. I., Soloviev, A. A., Allègre, C. B., Sobolevskii, A. N. and Intriligator, M. D. "Patterns of macroeconomic indicators preceding the unemployment rise in Western Europe and the USA", *Pattern Recognition*, Vol. 38, no. 3, pp. 423–435, 2005.
26. Rauch, C. "AI for good—how artificial intelligence can help sustainable development", 2018. [Cited 2020 April 25]. Available: https://medium.com/@C8215/ai-for-good-how-artificial-intelligence-can-help-sustainable-development-58b47d1c289a.
27. Skiba, M., Mrówczyńska, M. and Bazan-Krzywoszańska, A. "Modeling the economic dependence between town development policy and increasing energy effectiveness with neural networks. case study: the town of Zielona Góra", *Applied Energy*, Vol. 188, pp. 356–366, 2017.
28. Liu, K. F.-R. and Yu, C.-W. "Integrating case-based and fuzzy reasoning to qualitatively predict risk in an environmental impact assessment review", *Environmental Modeling & Software*, Vol. 24, no. 10, pp. 1241–1251, Oct. 2009.
29. Price Economics Data Studio, "Which industries are investing in artificial intelligence?" November 2018. [Cited 2020 April 28]. Available: https://priceonomics.com/which-industries-are-investing-in-artificial/.
30. Harkut, D. G., Kasat, K., and Harkut, V. D.. "Introductory chapter: artificial intelligence-challenges and applications". *Artificial Intelligence-Scope and Limitations*. Intech Open, pp. 1–5, 2019. DOI: http://dx.doi.org/10.5772/intechopen.84624.
31. Techutzpah, "Artificial intelligence benefits and challenges – a double-edged promise" February 2019. [Cited 2020 April 26]. Available: https://blockdelta.io/artificial-intelligence-benefits-and-challenges-a-double-edged-promise/.
32. Tag, L. "Artificial Intelligence: Challenges, Benefits, and Risks" April 2019. [Cited 2020 April 26]. Available: https://www.luxtag.io/blog/artificial-intelligence-challenges-benefits-and-risks/.

13

Proposed Model of Agriculture Big Data for Crop Disease Classification and Recommendation

Raghu Garg and Himanshu Aggarwal

CONTENTS

13.1 Introduction

Farming requires significant enhancement to withstand the changing circumstances of the Indian economy. A highly specialized procedure is required for systematic monitoring of harvest. Crop disease indirectly affects the reduction of both the quality and quantity of agrarian stocks. A multitude of pesticides are accessible to prevent diseases and improve harvest, but discovery of modern disease and appropriate pesticide to monitor the infected disease is troublesome and requires professional advice, which is time-consuming and rare. The existence of disease on the plant is indicated by symptoms on leaves. This calls for a computerized, detailed, and slightly less expensive system for the detection of diseases and proposal of pesticides. This chapter recommends a system for crop disease restraint that will help researchers and agricultural authorities in decision making based on past data, with the assistance of big data analytics. If big data analytics is utilized in agriculture, it will not only be an enormous modernization in the history of agriculture but also a pioneering work in human history. In our research, we worked on diseases of paddy, cotton, and wheat. The diseases that infect wheat plants are stem rust, leaf rust, powdery mildew, and yellow rust (Huang et al., 2014). Some of the cotton leaf diseases are bacterial blight caused by "Xanthomonas Campestrispv. Malvacearum" bacteria (Rothe and Kshirsagar, 2015), Alternaria, Cerespora, Grey Mildew (Revathi and Hemalatha, 2012), and Fusarium Wilt (Rothe and Kshirsagar, 2015). Paddy diseases include rice leaf blast disease (BD), brown-spot disease (BSD), and narrow brown-spot disease (NBSD) (Kurniawati, Abdullah, Abdullah, and Abdullah, 2009). To fully classify crop diseases and recommend solutions to save the plants, this chapter proposes two machine learning techniques—Naïve Bayes and support vector machine (SVM) in text categorization. For Naïve Byes experiment configuration, three nodes, Hadoop cluster with Hadoop 2.7 receptacle, and mahout 0.7 machine comprehending archive have been wielded in the MapReduce programming model. Here, eclipse IDE is employed for the programming habitat. Data is compiled from TATA chemical laboratory and agriculture websites. Text categorization is the process of filtering text records into one or more predefined classifications or degrees of similar documents. Disparities in the outcomes of such categorization originate from the outline set elected to establish the coalition of an allotted document with a given classification. Moreover, researchers have examined the benefit of machine learning strategies to automatically associate reports with initial categories by using a training set to adapt the classifier to the feature set of the document. The machine learning process starts with the inspection of specimen documents to deduce the least aspect set that generates the anticipated categorization outcomes. This training stage may or may not be supervised. In both trials, a set of classification has been distinguished, unlike in clustering which formulates sectors based on characteristics of the original documents. The unsupervised learning techniques utilize elements of the training documents to let the algorithm determine the grade each document belongs to. Supervised learning techniques use a batch of qualifying documents that have been correlated to differentiate which feature set of the statements will stimulate required conclusions. Machine learning techniques successfully delivered document sets over the definitive vector space prototype. In these experiments, only the SVM and Naïve Bayes methods are selected. In the paper (Basu, Walters, and Shepherd, 2003), SVM and ANN are compared; the SVM algorithm is comparatively less complex than ANNs because the parameter α that establishes the hyperplane is very insignificant, and α can be predicted to be minor because it is linear. In another paper (Kang, Yoo, and Han, 2012), the examinations administered to gauge the efficiency of SVM, Naïve Bayes, and ANN. SVM and Naïve Byes give comparative results more than ANN. The author (Luo, Li, and Cao, 2016) has also shown that SVM gives more promising results than Naïve Bayes. So, in our recommended experiments, we prefer Naïve Bayes using the MapReduce programming model over the Hadoop environment and SVM.

The remainder of the paper is orchestrated as follows: in Section 13.2, big data in soil is described. The proposed material and methods have been derived in Section 13.3.

Discussion of the crop disease classification system operating machine learning comprising their performance is presented in Section 13.4. A comprehensive exploratory survey for crop disease classification and solutions are presented in Section 13.5. Section 13.6 concludes the chapter.

13.2 Big Data in Soil

Big data depicts complex, variable, and high-velocity data that demands progressed networks and technologies to organize storage, handling, and inspection of information.

13.2.1 Volume

The 'big' in big data itself defines volume (Chi, 2016). Agricultural data not only generates historical data but also amorphous data from cloud computing, digital technology, Internet of Things (IOT), professional's information, and remote sensing. These data are raw, undeveloped, and semi-structured, which is hard to oversee through existing traditional systems.

13.2.2 Variety

The volume correlated with the big data phenomena brings along new challenges for data centers trying to deal with its variety (Kamilaris, Kartakoullis, and Prenafeta-Boldú, 2017). With the fortune of smart devices such as sensors, digital technology in agriculture has become complicated as it encompass not only chronological data but also semi-structured, non-structured, and raw data from sensors, agricultural expert documents, e-mail data, and so on.

13.2.3 Velocity

Velocity in big data is the knowledge of data speed that comes from many sources. This is not limited to the speed of incoming data but also the speed of data streams (Zikopoulos and Eaton, 2011). For example, data from sensor tools are frequently moved to the depository of the database, but this data is not sufficient. In this way, our traditional procedures are not skilled in evaluating data that is continuously changing positions.

13.2.4 Variability

The unexpected data progression is examined by variability. The rise in usage gives challenges to sustain burden that usually results in peak load on some occasions. Modifications to big data refer to a few distinct elements, one of them is the amount of inconsistencies. For any significant estimation to come about, they need to be inspected through significant analytics and investigation tools. Big data is also inconsistent because numerous data sizes emerge from various data types and sources.

13.3 Material and Methods

13.3.1 Naïve Bayes Classifier

Naïve Bayes is a simple and practical machine understanding technique in earlier text classification research. This is actually optimal in some circumstances (Lewis, 1998; Domingos and Pazzani, 1997; Liu, Blasch, Chen, Shen, and Chen 2013).

Assume there are m possible classes $C = \{c1, c2, \cdots, c_m\}$ for a domain of documents $D = \{d1, d2, \cdots, d_n\}$ Let $W = \{w1, w2, \cdots, w_s\}$ be the set of distinct words, each occurring at least once in one of the documents in D. The probability of a document d occurring in class c can be evaluated using Bayes' rule:

$$P(c|d) = \frac{P(c)P(d|c)}{P(d)}.$$

(13.1)

Here, the denominator in the equation above is normally not computed for parametric statistical situations, and $P(d)$ is a constant. The word w_k appears unassisted in the document which provides the class c. Consequently, Equation (13.1) is now:

$$P(c|d) \propto P(c) \prod_{k=1}^{n_d} [P(w_k|c)]^{t_k},$$

(13.2)

where n_d is the number of unique words in document d and t_k is the regularity of each word w_k. To avoid drifting point underflow, we use the identical equation:

$$log \ P(c|d) \propto \ log \ P(c) + \sum_{k=1}^{n_d} [t_k \ log \ P(w_k|c)].$$

(13.3)

Here, d is determined as the class, and $c*$ picks up the maximum probability

$$c* = argmax_{c \in C} \left\{ log \ P(c) + \sum_{k=1}^{n_d} [t_k \ log \ P(w_k|c)] \right\}$$

(13.4)

When referring to the Naïve Bayes classifier (NBC), we can calculate $P(c)$, $6P(w_k|c)$ as:

$$\hat{P}(c) = \frac{N_c}{N} \ and \ \hat{P}(w_k|c) = \frac{N_{w_k}}{\Sigma_{w_i \in W} N_{w_i}}$$

(13.5)

where N is the total number of text files, N_c is the total number of documents in class c and N_{w_i} is the regularity of a word w_i in class c. These equations make MapReduce an applicable framework for the execution of NBC in large-scale datasets.

13.3.2 SVM Classifiers

For disease identification analysis, the linear SVM has been used. In the binary division, the fundamental vision is to discover a linear hyperplane; characteristics are categorized by linearly segregated hyperplane with unfavorable and favorable categories. The best distinguishing hyperplane difficulties can be reflected in Equation (13.6):

$$\min \varphi(w) = \min_{w,b} \frac{1}{2} \|w\|^2 = \min_{w,b} \frac{1}{2}(w^T w) \tag{13.6}$$

Two sorts of linear specimen can be detached if it fulfills the necessities exhibited in Equation (13.7):

$$(w \cdot x_i) + b \geq +1 \text{ for } y_i = +1$$
$$(w \cdot x_i) + b \leq -1 \text{ for } y_i = -1 \tag{13.7}$$

If $y_i = 1$ denotes the favorable categorization to which the point .. belongs, $y_i = -1$ denotes the unfavorable categorization. We want to locate the maximum margin hyperplane that splits up the points possessing $y_i = +1$ from those having $y_i = -1$. Here, w denotes the normal vector to the hyperplane.

13.3.3 Mean Average Precision (*mAP*)

The accomplishment of our proposed method is calculated using precision $P(N)$ and recall $R(N)$ for obtaining top N good recommend explanation established on machine learning algorithms, which is interpreted by

$$P(N) = \frac{I_N}{N}, \tag{13.8}$$

and

$$R(N) = \frac{I_N}{M}, \tag{13.9}$$

where I_N is the number of suitable fetched results from top N positions. In our investigations, we have utilized top $N = 10$. $N = 1$, also known as top-1 accuracy, and M, the total number of disease solutions in the dataset that are identical to the questioning done by farmers, agriculture experts, and so on. The standard accuracy of a single questioning .. is the mean of all precision values $P(n)$, $n = 1, 2, \ldots, N$, i.e.

$$\bar{P}(q) = \frac{1}{N} \sum_{n=1}^{N} P(n). \tag{13.10}$$

The mean average precision (*mAP*) is the mean of the average score's overall inquiries Q:

$$mAP = \frac{1}{Q} \sum_{q=1}^{Q} \bar{P}(q). \tag{13.11}$$

The *mAP* measure contains both the precision and recall information and depicts the whole ranking.

13.4 Crop Disease Classification System Using Machine Learning

Our proposed model is applied to crop disease classification and recommendation solutions. The recommendation system uses past data available to identify wheat, paddy, and cotton diseases, and recommend the best remedy based on symptom similarity using Naïve Bayes and support vector machine (SVM) algorithm. The first process of the proposed model is extracting useful information from the collected dataset and storing it on a distributed system. A vector data structure is used to store crop disease symptoms and crop names. Here, the disease name is used to classify data using discussed algorithms, with the help of a ten-fold cross-validation method. The mean average precision (*mAP*) is used for performance evaluation. After the training process, the proposed model will process existing statistics to identify the disease name and suggest the right pesticide to aid in crop production. Figure 13.1 shows the crop disease identification system using the Naïve Bayes machine learning method in big data. The implementation process using Naïve Bayes and support vector machine (SVM) algorithm system follows.

13.4.1 Implementation Process of Naïve Bayes

The execution and development of building the Naïve Bayes classifier using the MapReduce programming framework consists of important steps such as (a) data clearing and formatting, (b) convert formatting of data into vectors (training and second for testing) and storing on Hadoop cluster, (c) training the classification model using Naïve Bayes algorithm with regime dataset and (d) calculating classifier model performance using the test dataset. In the data pre-processing phase, the data set is divided into two parts: the first part of the data is used for model training and the other is treated as "unknown" data for model testing. If there are continuous variables available in the dataset, a pre-processing MapReduce job is performed to discretize the continuous

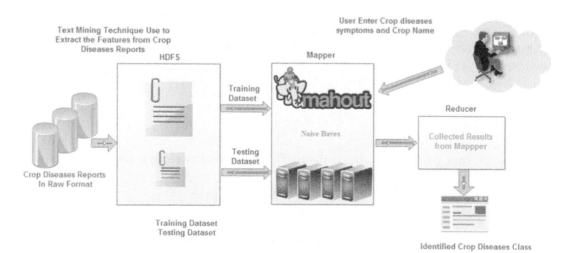

FIGURE 13.1
Crop disease identification system using Naïve Bayes.

variables. After pre-processing, the researcher loads the pre-processed data into HDFS and performs MapReduce tasks against the data.

a. *Data cleaning:* Data cleaning is the assembly of data for calculation by eliminating incomplete, inaccurate, irrelevant, duplicated, or improperly formatted data not beneficial in evaluation, as it obstructs the process and provides inaccurate results. Firstly, data is accumulated from various resources such as agriculture websites, lab reports, etc. The collected data is called raw data because it contains unwanted information. Then, sanctification of data is done to extract useful information from raw unstructured data, and this data is stored on HDFS. The Name Node of the Hadoop allocated file system tracks how the records are broken down into file blocks and which nodes shelter those slabs. The clients communicate promptly with Data Node to refine these local files corresponding to the blocks. The important data sources for the agricultural sector are laboratory test reports and agriculture statistics websites. Data cleaning is not about wiping out information to create room for new data but finding a means to maximize a dataset's accuracy without erasing information. It encompasses activity other than demolishing data—rectifying errors such as empty fields, pointing out duplicate data points, and converting data into proper format (such as text format) to improve data quality. Now, the file converts text data into vector format because the model can only examine sequential data.

b. *Dividing sequential data:* After data conversion into sequential form, they are split up into ten parts. Cross-validation methods (leave-one-out and ten-cross validation) are used to measure classifier accuracy. In these techniques, the training set is divided into mutually exclusive and proportional subsets; each classifier is trained on all the other subsets. Out of the ten subsets, one is utilized for testing and the rest for training. This process is repeated ten times. Nine subsets are used to train the model and one subset is used to test the model.

c. *Trained the training and testing model:* Next is training in the proposed model to recommend crop diseases solution using the Naïve Bayes machine learning algorithm. After training the model test, data is utilized to examine the execution of the recommended prototype. The primary objective of the train and test phase is to enhance the accuracy of the developed model.

d. *Design performance matrix:* In this matrix, we measure the number of instances correctly and wrongly categorized and obtain model accuracy.

13.4.2 Implementation Process of Support Vector Machine (SVM)

Like Naïve Bayes' implementation discussed above, data clearing and formatting and formatted data conversion into vectors (training and testing) are the same. Next, feature elements are weighed with Term Frequency and Inverse Documentation Frequency (TF-IDF) and disease symptoms (text) are exemplified with the vector space model (VSM). Then, a classifier with a support vector machine (SVM) is built. Lastly, the classifier for disease classification of test data is utilized. In this technique, the fundamental strategies of belief examination involve characteristic item weighting, feature choice, text articulation, and classifier algorithm designation.

13.4.2.1 Text Categorization

Text categorization intends to establish reports into predetermined stabilized sectors (Joachims, 1998). Modifying documents into a reasonable expression for the understanding algorithm and the classification task is the initial step in text categorization. Every unique term w_i in documents that come for a specific number of amounts is related to a feature. The term w_i is evaluated as feature if it seems in the training set at least 3 times and not like "and", "or", etc. According to Zipf's Law (Moreno-Sánchez, Font-Clos, and Corral 2016), there is a minimum amount of words that repeats frequently for every frequency distribution. Moreover, if one ranks words by their term frequency, the r-th most frequent word appears roughly $1/r$ times the term frequency of the vastly frequent words.

13.4.2.2 Feature Selection

Feature selection is an unavoidable fraction of disease examination. Its goal is to collect a small subset of features from the problem domain while retaining high accuracy in representing the original features. In recent years, a ton of feature selection techniques have been formulated where Chi-square (*CHI*) (Galavotti, Sebastiani, and Simi 2000) method has been considered. As a statistical test, it is recognized to conduct haphazardly for small anticipated counts familiar in in-text division because of having barely arising word features and occasionally few favorable training examples for a notion. The *Chi*–square difference between Positive and Negative Categories (*CDPNC*) is expressed in the Equation (13.12):

$$CDPNC(t_n, c_n, c_p) = p(t_i) * |CHI(t_i, c_n) - CHI(t_i, c_P)| \qquad (13.12)$$

In Equation (13.12), $p(t_i)$ is the regularity of word t_i in the training dataset.

13.4.2.3 Text Representation

The conventional vector space model (VSM) is utilized for text articulation in-text subject classification. The fundamental notion of VSM is to formulate each text into a vector. Every feature word of the text $D(t_1, t_2, ..., t_n)$ is assembled in words which can be each dimension of complementary vectors. The value of each feature item corresponds to a numerical manifestation of the text representation. Thus, the document $D(t_1, t_2, ..., t_n)$ is a vector and $(w_1, w_2, ... w_n)$ are the coordinate merits. For our system, the VSM model is exemplified as $D(t_1, w_1, t_2, w_2, ..., t_n, w_n,)$. Every feature of the document is assembled in phrases, which can be detected as each dimension of the complementary vectors text $T(t_1, t_2, ..., t_n)$. The burden of each characteristic commodity corresponds to a numerical representation of the text representation.

13.5 Experiment Analysis of Machine Learning Algorithms

In this examination setup, private Hadoop 2.7 infrastructure with composition master node of 8GB RAM, i7 CPU, and two data nodes with 3 GB RAM and i3 CPU, have been utilized. Data is accumulated from TATA chemical laboratory and agricultural websites. Subsequently, the feature extraction dataset contains comparative 5,000 records related to paddy, wheat, and cotton related diseases. Data is comprised of crop name, disease name, disease type, disease detail, location, disease symptoms, solution ID, etc. Eclipse IDE is used to formulate an application using Java. For this, we determined the vastly commonly used machine learning text classification techniques—Naïve Byes and support vector machine (SVM) for crop disease classification data with the help of agriculture experts. In this investigation, the data is divided into two parts: training and testing—70% for training, and the rest for testing.

13.5.1 Performance Comparison of Machine Learning Algorithms

The experiment compares the performance of SVM using a polynomial kernel with a Naïve Bayes classifier. The median average precision (mAP) values and their average of several string similarities are illustrated in Table 13.1 on wheat leaf diseases such as leaf rust, powdery, stem rust. In Table 13.1, it is shown that for disease leaf rust, the machine learning method SVM gives 85.89% mean average precision (mAP) value but the Naïve Bayes using Hadoop framework provides 87.99% accuracy. In the case of powdery disease, Naïve Bayes performed better then SVM; the Naïve Byes gives 90.34% mAP and the SVM gives 89.45%. A similar trend also follows in the case of stem rust disease—Naïve Bayes gives 89.45% mAP and SVM gives 87.23% mAP. In average mAP, the Naïve Bayes comes before the SVM.

We are performed experiments on cotton leaf diseases such as Malvacearum, Alternaria, Cerespora, Grey Mildew, and Fusarium Wilt using Naïve Bayes and SVM machine learning algorithms. In Table 13.2, for Malvacearum disease, Naïve Bayes gives an absolute mAP rate of 86.90% followed by SVM with 85.87%. In Alternaria cotton leaf disease, Naïve Bayes gives an mAP rate of 91.87%; SVM with 88.90%. In the case of Cerespora disease, SVM gives a higher than Naïve Bayes. The highest mAP is in Cerespora disease is by SVM at 91.64% and Naïve Bayes at 89.02%. In Grey Mildew disease, Naïve Bayes has 94.87% and SVM has 90.23%. The highest mAP in Fusarium Wilt disease by SVM is 87.29%; hamming at 90.34%. The highest average rate of Naïve Bayes is 90.06%; SVM has 88.78%.

The mAP values and their various string similarities are displayed in Table 13.3 on paddy rice diseases such as rice leaf blast, brown-spot, narrow brown-spot. In rice leaf blast, Naïve Bayes gives higher mAP (89.78%) followed by SVM (84.23%). In brown-spot

TABLE 13.1

Mean Average Precision (mAP) for $N = 10$ Obtained by Naïve Bayes and SVM in Wheat Leaf Diseases

Methods → Diseases ↓	Naïve Bayes	SVM
Leaf rust	87.99	85.89
Powdery	90.34	89.45
Stem rust	89.45	87.23
Average (mAP)	89.59	87.52

TABLE 13.2

Mean Average Precision (*mAP*) for $N = 10$ Obtained by Naïve Bayes and SVM in Cotton Leaf Diseases

Methods → Disease ↓	Naïve Bayes	SVM
Malvacearum	86.90	85.87
Alternaria	91.87	88.90
Cercospora	89.02	91.64
Grey mildew	94.87	90.23
Fusarium wilt	90.34	87.29
Average (*mAP*)	**90.06**	88.78

TABLE 13.3

Mean Average Precision (*mAP*) $N = 10$ Obtained by Naïve Bayes and SVM in Paddy Rice Diseases

Methods → Disease ↓	Naïve Bayes	SVM
Rice leaf blast (BD)	89.78	84.23
Brown-spot (BSD),	90.23	89.45
Narrow brown-spot (NBSD)	89.45	84.78
Average (*mAP*)	**89.82**	86.15

disease the accuracies of 90.23% for Naïve Bayes and 89.45% for SVM are achieved. The highest *mAP* is achieved in narrow brown-spot disease by Naïve Bayes at 89.45%, followed by SVM at 86.15%. The highest average *mAP* rate of Naïve Bayes is 89.82%, while SVM is at 86.158%.

13.6 Conclusion

In this chapter, we have proposed a system to test cotton, wheat, and paddy disease; the results suggest solutions that can help control crop disease. The proposed task is a solution based on historical data. The objective of the current research is to formulate a big data analytics suggestion framework to control crop disease that assists agriculture administrators and researchers. Here, we propose a technique for disease classification and solution recommendation using machine learning methods based on historical data. In the experimental setup, data is collected from TATA chemical laboratory and agricultural websites. After the characteristic extraction, the dataset contains around 5,000 records associated with paddy, wheat, and cotton-related diseases. We analyzed that Naïve Bayes machine learning disease classification algorithms in the MapReduce programming model on the Hadoop environment are better than the support vector machine (SVM).

References

Liu, B., Blasch, E., Chen, Y., Shen, D. and Chen, G., "Scalable sentiment classification for big data analysis using Näive Bayes classifier," In *2013 IEEE International Conference on Big Data*, 2013, October, pp. 99–104, IEEE.

Lewis, D. D., "Naive (Bayes) at forty: the independence assumption in information retrieval," In *European conference on machine learning*, 1998, April, pp. 4–15, Springer, Berlin, Heidelberg.

Domingos, P. and Pazzani, M., "On the optimality of the simple Bayesian classifier under zero-one loss," *Machine Learning*, vol. 29, no. 2–3, pp. 103–130, 1997.

Joachims, T. Text Categorization with Support Vector Machines: Learning with Many Relevant Features, In *European Conference on Machine Learning*, 1998, pp. 137–142. Springer, Berlin, Heidelberg.

Moreno-Sánchez, I., Font-Clos, F. and Corral, Á., "Large-scale analysis of Zipf's law in English texts," *PloS one*, vol. 11, no. 1, 2016.

Luo, F., Li, C., and Cao, Z., "Affective-feature-based sentiment analysis using SVM classifier," In *2016 IEEE 20th International Conference on Computer Supported Cooperative Work in Design (CSCWD)*, 2016, May, pp. 276–281, IEEE.

Basu, A., Walters, C., and Shepherd, M., "Support vector machines for text categorization," In *36th Annual Hawaii International Conference on System Sciences, 2003*. Proceedings of the, 2003, January, pp. 7–pp, IEEE.

Kang, H., Yoo, S. J. and Han, D., "Senti-lexicon and improved Naïve Bayes algorithms for sentiment analysis of restaurant reviews," *Expert Systems with Applications*, vol. 39, no. 5, pp. 6000–6010, 2012.

Huang, W., Guan, Q., Luo, J., Zhang, J., Zhao, J., Liang, D., Huang, L., and Zhang, D., "New optimized spectral indices for identifying and monitoring winter wheat diseases," *IEEE Journal of Selected Topics in Applied Earth Observations and Remote Sensing*, vol. 7, no. 6, pp. 2516–2524, 2014.

Rothe, P. R. and Kshirsagar, R. V., "Cotton leaf disease identification using pattern recognition techniques," In *2015 International Conference on Pervasive Computing (ICPC)*, 2015, January, pp. 1–6, IEEE.

Revathi, P. and Hemalatha, M., "Classification of cotton leaf spot diseases using image processing edge detection techniques," In *2012 International Conference on Emerging Trends in Science, Engineering and Technology (INCOSET)*, 2012, December, pp. 169–173, IEEE.

Kurniawati, N. N., Abdullah, S. N. H. S., Abdullah, S., and Abdullah, S., "Investigation on image processing techniques for diagnosing paddy diseases," In *2009 International Conference of Soft Computing and Pattern Recognition*, 2009, December, pp. 272–277, IEEE.

Chi, M., "Big data for remote sensing: challenges and opportunities," *Proceedings of IEEE*, vol. 104, no. 11, pp. 2207–2219, 2016.

Kamilaris, A., Kartakoullis, A., and Prenafeta-Boldú, F. X., "A review on the practice of big data analysis in agriculture," *Computers and Electronics in Agriculture*, vol. 143, pp. 23–23, 2017.

Zikopoulos, P. and Eaton, C., Understanding Big Data: Analytics for Enterprise Class Hadoop and Streaming Data. McGraw-Hill Osborne Media, 2011.

Galavotti, L., Sebastiani, F., and Simi, M., "Experiments on the use of feature selection and negative evidence in automated text categorization," In *International Conference on Theory and Practice of Digital Libraries*, 2000, September, pp. 59–68, Springer, Berlin, Heidelberg.

14

Machine Intelligence versus Terrorism

Piali Haldar and Ashok Singh

CONTENTS

14.1 Introduction

Machine Intelligence (MI) is one of the domains of artificial intelligence (AI). The role of MI in AI is gaining importance in the industry all over the world. There is a radical shift in the use of MI in business as well as other domains like security, physics, biotechnology, robotics, etc. Currently, most developed countries use MI to combat terrorism, as available technology and resources are not enough. The rate of terrorist attacks in India is higher than other developed nations like USA, Russia, Japan, and Germany, which calls for an urgency to combat it. ('What Is Machine Intelligence? | Shield AI' 2018)

The probability of a terrorist attack in India is higher compared to other developed countries. One of the reasons for this is that India shares boundaries with Pakistan, China, Nepal, Bangladesh, Afghanistan, Sri Lanka, Bhutan, and Myanmar, which gives rise to cross-border terrorism. Since terrorism is unpredictable, human capabilities are limited in anticipating the time, place, and nature of the attack. Security issues are becoming a severe problem daily as terrorist groups continuously use the latest technology in exchanging data and information. For this, MI plays a significant role in managing big data.

A report by the Congress's Joint Inquiry states that US intelligence agencies could have prevented the terrorist attack at the World Trade Center on September 11, 2001 if they were well equipped with information technology.

('House Permanent Select Committee on Intelligence, Report, Counterterrorism Intelligence Capabilities, and Performance Prior to 9–11, July 2002, Unclassified, HPSCI.' 2020)

In September 2019, Prime Minister Shri Narendra Modi has implied that Pakistan is the center for terrorism. He mentioned that both 9/11 (USA) and 26/11 (India) incidents share the same ground, and that it is time to battle terrorism and those who encourage it (Writer 2019).

One of the problems is information-sharing between departments. To combat terrorism, there is a need for flawless information dissemination through real-time data. It is possible to resist terrorist attacks through a collaborative effort of departments, with help from the latest technology.

14.1.1 The Role of Collaboration in Counterterrorism

Collaboration between departments is needed for better counterterrorism strategies; there is an edge in a quick response to any threat of terrorist activity. To develop a counterterrorism strategy, there should be a collaboration between government departments and counterterrorism communities, human wisdom and machine intelligence, and real-time and periodic data. The only way to effectively resist terrorism is through integration — when they act as a single unit. Not only does it create cooperation, but also provides better understanding of the current situation. Information Technology (IT) is the platform that allows us to implement Decision Support Tools (DST), which let humans solve complex problems accurately, efficiently, and effectively. This tool requires a massive amount of data provided by the government's agencies, counterterrorism communities, etc. Thus, collaboration between different agencies is required to make the system more accurate. All information stored in big data is analyzed through data mining, which gives valuable interpretation of available data that leads to identified previous terrorist activities, their patterns, locations, and types of people involved. (Figure 14.1).

14.2 Machine Intelligence

Machine intelligence is defined as a form of intelligence different from human and animal intelligence (Figure 14.2). Modern machine intelligence is a combination of imitation (i.e. artificial intelligence), self-learning, retrospection, and introspection. Although artificial

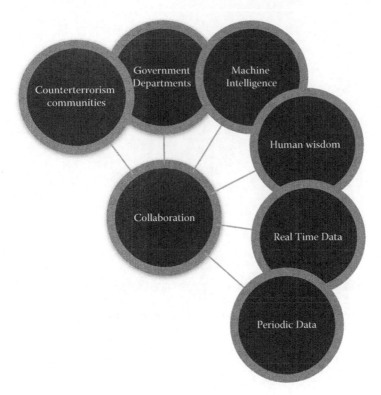

FIGURE 14.1
Collaboration from different department and specifications.

intelligence has become a prominent subject of research in the field of academics in recent years, it has been a subject for several years — lots of movies with this theme were screened in Hollywood in 1972.

14.2.1 Types of Machine Intelligence

There are four branches of Machine Intelligence (Figure 14.3):

- Cognitive Computing
- Artificial Intelligence
- Deep Learning
- Machine Learning

14.2.2 Cognitive Computing

Cognitive computing is the sensory branch of machine intelligence. Using sensors and algorithms, computers can "see," "hear," and "feel" (there have been strong efforts to address "smell" and "taste").

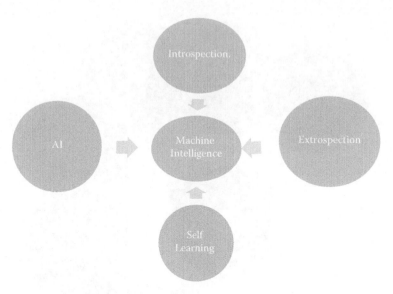

FIGURE 14.2
Conceptual diagram of machine intelligence with respect to its elements.

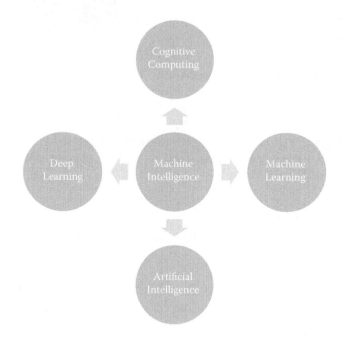

FIGURE 14.3
Author's contribution 3: 'Conceptual diagram of machine intelligence with respect to its individual branches'.

Cognitive computing develops human capability and makes the computer or machine think, behave, and act like a human being.

Image sensors provide sight to the machine and a microphone helps them hear. Text-to-speech and speech-to-text technologies empower them to communicate with human beings using natural (human) language. Some examples are Alexa, Siri, Cortana, and Google Assistant.

Adding cameras and microphones to computers isn't a new concept, but now a brain has been added to a computer. Cognitive computing is about adding artificial sensory capabilities and a brain to computers—this makes computers think, behave, and act like humans.

14.2.3 Artificial Intelligence

AI is not a new technology—one has been using it in their day-to-day life, like online shopping, Google, Facebook photo tagging, intraday share market, etc. It helps in decision making progress while implementing machine learning algorithms. In the past, it was used in limited areas, but cloud computing, decreasing price of storage devices, and fast processing units have contributed to the growth of this technology. Think of AI as the brain behind cognitive computing—cognitive computing oversees sensory capabilities, but AI can exist without them. There are no sensory limits to it; it's just an intelligent recommendation.

Some inventions that have emerged are the Tesla Driverless Car and Sophia the Human Robot (UAE citizen).

14.2.4 Machine Learning

Machine learning refers to learning from past data, historical trends, patterns, and predicting future trend or conditions. Machine learning helps through vast amounts of data, empowering the tool to predict the uncertainty more accurately in the future.

The classic machine learning training is teaching a computer to differentiate between cats and dogs, or different breeds of cats and dogs. Such capabilities are now being used to identify objects and individuals in criminal investigations. Meanwhile, some of the enterprises are using predictive aspects to improve customer service, security, and business efficiencies to maximize profit.

Based on city crime reports, this technology helps in developing different patterns of crime.

14.2.5 Deep Learning

The concept of deep learning is obtained out of machine learning, where computers learn from historical data, and then applying the knowledge the way a human does. Thus, deep learning uses neural science and neurological techniques. By repeating the same task, it gains experience (hence, the term deep learning). For example, if the machine repeats the same task for four times, it is called 4 neural network learning system; if the machine repeats the same task 40 times, then it is called 40 neural network learning system. Generally, more than 40 neural learning system are acceptable to incorporate.

Deep learning is the most advanced form of machine learning, and it is becoming the ideal way of training computers. Deep learning uses neural networks that mimic the physiology and functions of a human brain. Neural networks include several layers of neurons, leading to the use of the term "deep learning".

14.2.6 Intelligence

Intelligence has been described as the ability to perceive or infer information, and to retain it as knowledge, applied towards adaptive behaviors within an environment or context. It can be described in many ways—logic, understanding, self-awareness, learning, emotional knowledge, reasoning, planning, creativity, critical thinking, and problem-solving.

14.2.7 Types of Intelligence

The figure below shows that intelligence is not restricted to a human being, but also widely present in non-humans—animals (birds, fish, etc.), plants, and gadgets and machines (computer, smartphone, machine learning, artificial intelligence, deep learning) (Figure 14.4).

14.3 Relationships between AI, MI, BI, ML, and Big Data

Artificial Intelligence (AI), Machine Intelligence (MI), Business Intelligence (BI), and Machine Learning (ML) are unique from one another. Since they are in the developing phase, lots of progress is required to achieve a certain level for their unique identity. (Figure 14.5).

14.4 Big Data

Big data is the backbone of every module or technique. The process of AI is developing at a slow pace due to the complex nature of the problem and because of the non-availability

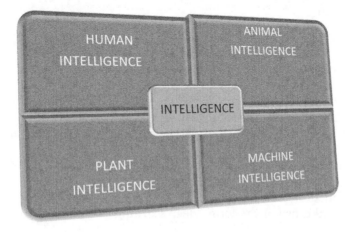

FIGURE 14.4
Author's contribution 4: 'Conceptual diagram of intelligence with respect to types of available intelligence'.

FIGURE 14.5
Author's contribution 5: 'The venn diagram with the relation of AI, MI, BI, ML, and BIG DATA'.

of required technology. Since AI is the process or philosophy of human-level intelligence in the digital world, it requires resources and various specialized teams to achieve it. First, every computer ideally works in a controlled environment (static in nature). All information is available in 0 and 1 format (binomial digit)—there is hardly a scope of fuzzy data, but in the real world, for any simple or complex task, a series of influential factor (dynamic in nature) directly or indirectly affects our current situation and human act and solve that particular problem in an effective way. This is the main key to the survival of human beings (since inception). Humans have acquired extensive knowledge over a period through experience, which transfers from one generation to another, and stored in the form of books and folk tales.

When we reached the moon on July 20, 1969 (National Aeronautical and Space Administration official website) with help of basic computing and with minimum resources (in terms of computing advancement), we created a miracle—there was no Object Oriented Programming Language introduced at that time, and the cost of computer was very high compare to today's computer peripherals (more affordable and more advanced in processing speed and memory storage). In the era of personal computer production and smartphone manufacture, companies achieve economies of scale, making advanced technology more affordable and widely available allowing Machine Intelligence (MI), Artificial Intelligence (AI), Business Intelligence (BI), and Machine Learning (ML) to become reality.

The cost of computer equipment has become affordable, making it useful for managing huge data in the form of big data (also known as four Vs).

14.4.1 Velocity

Big data are continuous in nature and could be achieved with the help of velocity, which arranges data sequentially and continuously in nature.

There are two types of velocity:

1. Frequency of data generation; and
2. Frequency of data handling, recording, and publishing.

14.4.2 Veracity

Veracity has been defined as data quality and the data value in big data (Onay and Öztürk 2018). Since analysis depends on the accuracy of the data, its quality matters a lot.

To make the data meaningful, one must process it using specific algorithms. It has been observed that supervised and unsupervised learning plays a vital role in helping a machine learn different tasks—like segmentation of population—based on available sample of huge data.

14.4.3 Variety

Variety in data helps connect missing pieces of information, as big data contain manuscript, imagery, audio-video, and other exogenous inputs through data fusion.

14.4.4 Volume

Volume is important in big data analysis because more data produces higher accuracy of prediction. Thus, the volume of the data determines the value and potential insight—whether it qualifies to be big data or not.

Big data pulse dynamic algorithm frame will not only be able to achieve the correct interpretation from available data, but also predict the situation and develop a prevention mechanism on its own.

In the context of AI, the scope of human involvement directly with data is limited, so privacy issue can be resolved easily.

14.5 Terrorism

Terrorism is one of the most heinous activities in the world. The term *terrorism* has been derived from the French word *terrorisme*, based on the Latin verb *terrere* (to cause to tremble). Jacobins had mentioned about the Reign of Terror for the first time during the French Revolution. Later, "terrorist" became a term of abuse that represents violence. At present, terrorism refers to the killing, by a group of people, of a common citizen to gain media attention. The United Nations Security Council in November 2004 has pointed out terrorism as any act "intended to cause death or serious bodily harm to civilians or noncombatants with the purpose of intimidating a population or compelling a government or an international organization to do or abstain from doing any act." In many countries, acts of terrorism have been distinguished from criminal acts in legal terms for several purposes.

14.5.1 Terrorism in India

Terrorism is not new to Indian people; dealing with incidents like this has become a habit. It is hard to determine the starting point of terrorism in India. The incidence of terrorism has been reported and recorded from the year 1980 and is still active until today. Most of the states are affected by terrorist activities, especially Jammu and Kashmir, Punjab, Gujarat, Delhi, Bihar, and Maharashtra. The northeast side of the country and border areas are the primary target of terrorists. Some incidents listed by the Union Territory New Delhi can be seen in Table 14.1, and the incidences of terrorism are plotted in the map in Figure 14.6.

14.6 Machine Intelligence versus Terrorism

There are developments taking place in the field of counterterrorism, especially in developed countries that have invested in AI technology to gain an advantage.

TABLE 14.1

List of Terrorist Incidents in India in 2020

Sr. No	Date	Incidence and Descriptions	Location
1	21/05/1996	Lajpat Nagar blast	Delhi
2	22/12/2000	Red Fort attack	Delhi
3	13/12/2001	Indian Parliament attack	Delhi
4	29/10/2005	Three powerful serial blasts in Delhi	Delhi
5	13/09/2008	Five bomb blasts in Delhi	Delhi
6	27/09/2008	Bomb blast in Mehrauli and Delhi Flower Market	Delhi
7	07/09/2011	Delhi Bomb Blast	Delhi
8	13/02/2012	Israeli Diplomat	Delhi

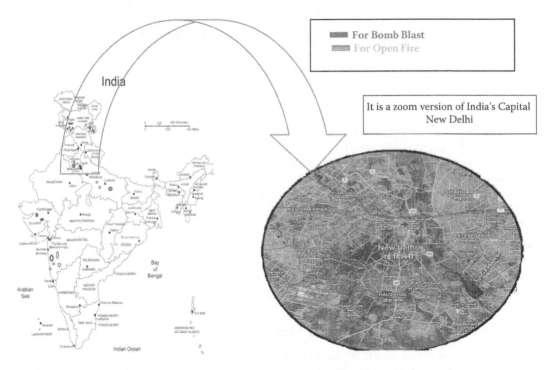

FIGURE 14.6
Author's contribution 6: 'Plotting the terrorist attack on the map of India as well as zoom version New Delhi Capital of India'.

An Early Model-Based Event Recognition using Surrogates (EMBERS) system (Tutun, Khasawneh, and Zhuang 2017) is used to predict and forecast unexpected events like civil riots, unforeseen diseases, etc. US Intelligence Advanced Research Projects Activity (IARPA)'s Open Source Indicators Program is a collaborative project between corporations and the academe, sponsored by the US government. The IARPA model takes the inputs from RSS feeds like social media, websites, and blogs. Based on these data, we can predict the next place of target and what time it might be.

However, it requires the involvement of:

- **Government** (permission, funds, task forces, etc.)
- **Scientists/Researchers** (data and algorithm development, other frameworks, etc.)
- **IT Companies** (IT infrastructures and data)
- **Corporations** (who are willing to share their customers' data to secure the nation)
- **Public** (cooperation, willingness, dedication, and participation, etc.)

14.6.1 The Role of Machine Intelligence in Preventing Terrorism

Information technology (biometrics, categorization, and clustering) is used to combat terrorism. Some of the tools and techniques are given below.

With the help of biometrics, technology can identify and verify whether someone is a terrorist (or included in a watch list) using 2D and 3D modeling. Some of the inputs used in biometrics are signature, face, gait, iris, fingerprint, voice, etc.

With the help of categorization and clustering technology, one can use numerous technical approaches like natural language processing, AI, machine learning, pattern recognition, statistical analysis, probabilistic techniques in extracting meaning and key concepts from (un)structured data.

All database processing is certified from different platforms like cloud server, local server, and centralized server that helps in syntactic and semantic consistency and interoperability of primary and secondary data.

Similar technologies are used collaboratively to combat terrorism—event detection, location sharing, information management system and filtering options, infrastructure advancement of 4G and 5G technologies, knowledge-based management, context development, predictive modeling, and prevention management.

Since a terrorist may look like a regular citizen, it is hard to label someone as one.

To allow machine intelligence to operate in terrorism, one must determine a terrorist by keeping a close eye on their activities—scout their residence, tap their phone, track their financial transactions like vehicle registration and businesses, inspect their education, social circles, and religious beliefs—and turn the information into big data to predict any form of illegal or terrorist activity.

14.6.2 A Conceptual One Level Data Flowchart

A conceptual one level data flowchart is given a detailed description in Figure 14.7. Some of the database input descriptions are given in bullet-point format.

- **Phone Call Conversation Database (P.C.C.D.B.):** arrange to record each voice conversation so that all conversations can be analyzed by the machine learning environment.
- **All Local Police Station Real-Time Database (A.L.P.S. R.T.D.B.):** All local police station should have access to real-time data (that can be analyzed by machine learning environment) that will identify terrorist activity.
- **Central Hazard Material Real-time Inventory Database (C.H.M.R.T.I.D.B):** Keep a real-time inventory system for prohibited chemicals and raw materials used in producing explosives. Such inventory should be kept on close

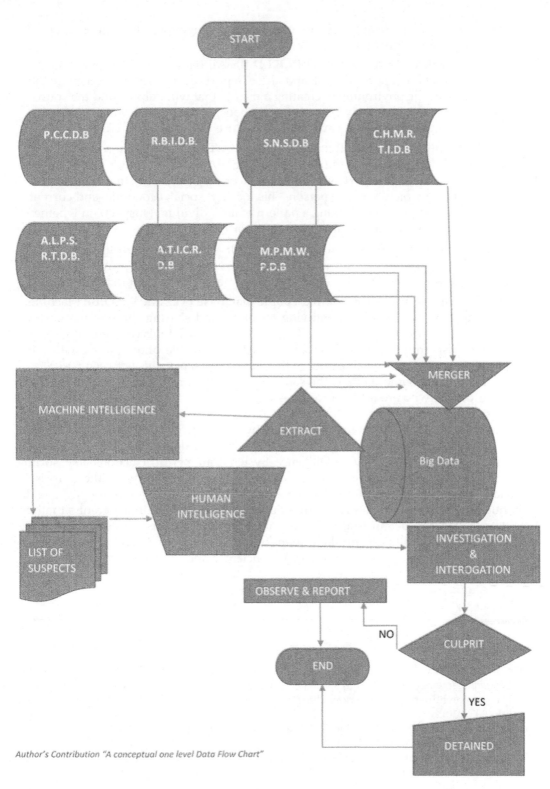

Author's Contribution "A conceptual one level Data Flow Chart"

FIGURE 14.7
A conceptual one level data flow chart.

observation and all inventories should have proper tagging so that one can report to the central information system.

- **Reserve Bank of India Database (R.B.I.D.B):** All banks should provide suspicious transaction reports to RBI and these reports should be shared with the machine learning environment, creating a trigger that will help us find the source and prevent other money-related fraud, boosting the Anti-Money Laundry System in implementing its cause and procedure efficiently and effectively.

- **All the Identification Card Related Database (A.T.I.C.R.D.B):** There should be a centralized database for identification number (PAN Card, Aadhar Card, Ration Card, Voter Card, passport with their latest photograph, etc.) that will help in getting an exact picture of the person—his locality, social, economic, and current professional status—and creating a pattern of an individual (suspect) on whether they participate in terrorist activity actively or otherwise.

- **Social Networking Site Database (S.N.S.D.B):** Most terrorist groups use social networking sites for recruitment. So, machine learning tools can be used to prevent terrorist activities by impeding posts made by the terrorist groups.

- **Missing People and Most Wanted People Database (M.P.M.W.P.D.B):** Machine learning tools will help in identifying terrorists and sharing the information to global anti-terrorist organizations. By using big data, ML tools can help single out the terrorist from society. ML will try to match available photographs with the population; once the facial feature of the photographs matches between 60-100%, then one can assume them as the same person. This process will help in identifying people who are a threat to our society.

A model where a dynamic database is created by merging data available from different sources has been developed. The government can use big data to identify the terrorists living in society. The Machine Intelligence System can perform actions like sorting, analyzing, clustering, fuzzy logic, probability testing, etc. in identifying the terrorist. It can also prepare documents on the list of suspects that makes the job of the investigator easy; humans can continue to probe, investigate, and interrogate in different situations. The interrogator can detain (once they are found guilty), release, or put them under vigilance. Thus, MI will not only help identify terrorists easily, it will help preventive action and reduce the incidence of terrorism efficiently and effectively in India.

References

Writer, S. 2019, "Howdy, Modi!' Event: India has given farewell to Article 370, says PM Modi," *Livemint*. September 22, 2019, https://www.livemint.com/news/india/howdy-modi-in-houston-live-pm-narendra-modi-in-usa-donald-trump-latest-news-updates-1569158613377.html (Accessed July 30, 2020).

Barngrover, C., 2018, What Is Machine Intelligence? Shield AI. September 13, 2018, https://www.shield.ai/content/2018/9/13/what-machine-intelligence (Accessed July 30, 2020).

Wikipedia 2019, List of Terrorist Incidents in India, https://en.wikipedia.org/wiki/List_of_terrorist_incidents_in_India (Accessed July 30, 2020).

Tutun, S., Khasawneh, M. T., and Zhuang, J., "New framework that uses patterns and relations to understand terrorist behaviors," *Expert Systems with Applications*, vol. 78, pp. 358–375, 2017.

House Permanent Select Committee on Intelligence on Intelligence Subcommittee, 2017, Counterterrorism Intelligence Capabilities and Performance Prior to 9–11, https://fas.org/irp/congress/2002_rpt/hpsci_ths0702.html (Accessed July 30, 2020).

Onay, C., and Elif Öztürk, "A review of credit scoring research in the age of big data," *Journal of Financial Regulation and Compliance*, vol. 26, no. 3, pp. 382–405, 2018.

15

IoT Crypt – An Intelligent System for Securing IoT Devices Using Artificial Intelligence and Machine Learning

Aakriti Singla and Anand Sharma

CONTENTS

15.1 Introduction

With increasing data released from various sources and different applications being introduced to the world, various organizations have started to adopt innovative technologies to solve complex problems. With lots of data generated, risk factors and threats increase towards this data and grows the need for cybersecurity to protect data from any sorts of vulnerable attacks. Many algorithms and technologies can be applied to solve these cybersecurity issues with more automation power, and better results lead to enhanced ways to prevent attacks on applications. Recent technologies used worldwide to solve any form of complex problem or carry out any task are artificial intelligence; in cases where large datasets are involved—machine learning (supervised, unsupervised, reinforcement learning) and deep learning—big data comes into the picture (for data visualization and data analytics). These technologies are used to build any form of software and program them according to your needs. An example is the development of intelligent systems. These systems are technologically automated—advanced machines that interpret in a particular way and behave accordingly.

When lots of data are introduced and lots of systems are designed with a regular flow of data, it becomes obvious that data threat is a major concern for the organization—this is where issues of cybersecurity plays its role. For our introduction of these technologies, we have used machine learning algorithms and artificial intelligence to build up an intelligent system software capable to protect IoT system applications from third-party threats and other cybersecurity issues. This system will analyze the devices connected, other users' access, and, finally, generate the report for the organization.

15.1.1 Building a Foundation for the Internet of Things

The Internet of Things is built on a concept that devices, sensors, and other hardware objects are connected to form interconnected devices, stream data over the internet, and help in smarter decision making. This is changing the way businesses and enterprises use technology to carry out functional tasks. The devices constructed using this technology contain data from sensors and various devices connected in the system and the cloud. Different devices and sensors—even microcontrollers—relate to performing functional tasks to address a problem. Base knowledge and other data are already given to the system, creating the foundation for the Internet of Things (Figure 15.1). The flow of data helps organizations efficiently pursue opportunities and earn maximum profits, giving efficient innovative solutions in less time. Reliable, stable, and secure infrastructures are required to make a complex system of devices communicate with one another in a meaningful—and profitable—way.

As this technology enter with an empowering force to change the way of handling tasks in the corporate world, there are a few challenges faced by organization—data security handled by the Internet of Things, cost budget analysis, downtime cut execution of complex tasks. Some other challenges are listed below:

1. Using business intelligence and artificial intelligence in predictive data analytics solutions to make decisions for real-time data generated.
2. Storing large volumes of data in a system of interconnected hardware devices and software that often leads to the vulnerability of cybersecurity.
3. Using predictive data analysis or visualizations based on historical data.
4. Handling high volume streams of information from devices.

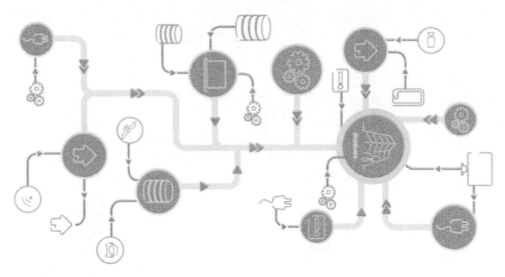

FIGURE 15.1
The foundation of Internet of Things.

15.2 IoT Architecture

The IoT architecture is a well-constructed design combined with various hardware devices, gateways, sensors, control, and user applications to give authenticated permissions to devices and applications, and data warehouse or storage for storing and streaming of data continuously (Figure 15.2). Additionally, architecture includes network cloud or connectivity over a network for communication and transfer of data over devices. These components are the building blocks of any IoT infrastructure, and the applicability and effectiveness of these systems enhance the quality of the applications and the way they communicate with each other.

15.2.1 IoT Components

- **Devices**
  The devices in IoT architecture are the primary components equipped with sensors that are responsible for connectivity and communication to gather data and transfer it to other connected devices or network and allow actuators to act in infrastructure.

- **Gateways**
  A gateway is a component in the IoT architecture that devices and sensors are connected to the cloud for IoT solution to be provided.

- **Cloud Gateway**
  The cloud gateway is a block component of IoT architecture or infrastructure that provides streams of data collected from sources; ensures efficient and secure data transmission between gateways and IoT cloud servers connected with different hardware and devices.

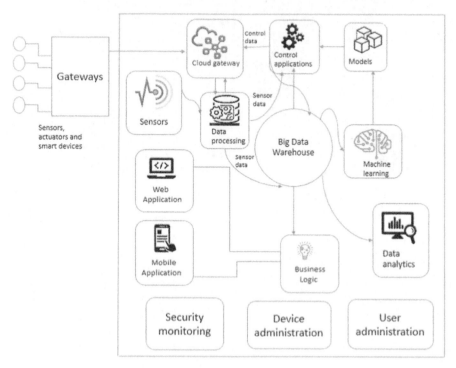

FIGURE 15.2
The Internet of Things (IoT) architecture.

- **Streaming Data Processor**

  This ensures effective transition of input for streaming unstructured data received from hardware devices and sensors, and control application data to a warehouse without data loss or corruption risk.

- **Big Data Warehouse**

  Another vital component involves big data warehouse that ensures collecting preprocessed and filtering of data required for meaningful insights. This data could be extracted from a data lake (large bag of data) to a big data warehouse whenever needed.

- **Control Applications**

  Control applications are the applications that work on commands sent by devices. These applications are programmed to help monitor the equipment involved—in case of detection of any sort of pre-failure situations, the IoT system generates an automatic message notification to the field engineers to handle the situation.

- **User Applications**

  User app lications are software components of an IoT system that can establish a connection between the users and the overall IoT system, an efficient communication network among all the devices. This feature gives an option to control and monitor the smart devices and sensors controlled by a centralized automated system, to automate user tasks.

15.3 IoT Security

IoT is a growing technology that formulates the base concept of different types of sensors and devices connected so they can communicate or pass information over the internet or cloud either by the users or the programs working with the devices that can help the system hide personal data given by the sensors or devices and help achieve useful objectives [1,2]. IoT (Internet of Things) consists of various devices and sensors that generate, process, and exchange enormous amounts of data; unauthenticated privacy-sensitive information are prone to various cyber-attacks [3]. The practical implementation of IoT applications consists platforms efficient in tracking of data, sensing data from various sources, communicating through various devices and sensors, knowledge processing, coordinating, and distributing data traffic across the system devices, etc. [4] One of the most important security credentials in an IoT application includes authentication control over the system, tracking of data across devices, information integrity, privacy, and digital signature, etc. With a high percentage of data generated for computational sensing, decision making, and communication are assumed to carry out all these functional tasks in data centers, and creates a need for ensuring security in data centers as well as maintaining security between data centers and different IoT devices and applications (Figure 15.3) [5].

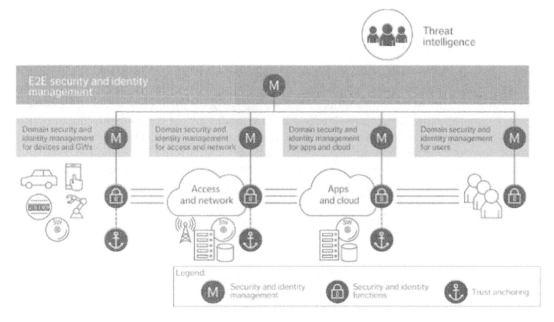

FIGURE 15.3
End-to-end security management in an overall IoT application.

15.4 Artificial Intelligence, Machine Learning, and Deep Learning

15.4.1 Artificial Intelligence

Artificial intelligence or AI is defined as a branch of computer science that makes a machine, or a system, artificially trained to perform elevated levels of computational and complex problems without being explicitly programmed [6]. It can also be the study and design of an artificial intelligence system consisting of some base training data stored to the system and intelligent agents, overall forming an intelligent system that perceives its environment and decides accordingly to reach the appropriate result [7].

15.4.2 Machine Learning

Machine learning is a field in AI technology that trains the machine to improve its performance based on past experiences or previous results through various supervised, unsupervised, or reinforced techniques, which makes the machine capable and efficient enough for prediction and analysis without being programmed. In other words, it is a way of making a machine think and act like a human brain and make appropriate predictions or decisions of outcomes based on the training data and knowledge base provided to the system. Machine learning methods enable computers to learn without being programmed; trained based on defined datasets of the domain [8]. ML has derived its roots from statistics and mathematical optimization areas and can be used independently in other AI or data analytics technologies. Various machine learning algorithms are used in many solution aspects to look for recognition, familiarity, or patterns in data collected.

15.4.3 Deep Learning

Deep learning (deep neural learning or deep neural network) is an advanced research field of artificial intelligence technology that focuses on getting its system artificially trained to perform high computational tasks and works with a base concept of neural networks (just like the nervous system in a human body) by forming a complete network architecture consisting of various nodes connected altogether [9]. Deep learning is capable of learning unsupervised algorithms from unstructured or unlabeled data and forming a trained dataset with each node connected to other nodes, passing relevant information throughout the system. The artificial neural networks in a deep learning model are built like the human brain with neuron nodes, to work on high computational power and predict better decisions (Figure 15.4).

15.5 Building an Artificial Intelligent System

15.5.1 Intelligent Systems

An intelligent system is a PC-based automated framework based on the idea of complete algorithms and artificial intelligence capabilities to interpret, represent, and analyze data fused from past data. Based on information received, these frameworks are planned clever enough to become familiar with the structure of the data, determine new data, distinguish

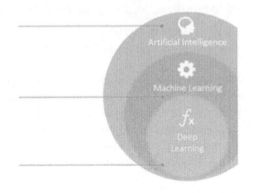

Artificial Intelligence
Any technique which enables computers to mimic human behavior.

Machine Learning
Subset of AI techniques which use statistical methods to enable machines to improve with experiences.

Deep Learning
Subset of ML which make the computation of multi-layer neural networks feasible.

FIGURE 15.4
AI vs. Machine Learning vs. Deep Learning.

systems, identify strategies and standards of conduct, and follow up on the aftereffect of its investigation. Intelligent systems can perform search and enhancement mechanism with scarce learning capacities fused in them. These frameworks perform complex undertakings with automated systems, unexpected to be done through conventional figuring methods. A few ML algorithms—for example, unsupervised learning, supervised learning, and reinforcement learning—can be effectively joined in planning intelligent systems (Figure 15.5).

Applications of intelligent systems consist of various diagnostic, robotics, and engineering systems that are developed because of intelligent procedures implemented in Intelligent Systems Design. Here is a list of some intelligent systems:

a. Expert systems

b. Fuzzy systems

c. Artificial Neural Networks

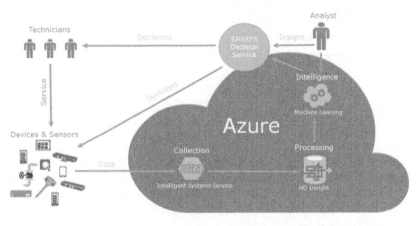

FIGURE 15.5
IoT-based intelligent system platform.

    d. Genetic Algorithms and Evolutionary Programming

    e. Swarm Intelligent Systems

    f. Knowledge-Based and Rule-Based Systems

For our work, we focused in designing an expert system that provides cybersecurity to our IoT applications. We will discuss expert systems briefly before moving forward.

Intelligent systems or expert systems equipped with artificial intelligence are developed to behave like humans, solve large complex problems with high computational power, and reach decisions or predictions for a certain problem along with the help of the training data and knowledge base data to the system. Some of the characteristics of an intelligent system are:

- Logical behavior
- Ability to solve complex problems
- Responsive and adaptive nature
- Ability to provide non-linear program navigation
- Effectively uses existing information
- User-friendliness and high interactivity
- Reliability

15.5.2 Expert Systems

Expert systems are an application of artificial intelligence designed to make the decision according to a problem or situation, depicting the behavior of a human expert. These intelligent systems designed using artificial intelligence concepts, tools, and technologies possess expert knowledge in a particular domain, so efficient in solving complex problems by reasoning through bodies of knowledge, that they give better results and appropriate decisions than conventional procedural code [10,11].

Expert systems can take human decisions with the help of experts' knowledge (called a knowledge base). It contains accumulated experience that has been loaded and tested. Unlike other intelligent systems, expert systems knowledge is enhanced by providing additional rules and regulations to the knowledge base, helping the system make a better decision; with more experience, the system can improve its performance (Figure 15.6). Few characteristics of expert systems are:

- Understandable
- Reliable
- High performance
- Highly responsive

Figure 15.6 shows the architecture of an expert system and the most important module of a rule-based expert system. The user interacts with the expert systems through a user interface that makes access more comfortable for humans and hides much of the system complexity. Expert systems employ a variety of interface styles such as interactive, menu-driven, and graphical user interfaces.

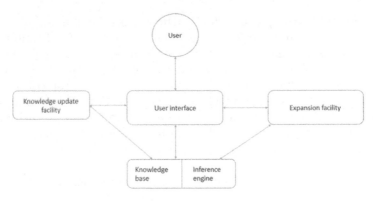

FIGURE 15.6
Architecture of an expert system.

15.5.3 Machine Learning for Security of IoT Applications

As various IoT devices are continually used in different areas, low-end computing power, storage capacity, and extended security solutions have become important. IoT applications now face new security risks and vulnerabilities, botnets, etc. It is easy for malicious attackers to hack into IoT devices—they generate lots of data through machine learning (that analyze data for security-related cases like safe device behavior, general usage patterns) and block abnormal activity and potentially harmful behavior by devices. Now, this technology forms the base concept to protect IoT system applications from cybersecurity threats using various machine learning or deep learning algorithms. These techniques enable a system to learn from experience and past data initiated to the system, to help them visualize the task and finally decide.

IoT applications consist of various physical hardware devices and other components, and are, therefore, more prone to cybersecurity threats and exposure to sensitive and personal data from the outside world. These devices generate all forms of data and personal information that can be secured through machine learning algorithms, protecting data from being exposed to third parties.

15.5.4 Some Machine Learning Methodsx

- **Supervised Learning Techniques** are used to analyze the network, data traffic, or app traces of IoT devices or applications and user's authentication patterns to build the classification or regression model to detect network intrusion, spoofing attacks, DoS attacks, and malware detections; and utilize neural networks to detect network intrusion. These techniques involve SVM (Support Vector Machine), KNN algorithm, Naïve Bayes, and DNN (Deep Neural Networks).

- **Unsupervised Learning Techniques** have a special characteristic of using unlabeled data and forming data clusters by grouping them into distinct collections to detect attacks at various vulnerable points in an application or system. IGMM, an unsupervised learning technique, can be applied in proximity-based authentication in the proximity without leaking the localization information of the devices.

- **Reinforcement Learning** is another machine learning method that enables a machine or a system to learn from experience with the help of training data fed into the system. Also, reinforcement learning works as a backup plan mechanism for systems in situations needing an alternative path to reach the output. This learning method enables a device to choose a security protocol and key constraints against various cyber-attacks to the application. Q-learning is a part of reinforcement learning techniques and works well in forming security provisions for IoT devices that has been used to improve the performance of devices by monitoring authentication and spoofing attacks.

Unlike knowledge-based systems, machine learning techniques used in supervising intelligent systems are preferred in applications where learning activity is performed by computer systems through extraction of relevant information to derive predictions and smart recommendations for an output. Some other machine learning techniques such as visualizations, object recognition, pattern recognition, analysis, or reinforcement learning also play a significant role in protecting IoT devices or applications from various cybersecurity threats and vulnerabilities. The most vulnerable cybersecurity factor to IoT applications include spam filtering, authentication access control or user monitoring, risk analysis, zero-day attack identification, etc. are all controlled using various machine learning or deep learning algorithms.

15.5.5 Intelligent Systems and the Internet of Things

IoT applications consist of various devices and sensors widely implemented in many organizations, usually in IT departments (deploying or constructing many applications, working on IoT technology with other software running parallel in infrastructure, and carrying out complex procedures and tasks). Due to increasing threats, risks and information prone to unauthorized access, it has become important for organizations to adopt new forms of protection and cybersecurity methods—like the ability to detect unauthorized access to IoT devices connected to their network.

The phrases "IoT" and "intelligent systems" are often used interchangeably by technology vendors. Both phrases refer to a new and rapidly evolving IT technology, using smart remote devices that automatically and securely transmit and receive information through the internet or cloud connection to one or more data centers. In data centers, business intelligence tools analyze data and generate reports that help businesses process more efficiently. The hardware devices' security proves to be a starting point for the implementation of IoT protocols and procedures because of their incredibly low area and energy requirements throughout application. They are also naturally more prone to side-channel and physical attacks; they enable the creation of a secure and trusted flow of information all over the system.

15.6 Proposed Work

In our research method, we proposed a mechanism to develop an artificial intelligence system with the help of supervised and reinforcement learning techniques, to prevent cybersecurity issues to the IoT system application. To begin designing an intellectual model, we need to extract features from data to learn insights, perform predictions, or train systems to solve a problem.

15.6.1 Formulate a Concept

The first step to design any model or system is to formulate the base of the system. This contains the objective of the problem and the task the system would perform, and then decide what product should be created. It should have a base concept or terminology to solve the problem efficiently—an artificial intelligence system.

In our work, our first step defines how we can make a base to detect malware attacks and unauthorized users access with the help of historical data and data obtained from devices. This step will create a foundation of the system requiring cybersecurity.

15.6.2 Make a Research

As soon as the concept is made and a base module is ready, we start our research. Explore as much data and mechanisms as you can figure out and list the ones you can include in our design. Collect more information about how a job is done for the problem. Start working on historical data presented in web analytics services or BI solutions of IoT applications—in this way, we can validate our target system or application. Transparency and communication are the main drivers of AI community and it is important to mention the copyright of the model or code you choose to use or modify for the design of our system. Cybersecurity issues and data need to be explored and collected to ensure the requirements needed for the development of the system.

15.6.3 Split the Problem

Here are a few criteria on how to split the problem for a complex system:

- Process Stages
- Sources of Information
- Conditions for Target Actions
- Associated Dynamics Behavior

After you cut a problem into parts, ensure that you still have all the necessary components to be completed. Using machine learning techniques, preferably supervised learning, formulate an algorithm according to the process stages (in the form of a split). Collect data from all the sources—devices including sensor data, cloud data, and even personal data—and form a combined dataset and train the algorithm accordingly.

15.6.4 Control for Consistency

Completing the third step, we jump to the written process and identify which level of expert decision goes best with each step and refine your initial process to control overall consistency. This helps automate, semi-automate, and optimize our overall decision. At the end of this step, make sure to review your final template or automated steps to guarantee that they are accurate in making correct decisions.

15.6.5 Map Out Key Components of Our Expert System for Refinement

Now that we have formularized our initial steps to design our expert systems, it's time to start developing with specific techniques, tools, and controls you need to enhance your system. For our IoT applications cybersecurity, it is important to design an algorithm that can control the flow of data from the system before it is exposed—this can be achieved by encoding and storing the data in the cloud. The visualizations or patterns of all forms of data would be done by the expert system using the Q-learning algorithm.

15.6.6 Re-evaluate the Expert System and Prioritize Issues for Enhancement and Refinement Quarterly

After the complete design and development process of the system, the testing process is carried out by providing raw data to the IoT system and checking for unauthorized access in quarters. Each quarter, we re-evaluate our expert system to prioritize the efficiency or performance of the next block; in case of errors, we refine the steps and check again until we achieve the accurate decision or output.

15.7 Experimental Analysis

An experiment was performed based on the proposed research method, and according to the analysis, the results were outstanding. An intelligent system was designed, with supervised machine learning algorithm (a bit of reinforcement learning technique was included to provide the system with options). The knowledge data was fed to the system and a thorough analysis was done through supervised learning mechanism. The system was introduced with the authorized devices of the system that made it work intelligently, differentiating between authorized and third-party devices approaching the system. The proposed methodology consists of training the system using a supervised learning mechanism where the training data and the data samples are introduced to the system; the sample data inputs are coupled with their desired outputs that make the machine learn a general rule to map inputs to outputs leading to a prediction.

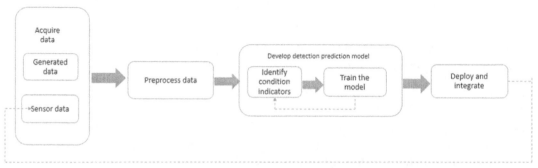

Sensor data from the IoT application on which the algorithm is implemented

FIGURE 15.7
The proposed methodology.

Any intelligent system designed with efficient supervised machine learning algorithms can detect any suspicious or unauthorized entry to the IoT application. The proposed intelligent system describes how machine learning or deep learning techniques can be employed in diverse ways to solve cybersecurity threats.

15.8 Conclusion and Future Work

A methodology to secure IoT application framework by building an intelligent structure dealing with cryptic methods to secure gadgets through different machine learning and deep learning approaches have been proposed in this chapter. The job of an intelligent framework in the cybersecurity field will proceed to develop and thrive. The advancement of these frameworks in various domains and associations will have positive and negative impacts on cybersecurity threats and issues as well as the IoT application development. With the growth of artificial intelligence and machine learning technologies in today's world, these algorithms prove to contribute in large towards protecting these applications and other hardware devices from vulnerable cybersecurity risks and threats.

Machine learning and deep learning are important fields of AI. These learning mechanisms can be used widely to develop intelligent systems to perform complex problems and achieve efficient results. The algorithms used in developing smart intelligent systems to provide cybersecurity help various malware attacks and unauthorized access to the system. Machine learning and deep learning ought to be significant tools in the cybersecurity toolbox, especially when the analytic tasks included require modeling a lot of information by complex relations between the framework's output and input.

References

1. Council N., "Disruptive civil technologies: six technologies with potential impacts on us interests out to 2025," in *Conference Report CR, 2008*.
2. Atzori L., A. Ierax, and Morabito G., "The internet of things: a survey," *Computer Networks*, vol. 54, no. 15, pp. 2787–2805, 2010.
3. Sicari S., Rizzardi A., Grieco L. A., and Coen-Porisini A., "Security, privacy and trust in internet of things: the road ahead," *Computer Networks*, vol. 76, pp. 146–164, 2015.
4. Juels A., "RFID security and privacy: A research survey," *IEEE Journal on Selected Areas in Communications*, vol. 24, no. 2, pp. 381–394, 2006.
5. Kong J. H., Ang L.-M., and Seng K. P., "Minimalist security and privacy schemes based on enhanced AES for integrated WISP sensor networks," *Journal of Communication Networks and Distributed Systems*, vol. 11, no. 2, pp. 214–232, 2013.
6. Merriam-Webster, https://www.merriam-webster.com/dictionary/artificial%20intelligence.
7. Oxford Dictionaries, https://en.oxforddictionaries.com/definition/artificial_intelligence.
8. Fisher D. H., "Knowledge acquisition via incremental conceptual clustering," *Machine Learning*, vol. 2, pp. 139–172, 1987.
9. Jones M. Tim, "A beginner's guide to artificial intelligence, machine learning and cognitive computing," June 2017, https://www.ibm.com/developerworks/library/cc-beginner-guidemachine-learning-ai-cognitive/cc-beginner-guide-machine-learning-ai-cognitive-pdf.pdf.

10. Lucas P. J. F., Van der Gaag L. C. (1991). Principles of Expert Systems, Addison-Wesley, Wokingham, UK. [Textbook on expert systems that emphasizes knowledge representation and inference, including formal meanings of knowledge-representation formalisms.].
11. Singla, A. and Sharma, A., "Physical access system security of IoT devices using machine learning techniques (March 20, 2019)," In Proceedings of *International Conference on Sustainable Computing in Science, Technology and Management (SUSCOM-2019)*, February 26–28, 2019, Amity University Rajasthan, Jaipur, India. Available at SSRN: https://ssrn.com/abstract=3356785.

16

Intelligent Systems

Enhanced Security Using Deep Learning Technology

Satyajee Srivastava, Abhishek Singh, and Deepak Dudeja

CONTENTS

16.1 Introduction

Machine learning is one of the most trending and demanding skill in today's information-driven world. It is an application of the broader concept known as artificial intelligence and provides a system the ability to learn and improve automatically from experience without being programmed. It focuses on developing computer programs that can access and use data to learn. Machine learning can be used through various methods, but often are categorized as unsupervised and supervised methods. Let's have a brief introduction of some of these methods:

1. **Supervised Learning** – It is a kind of learning performed by machines where input variables use "x" and an output variable, "y" [1]. They just need to use an algorithm to learn the function for mapping input to the output.

$$y = f(x)$$

The goal is to estimate the mapping function in a satisfactory manner that whenever they are given new input data (x), they can predict the output variables (y). The algorithm repeatedly makes predictions on training data that we provide, and the learning terminates when the algorithm achieves an acceptable performance level [2]. Most of the world's practical machine learning uses supervised learning. (e.g., regression, classification, etc.)

2. **Unsupervised Learning** – It is a kind of learning performed by machines with only input data (x) and no corresponding output variables initially. The goal is to model fundamental or underlying structure distribution in provided data increasingly learn about [3]. This type of learning is called as such because no defined correct answers are there, therefore, no mapping mechanism. Algorithms used in unsupervised learning are left to their own decisions to discover and present the exciting and interesting underlying structure in the data. (e.g., clustering, association, etc.)

3. **Semi-Supervised Learning** – This kind of learning lies somewhere between supervised and unsupervised learning methods. Sometimes, there are problems where machines are provided with a large amount of input data (x) but only a small part of the complete data is labeled (y). In these situations, this kind of learning method proves handy and more efficient, making use of assumptions—continuity assumption, cluster assumption, or manifold assumption [4]. A mix of supervised and unsupervised method can be used to solve such problems.

4. **Reinforcement Learning** – It is a kind of learning method in which an agent interacts with its environment by performing certain actions and from there, discovers *rewards* and *penalty*. Whenever an agent acts on its environment, it receives some evaluation of its action but is not told which is the correct one. Here, the role of rewards and penalty comes into play [2]. Therefore, it is also known as learning through experience.

The different learning methods used in machine learning are useful in tasks, but regarding security concerns, machine learning alone cannot be trusted completely [5]. We need some advanced and more specific techniques like deep learning technologies.

16.2 How Deep Learning Techniques Differ from Machine Learning Techniques

Unlike traditional and long-established methods of machine learning, deep learning classifiers are trained with feature learning instead of task-specific algorithms—the machine can learn patterns within the pictures given instead of requiring the human operator to outline the patterns that the machine ought to search for within the image [6]. In the traditional setup of machine learning, one of the most typical problems is feature engineering. Feature engineering extracts suitable features from the data provided that could be used wisely in the model [7]. If features in data are less or incomplete, the model is said to be flawed or is a high bias model, and if the number of features is too much (all of them are not contributing to the output of the model), then it is said to be flawed or is a high variance model. Deep learning is based on "representational learning," also known as feature learning [2]. The deep learning model is composed of several layers of neural networks. Each layer receives input from the previous layer's output and after processing, passes them off to the next neural network layer. The more the number of layers, the deeper the model is (Figure 16.1).

The only area of concern in the deep learning model is that it requires an exceptionally large dataset compared to machine learning models [8]. As the size of data increases, deep learning technology outperforms machine learning technology tremendously. Let's understand the terminologies above in detail and have some deeper insights about deep learning.

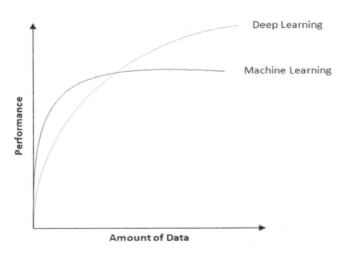

FIGURE 16.1
Deep learning vs. machine learning.

16.3 Deep Learning and Neural Networks

Neural Networks, also known as artificial neural networks or ANNs, are a subset of ML techniques, loosely impressed by biological neural networks. These networks don't seem like realistic models of the brain and model tough problems using robust/sturdy algorithms and data structures. They sometimes delineate as a set of connected units, known as artificial neurons, organized in layers. Layers incomplete neural networks can be classified into three categories: input layers, middle layers (hidden layers), and output layers [9]. The more the number of hidden layers, the deeper the model is. The capability of prediction of neural networks comes from this gradable multi-layered structure [10]. Through correct training, the network will learn the ways to optimally represent the inputs as features at completely different scales or resolutions, mix them to form higher-order feature representations, and relate them to output variables — learning ways to create predictions.

Deep Learning (DL) can be considered as a set of neural networks that form feasible multi-layer neural networks. Typical DL architectures are convolutional neural networks (CNNs), deep neural networks (DNNs), generative adversarial networks (GAN), continual neural networks (RNNs), and others [11].

DNNs are capable of learning high-order features with a lot of complexities and abstractions because of their considerable number of middle (hidden) layers compared to shallow neural networks [12].

Let us understand further concepts through a simple face recognition system built using deep neural networks.

16.4 General Outline of a Face Recognition System

Any face image is learned by our model in pre-defined ways and then gets stored in knowledge memory. While identifying the face of a human or any other object for which the model is built, previously stored values are taken into memory and used [13]. We can say that face recognition contains two phases:

1. Learning Phase
2. Recognition Phase

16.5 Block Diagrams

1. Block diagram of the Learning Process
2. Block diagram of the Recognition Process

The process of face recognition is depicted in the detail (Figures 16.2 and 16.3).

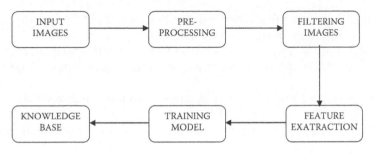

FIGURE 16.2
Learning process.

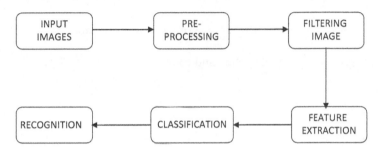

FIGURE 16.3
Recognition process.

16.6 Input Images

Images can be given as an input by various methods (preparing a dataset of collection of images or by collecting the images in a particular directory and read images from there, etc.) The former way of image input is just applying the image function to the image and arranging them in the form of an $M \times N$ array as shown in Eq. (1). Here, each element of array is a discrete quantity of images [14].

$$f(x, y) = \begin{pmatrix} f(0, 0) & f(0, 1) & \text{.......} & f(0, N-1) \\ f(1, 0) & f(1, 1) & \text{.......} & f(1, N-1) \\ .. & .. & & .. \\ f(M-1, 0) & f(M-1, 1) & \text{.......} & f(M-1, N-1) \end{pmatrix}$$

Eq. (1) – Representation of Digital images

16.7 Read Images

Once the image is given as an input, they need to be read first by the machine as they can't directly read images as humans do. However, you will be surprised to know that even in humans, there are pre-defined processes that happen for acquiring and understanding images [15]. Let's have a look at the steps to read images.

In Figure 16.4, we are taking images as inputs from the path specified, appending image names at the end of the file path, and then reading images one by one using a user-defined function.

For these purposes, we are using two libraries of python (Figure 16.5).

`import os` - "os" is used for directory related purposes (i.e. accessing certain system

path).

`import cv2` - OpenCV had released two major types of python interfaces, of which

"cv2" is the latest. It is used for reading, writing, displaying, and many

more image processing (image scaling and color conversion).

16.8 Face Detection

For face recognition, face detection needs to be done first. In this step, only regions in which faces are present are captured and taken into considerations for further processing [16]. The more accurate this step, the more precise your final recognition system will emerge. There are various algorithms for detecting faces like Haar-cascade's frontal face

```
path        = 'C:\\Users\\Desktop\\images'
filenames   = os.listdir(path)|

for filename in filenames:
    filepath    = os.path.join(path, filename)
    images      = read_images([filepath])
```

FIGURE 16.4
Input image.

```
def read_images(filepaths):
    images = np.zeros((len(filepaths), 256, 256, 3), dtype=np.uint8)
    for i, filepath in enumerate(filepaths):
        img = cv2.imread(filepath)
```

FIGURE 16.5
Reading image.

detection algorithm, MTCNN algorithm, and many more [17]. In this chapter, we'll be using the MTCNN detection algorithm.

```
face, no_face, more_face = detect_face_mtcnn(filepath)
```

The overall framework of our approach is shown in Figure 16.6 [18].

First, the candidate windows square measure is made through a quick Proposal Network (P-Net). After that, we refine these candidates through a Refinement Network (R-Net). In the third stage, the Output Network (O-Net) produces the final bounding box and facial landmarks position [11].

16.9 Pre-Processing

The most crucial and tedious task in any project is the pre-processing of raw data so that it can be converted into forms where features can be extracted, and models need to be applied

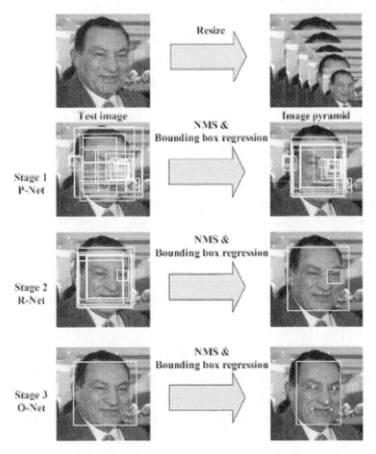

FIGURE 16.6
Overall pipeline of face detection using three-staged MTCNN.

[19]. Pre-processing itself contains many steps like face alignment, image pre-whitening, image resizing, image cropping, color conversion (BGR, RGB, and grayscale), etc.
Converting color RGB to BGR

```
img = cv2.cvtColor(face[0], cv2.COLOR_RGB2BGR)
```

Applying pre-whitening using FaceNet model

```
pre_white     = facenet.prewhiten(img)
```

Resizing image to 160 ×160

```
resized_img  = cv2.resize(pre_white[0], (160, 160))
```

There are other pre-processing steps, but it purely depends on the requirements and target (face recognition system).

16.9.1 What Is FaceNet and Why Is It Used?

FaceNet is one of the finest deep convolutional networks designed by Google, trained to resolve face verification, recognition, and agglomeration drawback expeditiously at scale.

1. FaceNet tries to directly learn mapping from images of faces to a compact Euclidean space. Here, distance measures correspond to measure of similarity of faces [20] (i.e. if we have an image X and we want to measure its similarity with images Y and Z — if remaining pre-processing steps have been done correctly — then, we can measure the distance between images X-Y and X-Z. The less Euclidean distance between these two pairs of images, the more similar they are [21].
2. It optimizes the embedding face recognition performance by using only 128-bytes per face [20].

16.9.2 Embeddings

An embedding is a kind of mapping of a discrete & categorical variable of continuous and easily readable numbers. Within the context of neural networks and deep learning, embeddings can be low-dimensional and learned continuous representation of vectors of discrete variables [22] (Figure 16.7).
   These embeddings have three primary purposes:

1. To find nearest neighbors in the whole embedding space.
2. Used as inputs to ML models for supervised learning.
3. Visualize different concepts and relations between various categories.

	0	1	2	3	4	5	6	7	8	9	...	118	119	120	121	12
0	-0.021412	-0.049293	0.079603	0.079617	0.033326	0.197778	-0.041095	0.034463	0.177045	-0.086410	...	0.033448	-0.085822	-0.015031	-0.186310	0.18418
1	0.053163	0.036084	-0.086167	0.150768	0.068212	0.246019	-0.119493	-0.120695	0.051318	0.017295	...	-0.016329	-0.126483	-0.041340	-0.060489	0.32661
2	0.179895	0.001523	-0.025659	-0.074045	0.008480	0.245909	0.099766	0.008621	-0.061269	0.015780	...	-0.071834	-0.035602	0.107031	0.009936	0.14028
3	0.080496	0.091929	-0.116010	-0.035320	-0.007765	0.205342	-0.121332	-0.092824	0.043167	-0.118300	...	0.121876	-0.038492	0.081920	0.131174	0.11953
4	0.069900	-0.031127	-0.133671	-0.037717	0.032219	0.019345	-0.008036	-0.023919	-0.067092	-0.014599	...	-0.125483	0.016435	0.053114	0.009534	0.06923
5	0.031348	-0.059008	-0.010179	-0.107743	-0.139914	-0.010513	-0.160733	0.112779	-0.032004	0.127036	...	-0.007522	-0.111971	0.204085	-0.103811	-0.03541
6	0.087230	-0.116812	-0.019746	0.118931	-0.137596	0.098613	-0.153682	-0.069303	0.068930	0.104526	...	0.059462	-0.110034	-0.060789	-0.117236	0.03908
7	0.071558	-0.015297	0.001701	0.042281	-0.122836	0.244570	-0.104704	-0.076886	0.009781	0.082183	...	-0.060231	-0.057067	0.003734	-0.061577	0.13449
8	-0.040520	-0.090272	-0.001473	0.053950	-0.103256	0.196921	-0.103252	0.076564	0.093886	0.122660	...	-0.004195	-0.087539	-0.154087	-0.062191	-0.02347
9	0.139139	0.152848	-0.089632	0.082474	-0.060107	0.158003	-0.003023	-0.052397	0.023601	0.052151	...	-0.076727	0.002475	0.030172	-0.167028	0.08267
10	0.071886	-0.032424	-0.070742	0.032944	-0.120346	-0.020780	-0.115071	-0.122006	-0.026071	0.156597	...	0.066634	0.004182	0.054095	0.036131	0.15413
11	-0.040082	0.005630	-0.085314	-0.082814	0.016002	0.074683	-0.057215	-0.075700	-0.068534	0.103363	...	0.021323	0.021573	0.089570	0.024662	0.19668
12	0.064147	0.050862	-0.055462	0.070230	0.032912	0.111457	0.055007	-0.193951	0.044372	-0.038804	...	0.112963	-0.039437	0.007473	-0.064227	0.23512

13 rows × 128 columns

FIGURE 16.7
Embeddings of 13 different images.

16.10 Image Filtering

16.10.1 Spatial Filtering

Spatial filtering is simply a process of using spatial masks for image processing. The masks used here are called spatial filters, and they can be linear or non-linear [23].

Figure 16.8 shows a general 3 × 3 spatial mask which denotes the gray level of pixels at any location by $y_1, y_2, y_3, ..., y_9$; for this, the response of the linear spatial mask is

$$R = w_1y_1 + w_2y_2 + ...+w_3y_3$$

16.10.2 Median Filtering

The filtering method above blurs the edges and other sharp details. So, if your objective is noise reduction and not blurring, this filtering method is an alternative for you [15].

16.11 Feature Learning

Deep learning focuses on representational learning also called feature learning. Feature learning implies a technique to learn features of given input [24]. It is done by

W_1	W_2	W_3
W_4	W_5	W_6
W_7	W_8	W_9

FIGURE 16.8
Mask of a spatial filter.

transforming raw data input into a representation that can be efficiently used for tasks like training model, checking similarity measures, etc.

It includes feature selection and feature extraction.

16.11.1 Feature Selection

It is a method of selecting or sub-setting limited (or specific) features from an available substantial number of features/variables from raw data input [25]. These selected features are what the learning algorithm should focus on.

Complete feature set
Identify useful features
Selected feature set

16.11.2 Feature Extraction

It is a method of transforming existing features/variables in raw input data to a lower-dimensional space [26]. Some examples of feature extraction algorithms are PCA (Principal component analysis), LDA (Linear discriminant analysis), etc. [25] (Figure 16.9).

16.12 One-Shot Learning

The major problem in deep learning model is the need for an exceptionally large amount of data to get more accurate results [22], but it will be convenient for models to learn from few data.

The main idea behind one-shot learning is to learn the class of an object using only a few data [27]. In face recognition, we want to recognize one person's identity by providing only one image of a person's face as an input to the system. This can be done with the help of Siamese neural networks [28].

The images in Figure 16.10 are good examples of face recognition using the Siamese network. We can see that in the first sub-network, the image is an input followed by a sequence of convolution, pooling, and fully connected layers, finally reaching a feature vector of 128 embeddings. For comparison, we need to calculate the distance d between

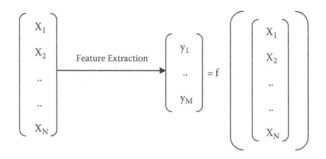

FIGURE 16.9
Feature extraction.

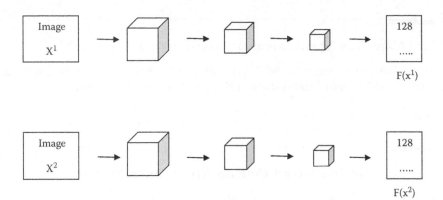

FIGURE 16.10
Face recognition using Siamese network.

encodings of these images (i.e. between $F(x^1)$ and $F(x^2)$). A threshold value is set up, and if the distance between their encodings are less than the threshold, then the two images are of the same person.

16.13 Triplet Loss

Triplet loss is a kind of loss function used in neural networks. Gradient descent can be applied on a triplet loss function. A triplet loss function is simply considered as a loss function using three images: first is an anchor image, second is a positive image P (same Figure 16.11 person as the anchor), and third is a negative image (another person from the anchor). It has a baseline as an input (an anchor) (as shown in Figure 16.11). It is compared with a positive input and a negative input [28]. The triplet loss minimizes the distance between an anchor (baseline) and a positive — having the same identity — and maximizes the distance between anchor (baseline) and a negative — having different identities.

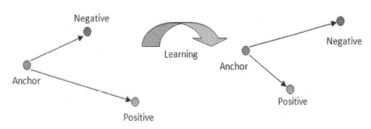

FIGURE 16.11
Training model using triplet loss.

16.14 How Can This Mechanism Be Made into a Product?

The above mechanism, along with add-ons, can be combined in sequence and converted to a software product. Some *Use-Cases* of the mechanism above are:

16.15 Face Recognition Based Online Attendance System

Face recognition based online attendance system can be proven as a smart approach in monitoring the attendance of students in schools and employees in companies. The steps above, if combined in sequence accordingly and used in building a deep learning model, can be used to detect and identify various identities [29]. The workflow is mentioned in Figure 16.12.

But this will not be the complete product; it's just a part of it. We need to prepare a pipeline from beginning to end (i.e. collecting images of different identities using CCTV cameras, preparing a database, pre-processing those images, applying the prepared model on images to identify the correct identity, and then marking the attendance of the

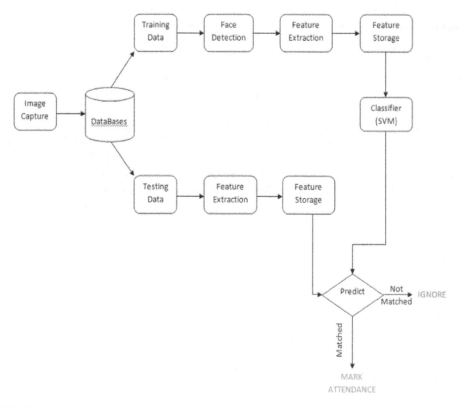

FIGURE 16.12
Workflow.

identified person in the organization's database) [30]. This project can be provided with many advanced functionalities (e.g., attendance using cell phone apps) but permitted only within a specified geo-location range, etc. In this way, a well-organized software product can have less human involvement and increased security.

16.16 Intent Prediction

Face detection and recognition is the first step of applying the intent prediction model. Intent prediction is the next important thing that can contribute to security concerns [31]. If professionals succeed in making a prediction model for this, then it can be integrated with our proposed face detection and recognition model, which can be used in public places where CCTV cameras can detect the faces of the crowd and try to figure out their intent [32]. If any suspect is found, immediate action can be taken. This achievement could prove to be an advanced security layer.

16.17 Face Recognition-Based Gate Access

Age restrictions on public places like bars, wine shops, etc. can use face detection and recognition technique to detect a person's age and correctly determine which person should be allowed to enter. Age detection by individual facial features is now possible [33]. This mechanism can be used at places, like wine shops, where there is an age restriction (e.g., in Delhi, the minimum age for purchasing liquor is 25 years; in UP it is 21). The product can be programmed accordingly.

16.18 Face Recognition-Based Payment Services

The day-to-day needs of the modern world (e.g., online payment service) can be connected to biometric security. Facial verification and authentication at the time of payment at POS can act as an added layer of security [34]. The finance sector is prone to hackers' attacks and needs the best possible security layers because it is related to money — if not handled with care, it can adversely affect the financial condition individually and nationally [35].

Conclusion

We have seen how deep learning techniques have emerged and contributed to the security concerns of the world. Using image recognition (face recognition, handwritten digit recognition, pattern matching, signature verification, etc.), deep learning has proven better than traditional machine learning techniques. A simple face recognition system can be easily built by anyone who has a good understanding of algorithms, structures, and a little bit of coding skills. With the use of deep learning and its various techniques and algorithms, we can build several real-time models that can help in daily security work and can save time. Technology should be made efficient. Our society can be provided with a secure environment using advanced deep learning techniques and software products built on the same architecture.

References

1. Sathya R., and AbrahamA., "Comparison of supervised and unsupervised learning algorithms for pattern classification, "*(IJARAI) International Journal of Advanced Research in Artificial Intelligence*, vol. 2, no. 2, pp. 34–38, 2013.
2. Nguyen G., Dlugolinsky S., Bobák M., Tran V., López García A., Heredia I. P. Malik, and Hluchý L., "Machine learning and deep learning frameworks and libraries for large-scale data mining: a survey," *Artificial Intelligence*, review 52, no. 1 , pp. 77–124, 2019.
3. Köstinger M., Wohlhart P., Roth P. M., and Bischof H., "Annotated facial landmarks in the wild: A large-scale, real-world database for facial landmark localization," in *IEEE Conference on Computer Vision and Pattern Recognition Workshops*, 2011, pp. 2144–2151.
4. Krizhevsky A., Sutskever I., and Hinton G. E., "Imagenet classification with deep convolutional neural networks," *Communications of the ACM*, vol. 60, no. 6, pp. 84–90, 2012.
5. Sun Y., Chen Y., Wang X., and Tang X., "Deep learning face representation by joint identification-verification," in *Advances in Neural Information Processing Systems*, 2014, pp. 1988–1996.
6. Yang S., Luo P., Loy C. C., and Tang X., "From facial parts responses to face detection: A deep learning approach," in *IEEE International Conference on Computer Vision*, 2015, pp. 3676–3684.
7. Hinton G., Osindero S., and Teh Y. W., "A fast learning algorithm for deep belief nets," *Neural Computation*, vol. 18, pp. 1527–1554, 2006.
8. Burgos-Artizzu X. P., Perona P., and Dollar P., "Robust face landmark estimation under occlusion," in *IEEE International Conference on Computer Vision*, 2013, pp. 1513–1520.
9. Cao X., Wei Y., Wen F., and Sun J., "Face alignment by explicit shape regression," *International Journal of Computer Vision*, vol 107, no. 2, pp. 177–190, 2012.
10. Zhong G., Wang L.-N., Ling X., and Dong J., "An overview on data representation learning: From traditional feature learning to recent deep learning," *The Journal of Finance and Data Science*, vol. 2, no. 4, 265–278, 2016.
11. Zhang K., Zhang Z., Li Z., and Qiao Y., "Joint face detection and alignment using multitask cascaded convolutional networks," *IEEE Signal Processing Letters*, vol. 23, no. 10 , 1499–1503, 2016.
12. Cootes T. F., Edwards G. J., and Taylor C. J., "Active appearance models," *IEEE Transactions on Pattern Analysis and Machine Intelligence*, vol. 23, no. 6, pp. 681–685, 2001.
13. Yu X., Huang J., Zhang S., Yan W., and Metaxas D., "Pose-free facial landmark fitting via optimized part mixtures and cascaded deformable shape model," in *IEEE International Conference on Computer Vision*, 2013, pp. 1944–1951.
14. Athanasiou L. S. , Fotiadis D. I. , and Michalis L. K., Atherosclerotic Plaque Characterization Methods Based on Coronary Imaging. Academic Press, 2017.
15. Dosovitskiy A., Springenberg J. T., Riedmiller M., and Brox T., "Discriminative unsupervised feature learning with convolutional neural network," *Advances in Neural Information Processing Systems*, 766–774, 2014.

16. Ahmad, F. Ahmad, A. and Ahmad, Z."Image-based face detection and recognition: "state of the art". arXiv preprint arXiv:1302.6379, 2013.
17. Chen D., Ren S., Wei Y., Cao X., and Sun J., "Joint cascade face detection and alignment," in *European Conference on Computer Vision*, 2014, pp. 109–122.
18. Zhang K., Zhang Z., Li Z. and Qiao Y., "Joint face detection and alignment using multitask cascaded convolutional networks," *IEEE Signal Processing Letters*, vol. 23, no. 10, 1499–1503, 2016.
19. Li H., Lin Z., Shen X., Brandt J., and Hua G., "A convolutional neural network cascade for face detection," in *IEEE Conference on Computer Vision and Pattern Recognition*, 2015, pp. 5325–5334.
20. Schroff F., Kalenichenko D, and Phibin J., "FaceNet: a unified embedding for face recognition and clustering,"in *Proceedings of the IEEE Conference on Computer Vision and Pattern Recognition*, 2015, pp. 815-823.
21. Zhang C., and Zhang Z., "Improving multiview face detection with multi-task deep convolutional neural networks," *IEEE Winter Conference on Applications of Computer Vision*, 2014, pp. 1036–1041.
22. Koehrsen W., Neural Network EmbeddingsExplained: How deep learning can represent War and Peace as a vector. October 02. Accessed July 12, 2020. https://towardsdatascience.com/neural-network-embeddings-explained-4d028e6f0526.
23. Xiong X., and Torre F., "Supervised descent method and its applications to face alignment," in *IEEE Conference on Computer Vision and Pattern Recognition*, 2013, pp. 532–539.
24. Zhang Z., Luo P., Loy C. C., and Tang X., "Facial landmark detection by deep multi-task learning," in *European Conference on Computer Vision*, 2014, pp. 94–108.
25. Samina K., Khalil T., and Nasreen S., "A survey of feature selection and feature extraction techniques in machine learning," in IEEE 2014 Science and Information Conference, pp. 372–378, 2014.
26. Liu Z., Luo, X. Wang, and Tang X., "Deep learning face attributes in the wild," in *IEEE International Conference on Computer Vision*, 2015, pp. 3730–3738.
27. Yang S., Luo P., Loy C. C., and Tang X., "Wider face: A face detection benchmark," in *Proceedings of the IEEE Conference on Computer Vision and Pattern Recognition*, pp. 5525–5533, 2016.
28. Guo H., "One-shot learning in deep sequential generative models," (PhD thesis), p. 2792, 2017.
29. Farfade S. S., Saberian M. J., and Li L. J., "Multi-view face detection using deep convolutional neural networks," in *ACM on International Conference on Multimedia Retrieval*, 2015, pp. 643 650.
30. Dubey N. K., Pooja M. R., Vishal K., Dhanush Gowda H. L. , and Keertiraj B. R., "Face Recognition based Attendance System," International Journal of Engineering Research & Technology (IJERT), vol. 09, no. 06, June 2020.
31. Ghiasi G., and Fowlkes C. C., "Occlusion coherence: detecting and localizing occluded faces," arXiv preprint arXiv:1506.08347. 2015.
32. Saleh K., Hossny M., and Nahavandi S. "Intent prediction of vulnerable road users from motion trajectories using stacked LSTM network," in *2017 IEEE 20th International Conference on Intelligent Transportation Systems (ITSC)*, 2017, pp. 327–332.
33. Jain V., and Learned-Miller E. G., "FDDB: A benchmark for face detection in unconstrained settings," Technical Report UMCS-2010-009, University of Massachusetts, Amherst, 2010.
34. Yang B., Yan J., Lei Z., and Li S. Z., "Convolutional channel features," in *IEEE International Conference on Computer Vision*, 2015, pp. 82–90.
35. Ranjan R., Patel V. M., and Chellappa R., "A deep pyramid deformable part model for face detection," in *IEEE International Conference on Bio-metrics Theory, Applications and Systems*, 2015, pp. 1–8.

17

Methods for Generating Text by Eye Blink and Eye-Gaze Pattern for Locked-In Syndrome Patients

**Priyanshu Singhal, Rahul Gupta, Pankul Agarwal,
and Deepak Sethi**

CONTENTS

17.1 Introduction

Patients with locked-in syndrome have difficulty in communicating with the outside world, locked inside the body. It is hard for the person who cannot speak to share their feelings and emotions to the one he wants to [1]. The only method of communicating is through their eyes, as all the other voluntary muscles are paralyzed [2]. The patient is fully dependent on the caretaker or the nurse in decoding their eye movement pattern and eye blink; if caregivers are not present, then they are unable to communicate with anyone. The patient waits for the caregiver to have a look at his eyes to understand what they are trying to say. Questions are asked verbally or by placards like, "do you need water/food?" The affected person moves the eye in a particular manner to answer the question with yes or no. The questions are limited and predefined; if the patient wants to convey something new, then it becomes hard for the caretaker [2]. The patient will be vulnerable in this circumstance. There is a need for a computerized apparatus so the patient can communicate freely with the outside world. The objective is to automatize the manual procedure of decoding eye movements and build an application for the patients to communicate independently.

17.2 Locked-In Syndrome

The term locked-in syndrome [1] was coined by two American neurologists, Jerome B. Posner and Fred Plum, in the year 1966 for a patient who lost mobility, but communication was still left with his cognitive power. Persistent vegetative state (PVS) [3] has close related symptoms with this syndrome; both have characteristics of partial consciousness. Later, it was found that their causes are different—damage to the lower part of the brain (pons) causes locked-in syndrome and trauma to the upper area of the brain causes PVS [3].

There are three types of locked-in syndrome [2]:

Classic LIS: Consciousness and eye movements are maintained.
Incomplete LIS: Like the Classic LIS with spontaneous actions of cheek muscles.
Total LIS: Only the consciousness is present with no movement.

This approach deals with the first two categories of LIS where voluntary eye movement takes place.

17.3 Brain-Computer Interface (BCI)

Scientists produced an efficient way for LIS patients to communicate with the outside world. The first effort was the brain-computer interface (BCI) [4] that facilitates the signals patients send with the help of brain activities to computers. The activity between neurons through electrical impulses is captured by the device. This method is known as electroencephalography [4]. An electrode cap is used and worn on the head to measure the electrical activity over different parts of the brain through brain waves of the neurons. This process was later equipped with Functional Near Infrared Spectroscopy (fNIRS) [5] with the means for communication of patients that suffer from motor paralysis with their whole consciousness. Brain hemodynamic responses are measured by it.

17.4 Challenges Faced by BCI

BCI (Brain Computer Interface) devices are very costly and cannot be afforded by every person. The training for the proper functioning of BCI is a time-consuming process and can be done in two phases: the user must learn to control their brain feedback signals in the first and the feedback signals can then be used in training the classifier during the second phase [6].

The precision of brain activity detection is measured by ITR but is not excellent because of lack of development.

Current BCI do not have a satisfactory information transfer rate (about 45–60 bits/min).

17.5 Face Detection

Yan, Kriegman, and Ahuja [7,8] have represented four categories of face detection methods.

Feature-based: The feature-based method extracts the features of the face, then are trained as classifiers to differentiate between the facial regions and the non-facial regions. Its accuracy is better than other methods.

Appearance-based: The method finds the model of faces based on a set of training faces. Characteristics of the face are found through statistical analysis and machine learning. This is much better than other ways of performing and is also used for facial recognition as it helps in the extraction of features.

Knowledge-based: This method is dependent on a set of rules based on the knowledge of humans to detect the face. The position and distance of the eyes and nose are considered for face detection. It is hard to develop a set of rules appropriately, as some are too general or specific that falsely detects the face.

Template Matching: The template matching method uses a pre-defined face template to detect and locate between the template and the input pictures using correlation.

Significant efforts have been put to make face detection and recognition more accurate. Michael Jones and Paul Viola [9] revolutionized and developed a real-time face detection framework with better accuracy.

17.6 Eye Detection

Eye detection is used in many applications, and some methods are:

Electrooculography: [10–13] this method uses the concept of the electric field present around the eyes and changes when the eye rotates. Electrodes and sensory devices are placed close to the eyes to ascertain the value of the electric field. This has some drawbacks as the potential changes itself without any movement of the eye, so it is not trustworthy.

Scleral search coils: Studies have shown that when a wired coil moves, emf is induced in a coil. A modified contact lens for the eye position detection that has small wired coils is inserted in the eyes [10].

Infrared oculography: [11] This method uses infrared light and is less noisy than electro-oculography. It is also an invasive method. The movement of the eyes measured using this technique is horizontal; the vertical method is limited.

Video oculography: This method has simplified and made cheaper complex and costly methods available. Most commercial eye trackers use a video-based method for eye tracking. Single or multiple cameras are used in this method for eye detection [14,15].

17.7 Detection of Eye Gaze

We know the direction a person is looking at by their gaze; it shows the attention of the person. Gaze direction has two applications:

Feature-based gaze estimation.

The features [16,17] of the human eyes are investigated for indicators of recognition.

Appearance-based gaze estimation

This method [16] tracks eyes based on what we can see in pictures. The data of the image is plotted on display coordinates for the detection of gaze direction. In this method, a direct mapping is done from the image without the need to calibrate cameras or other related information.

17.8 Convolutional Neural Network

Convolution Neural Networks characterize, investigate, and clarify each layer, understanding the genuine contrasts between a CNN and standard neural network. The primary advances accomplished in each layer and procedure have been sketched out, with an emphasis on the ones utilized for work.

In machine learning, it is the revelation of different degrees of circulated portrayals known as deep learning [18]. It depends on arrangement dependent on the chain of importance of the models to learn deep level reflections in the information. Diverse conventional machine learning ventures have been improved with the assistance of deep learning algorithms (e.g., semantic parsing, regular language handling, move to learn, and PC vision, among others).

Convolution Neural Networks were made as a constituent of deep learning algorithms to get a significant sense from pictures as people do. PC shows pictures as a linear array of numerical qualities. Yet, the significance of a picture is in the relationship between the pixels for state across diagonals, all over. When the picture is straightened by the PC into the linear array, this relationship is lost. That is the reason CNN was designed. As the name suggests, these networks subsume over the given picture as little square shapes. Taking in normal of the all-out zone secured by the square shape we get. The separation is known as a step. In some cases, a couple of more pixels are included to keep the size. This is known as cushioning. The distinct layers of CNN incorporate pooling (max, min, and so forth), convolution, and dropout, thick or completely associated formats [19,20]. The convolution layer incorporates associations among certain hubs to certain the hubs of another. Pooling layers plan to diminish the contiguous size of the information that is formed after convolution (see Figure 17.1). Dropout layers arbitrarily drop-out any hubs by considering the chance of each in the layer getting handled. Thick layers are associated; each layer and its hubs are associated with the hub of the following layer.

17.9 Haar-Cascade

Haar Cascades [21–23] is the assortment of picture grouping algorithms. The Haar-like portrayal is utilized for chronology and discovery of pictures. It portrays the different highlights that gives one-of-a-kind characters to a substance. As we have just clarified, PC sees pictures (Figure 17.2) as a gathering of algorithmic qualities. Haar-like highlights are utilized to secure the rectangular part of the total picture. It attempts to consolidate different pixels of changing forces. Now, we move to how they separate images.

How do people separate an article? When they see one, for example, an apple, they are informed that it is an apple. After some time, when they attempt to recognize it, they will have a general perception of such article. The same can be said about Haar-Cascades.

The methodology depends on machine learning where a model is prepared by given dataset comprised of two kinds of pictures—positive and negative pictures. After this course work, these images are utilized to perceive and separate articles in the test dataset that is comprised of different pictures. We are accepting an identification of countenances in this specific circumstance.

Presently, all dimensional and various bits are used to figure image details. Part of these features is advantageous for us, while others are not as they don't get a one-of-a-kind trademark. How do we pick important aspects from others? This can be done using

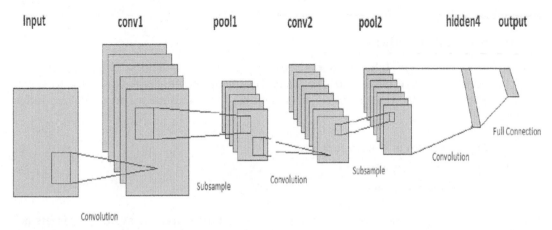

FIGURE 17.1
A sample CNN model.

(a)

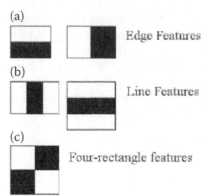

Edge Features

(b)

Line Features

(c)

Four-rectangle features

FIGURE 17.2
Different features of Haar-like structures.

Adaboost. We select each delivered incorporate and apply it on all the pictures present in the preparation dataset. Then, we register a feature that orders a picture of a face from various images without a face with an unrivaled edge. A part of these will be mis-classifications of specific images caused by a foggy picture, etc. We need not bother with a little subset of images to incline the classifier. That is the explanation we use only for aspects that lead up to the base bumble rate. This prompts the way that these aspects precisely group positive and negative images.

Given the circumstances, we can firmly say that an enormous part of the picture without a face is called a non-face region. It will spare a lot of calculation if we are able to check whether the rectangular portion belongs to a face region or not. If it is the non-face region, we must neglect it and pay more attention to the areas with pictures.

This prompts the ideal utilization of resources.

Presently, we have been utilizing OpenCV to recognize faces and the eyes in a picture. It is accompanied by a built-in Haar Cascade classifier that consists of a trainer and an identifier. It now includes the model trained for face and eye, so we don't have to utilize the trainer. We use the locator to recognize the facially desired landmarks and eye.

17.10 Product Functions

The communication with LIS is provided through this web application consisting of three modes operated by eye blink and eye gaze. The front screen displays "blink to select mode" and the three modes images scrolls whenever the user blinks. The available modes for use are:

1. Answer question in yes-no format.
2. Generate your own message.
3. Quick response messages.

Voluntary eye blink is monitored by the system constantly and the system redirects according to mode to a specific URL.

17.10.1 Mode 1 (Say Yes-No) Operation

To answer a question, the user blinks (yes), otherwise, it is considered as a no. Voluntary blinks are monitored by the system and once detected (Figure 17.3), then the answer yes is flashed on the screen. The reset button is present, clicked by the person who puts up the question to reset the answer. The same question must be asked more than twice to avoid incorrectly detected blinks

17.10.2 Mode 2 (Message Mode) Operation

The patient could note a message by himself with the help of eye blinking. 6 × 5 matrix consisting of characters in a particular cell is built. The matrix is shown in Figure 17.4 and the user blinks on the colored or highlighted row to select it. After the selection, it is highlighted for one second. The user blinks on the highlighted column to select the character. After selecting the character, it gets typed in the textbox under the matrix, which helps the user see the characters selected. If the user selects the wrong character, there is a way to erase or remove them (last or sixth row of the matrix).

To explain a flowchart, four variables are needed to be understood:

i: To count rows in the matrix, the counter variable is used.
N: Number of total rows (8).
j: To count columns in a matrix, counter variable.
M: It contains a total number of available columns (6/3) depending on the row.

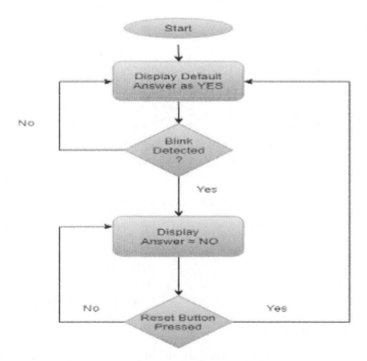

FIGURE 17.3
Flowchart of Mode 1.

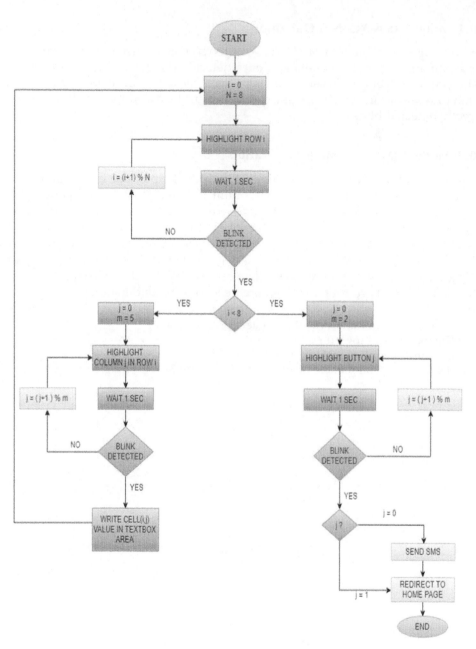

FIGURE 17.4
Flowchart of Mode 2.

17.10.3 Text Prediction

This technology assists the client in quickly noting down messages, as it predicts the words, saving time. The initial character is chosen by the user; with that given prefix (Figure 17.5), defined words from a dictionary are chosen and the top five are shown or

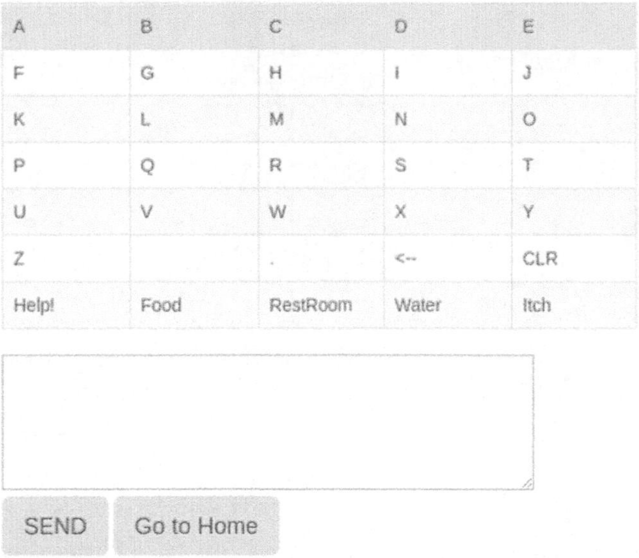

A	B	C	D	E
F	G	H	I	J
K	L	M	N	O
P	Q	R	S	T
U	V	W	X	Y
Z		.	<--	CLR
Help!	Food	RestRoom	Water	Itch

SEND   Go to Home

FIGURE 17.5
Matrix of alphabets used in Mode 2.

displayed in an extra row of the matrix. If none of the words in the dictionary matches the prefix, then the top five words are alphabetically displayed.

17.10.4 Mode 3 (Quick Response) Operations

This mode is used for regular activities like hunger, thirst, feelings of coldness or hotness, etc. to save time. The user can choose from the displayed messages; there is a slideshow of quick images that the user can slide through by using the pupils (Figure 17.6). The left-right movement of the eye manipulates the choices and blinking selects the message, sending it to pre-arranged recipients.

17.10.5 Send Message

The message typed or generated is sent to phone numbers as text messages. The message is sent using the Sinch API [34].

17.11 Proposed Model

The flowchart shows how the proposed model will run. Individual frames are extracted from the live video feed from the camera. The face is detected from the frame using haar-cascade, then it is passed to the facial landmark detection module to detect and generate facial landmarks. Eyes are extracted after getting the landmarks and are sent to three different modules (Figure 17.7).

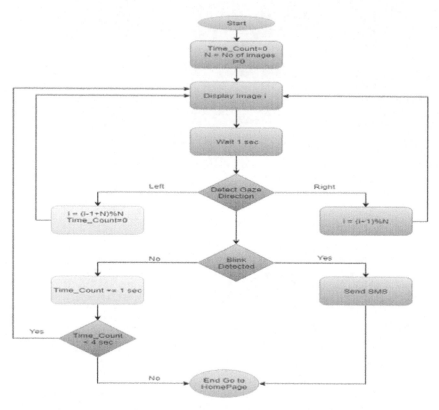

FIGURE 17.6
Flowchart of Mode 3.

17.12 Detection of Eye Blink with Facial Landmarks

Facial landmarks using OpenCV, Idlib [24,25]

The key regions of the face (mouth, eyebrows, nose, eyes, jawline) are shown by facial landmarks (Figure 17.8). The detection of landmarks is a two-step process: first is the detection using the haar-cascades model of the OpenCV library of python. After detection, facial landmarks are identified using the Python Idlib library [21,26].

The input image is detected by a pre-trained landmark detector of the Idlib library that gives a 68-point output of facial landmarks.

17.13 Eye Blink Detection

After the plotting of facial landmark, the eye blink in the video stream is detected. There are many eye blink detection methods but eye aspect ratio (EAR) [27] has the simplest calculations and is the most refined. The calculations are based on the distance between the plots of landmarks of the eyes. A single eye is represented by six points, each moving from left to right (Figure 17.9) (37–42, 43–48).

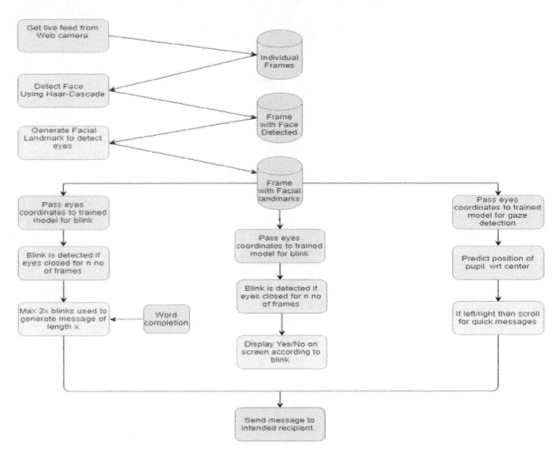

FIGURE 17.7
Flowchart for the proposed model.

In a research paper by "Soukupová and Čech" [27], eye aspect ratio (EAR) is derived. The equation of the eye aspect ratio consists of the numerator (the perpendicular distance between the eye base and eyelid) and the denominator (the horizontal distance).

$$EAR = \frac{|p2 - p6| + |p3 - p5|}{2|p1 - p4|} \tag{17.1}$$

During blinking, only the vertical distance changes as it is the distance between the eyelid and the eye base. On the left image, the eye is wide open, and the eye aspect ratio (EAR) is greater and constant with time; on right, the person is blinking and the vertical distance is approximately zero, resulting in the eye aspect ratio (EAR) of nearly zero. The plot of EAR with respect to time is represented in Figure 17.10. The EAR remains constant to around 0.25 when the eyes are open and the value drops to approximately zero when the person blinks.

FIGURE 17.8
Facial landmark plot.

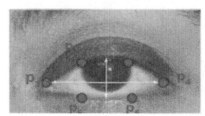

FIGURE 17.9
Six landmark coordinates of the human eye.

17.14 Eye-Gaze Detection

The direction an individual is looking at is determined by eye gaze. It also shows the attention level of a person. Detection of eye gaze direction (center, left, and right) is done by a machine learning model.

There are two established methods for eye gaze detection. The first one is the user calibration free system [28], and it does not require a pair of cameras to estimate the eye parameters, making it user friendly. The system is expensive as it employs two cameras and five illuminators [14]. The second method requires end-user calibration

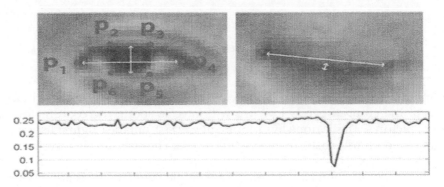

FIGURE 17.10
Plot of eye aspect ratio vs. time.

[16] that employs static markers that detect eye gaze by locating the center and edge of the iris. It can take a few moments to conduct calibration and get the coordinates upon display [14]. Both systems are costly and time inefficient; calibration processes and are slow for AR and MR applications but the algorithm we used has overcome these disadvantages.

17.14.1 Method of Working

Step 1 (Face detection): The face is extracted from the native image using Haar-Cascade classifiers of the OpenCV library, then it is reduced to 96 × 96 RGB image (that is converted to greyscale) for the detection of the landmark in our second step.

Step 2 (Facial landmarks of the eyes): Specific landmarks are required to detect eye gaze, as shown in Figure 17.11. The OpenCV library is used to find these landmarks.

Step 3 (Eye detection): The location of the eye is found through landmarks. Before we find the box bounded by the left eye, we initially locate the dimensions of the box:

$$"width = \max(left\_eyebrow\_inner\_end\_x - left\_eyebrow\_other\_end\_x,$$
$$left\_eye\_ineer\_corner\_x - left\_eye\_other\_corner\_x)" \tag{17.2}$$

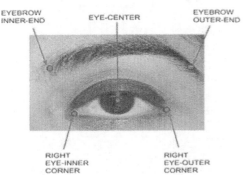

FIGURE 17.11
Separated facial landmarks [29].

and

$$\text{"height} = \max(left\_eyebrow\_inner\_end\_y - left\_eye\_inner\_corner\_y,$$
$$eft\_eyebrow\_other\_end\_y - left\_eye\_other\_corner\_y)\text{"} \tag{17.3}$$

We can find the coordinates of the box enclosing the eye from the extracted face. As the resolution of the cropped eye is low, we will have to locate the coordinates based on the original pictures. This is done by cropping the eyes from the original image, mapping the face image coordinates back to the original image. The eyes' image is resized to 42 × 50 for eye-gaze detection.

Step 4 (Eye gaze direction classification for a single eye): The eyes are cropped before the gaze direction classification. The classification model CNN [29] is modified to group the direction of eye gaze (Figure 17.12). The aim is to find an exact category of The Eye-Chimera database [30]. H191 ere, the CNN model consists of eight layers [31,32]. Two separate CNN models are trained by the separate right and left eye datasets.

Step 5 (Detection of eye gaze): The CNN model of the left and right eyes is then put together, detecting the direction of both the eyes (probability of each class). Then, the mean of probabilities is calculated. After that, the class that has the highest probability is selected.

17.15 Conclusion

The developed application is user-friendly and is designed to help patients diagnosed with locked-in syndrome, helping them become independent. The manual process was used, where the caregiver slides through a board containing all English language characters until the patient blinks to select. This process is repeated until a word is formed. This application is automated and can be used independently to communicate through blinking and pupil movement. This application can easily be shared and does not need high-end hardware, so

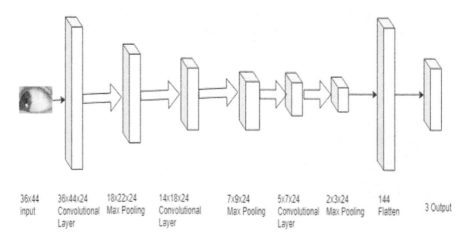

FIGURE 17.12
Eye gaze direction (CNN model).

it is cost-friendly. Further changes can also be done. This application helps LIS patients share their ideas and emotions to the world and prevent them from being locked inside. The independence of communication will help them live their life to the fullest.

17.16 Future Work

The potential features and improvements that can be added to the work are as follows:

- To prevent unwanted access to the application, a security feature can be added through face recognition of the patient, so that the application is run only by the intended patient.
- The application can speak as the user blinks and selects the character in the second mode. In the first mode, the application can declare the yes-no options selected, and in the quick mode, it can tell the message the user has selected.
- Eye wink can be used in many ways (e.g. for going back in the application, erasing the character selected in the text box, and switching between modes of the application).
- The EAR value calculated in eye blink detection should be less than the threshold value for detection. The threshold value is decided by the developer and can be made dynamic according to the situation.
- Mobile numbers of intended recipients for receiving the text message are fixed by the developer and cannot be modified. Modification to the list can be done by the user.

References

1. Casper S. T., "A History of the locked-in-syndrome: ethics in the making of neurological consciousness, 1880-present." *Neuroethics*, vol. 13, no. 2 , pp. 145–161, 2020.
2. Khanna, K., Verma A. and Richard B. ""The locked-in syndrome": Can it be unlocked?" *Journal of Clinical Gerontology and Geriatrics*, vol. 2.4, pp. 96–99, 2011.
3. Laureys, S., Owen A. M. and Schiff N. D., "Brain function in coma, vegetative state, and related disorders." *The Lancet Neurology*, vol. 3.9, p. 537546, 2004.
4. Kübler, A. et al. "Brain-computer communication: unlocking the locked in," *Psychological Bulletin*, vol. 127, no. 3, p. 358, 2001.
5. Chaudhary, U. et al. "Brain-computer interface–based communication in the completely locked-in state." *PLoS Biology*, vol. 15, no. 1, p. e1002593, 2017.
6. Hoffmann, U., Vesin J.-M. and Ebrahimi T., "Recent advances in brain-computer interfaces," In IEEE International Workshop on Multimedia Signal Processing (MMSP07), no. CONF. 2007.
7. Yang, M.-H., David J. K. and Ahuja N. "Detecting faces in images: a survey." *IEEE Transactions on Pattern Analysis and Machine Intelligence*, vol. 24.1, pp. 34–58, 2002.
8. Wu, Y. and Ji Q., "Facial landmark detection: a literature survey." *International Journal of Computer Vision*, vol. 127, no. 2, pp. 115–142, 2019.

9. Viola, P. and Jones M., "Rapid object detection using a boosted cascade of simple features." *CVPR*, vol. 1, no. 1, pp. 511–518, 2001.

10. Zhu, J. and Yang J., "Subpixel eye gaze tracking." In *Fifth IEEE International Conference on Automatic Face Gesture Recognition. IEEE*, 2002. pp. 131–136.

11. Chennamma, H. R. and Yuan X., "A survey on eye-gaze tracking techniques." arXiv preprint arXiv:1312.6410 (2013).

12. Vrânceanu, R. et al. "NLP EAC recognition by component separation in the eye region." *International Conference on Computer Analysis of Images and Patterns*. Springer, Berlin, Heidelberg, 2013.

13. Park, S.-W. et al. "Augmentative and alternative communication training using eye blink switch for locked-in syndrome patient." *Annals of Rehabilitation Medicine*, vol. 36, no. 2, p. 268, 2012.

14. Gwon, Su, et al. "Estimation of gaze detection accuracy using the calibration information-based fuzzy system." *Sensors*, vol. 16, no. 1, p. 60, 2016.

15. 16Jones E., Oliphant T. and Peterson P., "{SciPy}: Open source scientific tools for {Python}." 2001.

16. Kiat, Lim Choon, and Ranganath Surendra. "One-time calibration eye gaze detection system." *2004 International Conference on Image Processing*, 2004. ICIP'04. Vol. 2. IEEE, 2004.

17. Pfeuffer, Ken, et al. "Pursuit calibration: making gaze calibration less tedious and more flexible." Proceedings of the *26th annual ACM Symposium on User Interface Software and Technology. ACM*, 2013.

18. Alom M. Z. et al. "The history began from AlexNet: a comprehensive survey on deep learning approaches." arXiv preprint arXiv:1803.01164 (2018).

19. Sun, Y., Wang X. and Tang X., "Deep convolutional network cascade for facial point detection." Proceedings of the *IEEE Conference on Computer Vision and Pattern Recognition*. 2013.

20. Zarándy Á. et al. "Overview of CNN research: 25 years history and the current trends." 2015 IEEE International Symposium on Circuits and Systems (ISCAS). IEEE, 2015, pp. 401-404.

21. Wang, N. et al. "Facial feature point detection: A comprehensive survey." *Neurocomputing*, vol. 275, pp. 50–65, 2018.

22. Soo, S. "Object detection using Haar-cascade classifier." *Institute of Computer Science*, University of Tartu (2014): 1–12.

23. OpenCV, "Cascade classifier training — OpenCV 2.4.9.0 documentation," Available: http://docs.opencv.org/doc/user_guide/ug_traincascade.html.

24. King, D. E. "Dlib-ml: A machine learning toolkit." *Journal of Machine Learning Research*, vol. 10, pp. 1755–1758, July 2009.

25. Whitt, S. et al. "Sinch. Delegating web search from a mobile device"; https://www.sinch.com

26. Kazemi, V. and Sullivan J., "One millisecond face alignment with an ensemble of regression trees." Proceedings of the *IEEE Conference on Computer Vision and Pattern Recognition*. 2014.

27. Soukupova T. and Cech J., "Eye blink detection using facial landmarks." *21st Computer Vision Winter Workshop*, Rimske Toplice, Slovenia. 2016.

28. Model, D. and Eizenman M., "User-calibration-free remote eye-gaze tracking system with extended tracking range." *2011 24th Canadian Conference on Electrical and Computer Engineering (CCECE). IEEE*, 2011.

29. George, A. and Routray A., "Real-time eye gaze direction classification using convolutional neural network." *2016 International Conference on Signal Processing and Communications (SPCOM). IEEE*, 2016.

30. Florea L. et al. "Can your eyes tell me how you think? A gaze directed estimation of the mental activity." *BMVC*. 2013.

31. Chollet, F. "Keras documentation." (2015); Keras. io, retrieved from https://keras.io.

32. Pedregosa, F. et al. "Scikit-learn: machine learning in python." *Journal of Machine Learning Research*, vol. 12, pp. 2825–2830, October 2011.

18

Kinship Verification Using Convolutional Neural Network

Vijay Prakash Sharma and Sunil Kumar

CONTENTS

18.1 Introduction

A DNA test is thought to be the only choice to identify genetic similarities between human beings, but certain constraints are associated with it—court permission, lab setup, and money, etc. To find a reasonable and affordable solution digitally, researchers are working to establish kinship between two persons by alternative methods. It has been observed that the human face can act as a similarity feature to establish kinship between close family members. The theory is inspired by common observations—a child's nose is similar to his father's, or her eyes resemble her mother's." Facial features play a key role in establishing kinship through machine learning, deep learning, and AI. Kinship verification is used to find missing children, annotate images, or manage photo and social media applications automatically. It also has applications in the automation system—building a family database. Lately, lots of kinship verification methods have been proposed but it remains a challenging task to develop a method for real-world applications.

18.2 Methods of Kinship Verification from Images

Figure 18.1 shows the general kinship verification (KV) process from images. The basic approach for KV is extracting features from faces and applying some classification methods like SVM [1], KNN, etc. As technology progressed, approaches for solving kinship verification have also changed. Nowadays, convolution models are used instead of manual feature extraction methods, which provide more accurate results. Some researchers have also used metric learning and transfer learning approaches.

Fang, et al. [2] were the first researchers who worked on the kinship verification problem. They identified 14 facial features [3] (e.g. right eye color, eye to nose distance, left eye window, etc.). With the help of these features, they created a feature vector for parent and child. By matching these features using K-nearest neighbor or support vector machine, they were able to classify the kin relation between them.

Chergui, et al. [4] divided the complete process of kinship verification into four stages: first is the face pre-processing step that uses the Viola-Jones algorithm for eye detection, pose correction and face alignment. The second step is feature extraction that uses LBP and BSIF [5] algorithms. The third step is the feature selection step that uses Relief F, and the last step of classification uses SVM and KNN.

Convolutional neural network (CNN): A deep learning algorithm comprised of millions of connected neurons. Each neuron gets input from the previous neuron, performs operation on inputs received and gives output to the next layer. It takes an image as an input in the form of a matrix of pixels. CNN is used in areas like image classification, object detection, etc. CNN has four types of layers—convolution layer, pooling layer, flattened, and fully connected layer [6].

Convolution layer: It is the first layer of the CNN model used to extract feature from images; convolution operation (Figure 18.2) is performed between the input image and filter image. Filter image is a special type of pre-defined matrix. Several types of filters are available for different operations as mentioned in Table 18.1.

Convolution operation between two function f and g is the function $f * g$ defined by:

$$(f * g)(t) = \int_0^t f(u)g(t-u)du$$

In the convolution layer, multiple feature maps are prepared by different feature vectors. After training, the model decides which feature map is more useful (Figure 18.3).

FIGURE 18.1
Process for kinship verification from images.

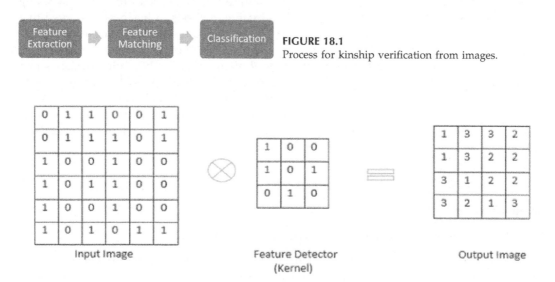

FIGURE 18.2
Convolution example.

TABLE 18.1

Operations and Filters

Operations	Filter
Identity	$\begin{bmatrix} 0 & 0 & 0 \\ 0 & 1 & 0 \\ 0 & 0 & 0 \end{bmatrix}$
Edge Detection	$\begin{bmatrix} 1 & 0 & -1 \\ 0 & 0 & 0 \\ -1 & 0 & 1 \end{bmatrix} \begin{bmatrix} 0 & 1 & 0 \\ 1 & -4 & 1 \\ 0 & 1 & 1 \end{bmatrix} \begin{bmatrix} -1 & -1 & -1 \\ -1 & 8 & -1 \\ -1 & -1 & -1 \end{bmatrix}$
Sharpen	$\begin{bmatrix} 0 & -1 & 0 \\ 1 & 5 & -1 \\ 0 & -1 & 0 \end{bmatrix}$
Normalized	$\frac{1}{9}\begin{bmatrix} 1 & 1 & 1 \\ 1 & 1 & 1 \\ 1 & 1 & 1 \end{bmatrix}$
Gaussian Blur	$\frac{1}{16}\begin{bmatrix} 1 & 2 & 1 \\ 2 & 4 & 2 \\ 1 & 2 & 1 \end{bmatrix}$

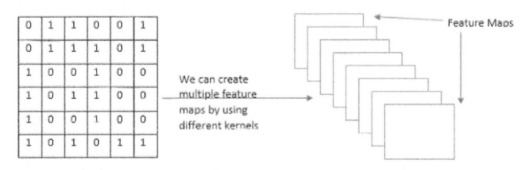

FIGURE 18.3
Multiple feature map.

Traditionally, convolution filters are handcrafted but CNN learns the kernel's features from examples. CNN learns these kernels/filters by initializing values to the kernel and calculating the error. Then, it updates these kernel values to minimize error. For more accurate results, CNN learns multiple kernels to find multiple feature maps.

Pooling layer: Pooling is used to normalize the image when we have lots of images of an object, but the object may not be present at the same location and of the same size in the image. All images do not have the same background and the same environment. So, when convolution layers extract features, these features are a bit destroyed. Pooling is used to recover such features. Different types of pooling are available—max pooling, sum pooling, min pooling. A max-pooling example with a box of 2 × 2 pixels is given in Figure 18.4.

Flattening: In the flattening layer, the pooled feature map is converted to a single-column matrix as shown in Figure 18.5.

FIGURE 18.4
Max-pooling process.

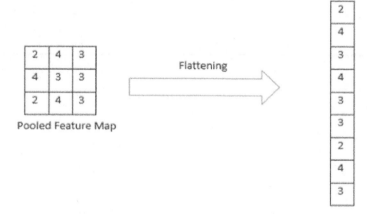

FIGURE 18.5
Flattening process.

Fully connected layer: The output of the flattening layer is fed into a fully connected (Figure 18.6) traditional neural network.

In Figure 18.6, X_1, X_2, X_3, X_4 are the outputs of the flattening layer. A fully connected model learns the weights and uses activation functions like Softmax and Sigmoid to classify the output. The complete process of CNN is shown in Figure 18.7.

Kinship verification using the CNN model: In a kinship verification problem, we must identify facial features and then match them. Identifying features is a tricky task and it requires a lot of knowledge to identify key features, and decide their weight and importance. Convolutional networks play a vital role in extracting the most relevant features for classification and verification. The results of CNN models are promising in the kinship verification problem.

Zhang, et al. [7] used a convolution neural network model and proposed a CNN architecture for kinship verification. The architecture is shown in Figure 18.8. This model has three layers: the first layer has 16 filters of the size 5 × 5 × 6; the second layer has 64 filters with the size 5 × 5 × 16; and the third layer has 128 filters of 5 × 5 × 64. ReLU

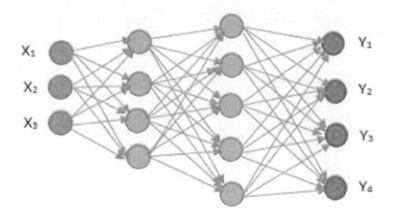

FIGURE 18.6
Fully connected model.

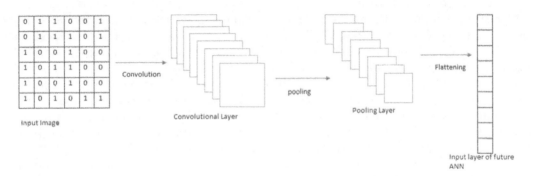

FIGURE 18.7
Complete CNN process.

Name	Input	Conv_1	Max pooling	Conv_2	Max Pooling	Conv_3	FC	Soft max
Dimension	64x64x6							
Filter Size		5x5x6	2x2	5x5x16	2x2	5x5x64		
Num		16		64		128	640	2
Stride		1	1		1			

FIGURE 18.8
Architecture of convolution module for kinship verification.

activation function is used in the internal layers and the Softmax classifier is used for classification.

The model is trained by backpropagation with a logistic loss function. Gaussian distribution is used for the initialization of weights. To improve results, they proposed a new structure called CNN point, which contains ten basic CNN models as shown in Figure 18.9.

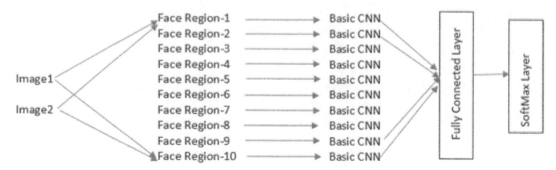

FIGURE 18.9
CNN point structure.

The face is divided into ten 64 × 64 regions and each face region-pair is fed to an independent CNN model. The output of all ten CNN models is combined and fed to the fully connected layer (Figure 18.10).

Nandy, et al. [8] used a special CNN model, Siamese CNN, shown in Figure 18.11. They used two squeeze net networks [9]. This network was pre-trained on the VGGFace2 data set. The results of both networks were combined by a similarity matrix (L1 norm, L2 norm, cosine Similarity) and fed to a fully connected network.

Instead of full-face, Yan and Wang [10] focused on the local parts of the face (e.g., mouth, nose, eyes, etc.). They proposed an Attention network, that consists of three convolution layers, two max-pooling layers, and one fully connected layer. After each convolution layer, an attention layer is added. They combined two RGB images (parent image and child image) and made an input data of 64 × 64 × 6. The first convolution layer contains 32 filters of 5 × 5 × 6, the second layer contains 64 filters of 5 × 5 × 32, and the third layer contains 128 filters of 5 × 5 × 64. From the third layer, they got an output size of 9 × 9 × 128. This output is fed to a fully connected network that contains 512 neurons and has a 6-channel binary classification result.

Haijun Liu, et al. [11] proposed a status aware projection learning (SaPL) method for kinship verification. They presented that the large age gap causes features to not match.

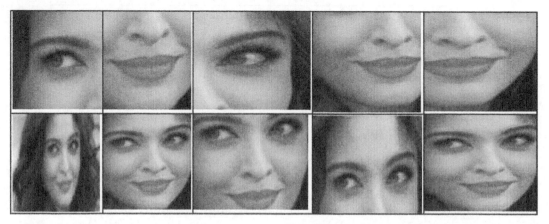

FIGURE 18.10
Ten different face regions.

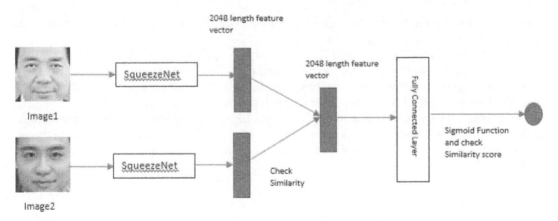

FIGURE 18.11
Architecture of siamese convolutional neural network.

So, they calculated Mahalanobis distances. SaPL is a combination of two components: one is common for both images, and the other a status specific component different for both parent and child. They used LBP and HOG for feature descriptions. Mahpod, et al. [12] used a supervised learning approach named Multiview Hybrid Distance Learning (MHDL). Haibin Yan, et al. [13] presented a new technique named Discriminative Compact Binary Face Descriptor (DCBFD) for kinship verification. Xiaoting, et al. [14] was the first researcher who stated that a child's skin color and eye color are inherited from the parents; they worked on color images and got better results.

Duan, et al. [15] proposed a new CNN architecture for kinship verification named Coarse-to-Fine Transfer (CFT). It has two components: coarse CNN (cCNN) and fine CNN (fCNN). cCNN was pre-trained with a large face recognition data set (CASIA WebFace database) used to find generalized facial features. fCNN trained with a small kinship dataset and used kin relation specific features. CFT consists of a convolutional layer, pooling layer, fully connected layer, and a softmax layer. In CFT, two convolutional layers are followed by one pooling layer. The architecture of CFT shown in Figure 18.12 (including the number of kernels for each convolutional layer).

Li, et al. [16] proposed a new framework for kinship verification named KinNet, a fine-to-coarse deep metric learning framework. In the framework, the network first pre-trained with the face recognition data set and then fine-tuned with the kinship data set.

Conv11-32	Conv12-64	Pooling	Conv21-64	Conv22-128	Pooling	Conv31-96	Conv32-192	Pooling	Conv41-128	Conv42-256	Pooling	Conv51-160	Conv52-320	FC1-512	FC2-10575

FIGURE 18.12
Architecture of CFT.

They ensemble four networks to improve performance. Figure 18.13 shows the complete architecture of the framework.

Dahan Eran, et al. [17] used VGG16 for kinship verification. At first, they used two VGG16 (Figure 18.14) modules for both images, and the results from these two modules were combined by the mask layer, and local and global filters were applied to the output. Avg Pooling is applied on the result and softmax was used for classification.

Some researchers worked on different concepts like Ertugrul, et al. [18] who used smile and disgust expressions to establish kin relation. Wu, et al. [19] proposed a deep Siamese fusion network for kinship verification that combines visual and voice information. Talking KINship [19] data set was used for this.

18.3 Kinship Verification from Videos

Lopez B Miguel, et al. [20] used videos for kinship verification. To extract faces, they used active shape models and extracted 68 facial landmarks. To describe the faces, they used two features: texture spatiotemporal features and deep learning features. For deep learning features, the VGG Face Network is used. The architecture of VGG-Face CNN is shown in Figure 18.15. The input of this network is an RGB face image of size 224 × 224. This network has 13 convolutional layers (Conv) each followed by the rectified linear unit layer (ReLU). Some of these ReLU layers are followed by the max-pooling layer (mpool), with two fully connected layers. To extract deep face features, they input video frames one by one to the VGG Face CNN model and collected the output of the fc7 layer.

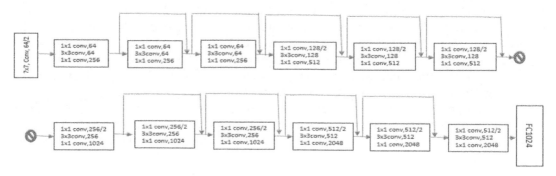

FIGURE 18.13
Architecture of KinNet Framework.

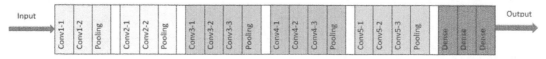

FIGURE 18.14
Architecture of VGG16.

Layer	0	1	2	3	4	5	6	7	8	9	10	11	12
Type	input	conv	relu	conv	relu	mpool	conv	relu	conv	relu	mpool	conv	relu
Name		conv1_1	relu1_1	conv1_1	relu1_2	pool1	conv2_1	relu2_1	conv2_2	relu2_2	pool2	conv3_1	relu3_1
Support		3	1	3	1	2	3	1	3	1	2	3	1
Filter dim		3		64			64		128			128	
Num filters		64		64			128		128			256	
Stride		1	1	1	1	2	1	1	1	1	2	1	1
pad		1	0	1	0	0	1	0	1	0	0	1	0

Layer	13	14	15	16	17	18	19	20	21	22	23	24	25
Type	conv	relu	conv	relu	mpool	conv	relu	conv	relu	conv	relu	mpool	conv
Name	conv3_2	relu3_2	conv3_3	relu3_3	pool3	conv4_1	relu4_1	conv4_2	relu4_2	conv4_3	relu4_3	pool4	conv5_1
Support	3	1	3	1	2	3	1	3	1	3	1	2	3
Filter dim	256		256			256		512		512			512
Num filters	256		256			512		512		512			512
Stride	1	1	1	1	2	1	1	1	1	1	1	2	1
pad	1	0	1	0	0	1	0	1	0	1	0	0	1

Layer	26	27	28	29	30	31	32	33	34	35	36	37
Type	relu	conv	relu	conv	relu	mpool	conv	relu	conv	relu	conv	softmax
Name	relu5_1	conv5_2	relu5_2	conv5_2	relu5_3	pool5	fc6	relu6	fc7	relu7	fc8	prob
Support	1	3	1	3	1	2	7	1	1	1	1	1
Filter dim		512		512			512		4096		4096	
Num filters		512		512			4096		4096		2622	
Stride	1	1	1	1	1	2	1	1	1	1	1	1
pad	0	1	0	1	0	0	0	0	0	0	0	0

FIGURE 18.15
Architecture of VGG Face CNN.

Yan Haibin, et al. [21] created a new database named Kinship Face videos in the wild (KFVW). First, they select frames, convert them into grayscale, and extract LBP. They used four distance metric learning methods, information-theoretic metric learning, KISS metric learning, cosine similarity metric learning, and side information based linear discriminant analysis. They also studied human observation on kinship verification and concluded that metric learning methods are not as good as human observations Summary of different kinship detection methods shown in Table 18.2.

18.4 Datasets

Five kinship image data sets are available for research. Images of these data sets were collected from the internet. In KinFace, W-I and KinFaceW-II images are captured in an uncontrolled environment. This means no restriction on the pose, background, lighting, age, etc. Most data sets have four relations: father-son (F-S), father-daughter(F-D), mother-don (M-S), and mother-daughter(M-D). The summary of these datasets is shown in Table 18.3.

18.5 Conclusion

Kinship verification is an emerging topic around computer vision. Lots of researchers are working and trying to provide solution of real-world application. Convolutional Neural

TABLE 18.2

Summary of Kinship Detection Methods

Authors	Method Name	Data Set	Accuracy				
			FS	FD	MS	MD	Mean
Wu et al. [19]	Voice-based recognition	Talking [19]	23	34	31	31	29.8(Error)
Dahan and Keller [17]	Selfkin module	FIW [22]	68.8	68.91	70.2	73.8	68.00
Chergui and Ouchtati [23]	BSIF+PML LBP+PML	Cornell KinFace [2]	-	-	-	-	86.71 83.56
		UB KinFace [24]	-			-	64.12 74.50
		KinFaceW-I [25]	-	-	-	-	78.89 76.36
		KinFaceW-II [25]	-	-	-	-	75.01 76.63
Zhang et al. [7]	Deep Convolutional Neural Network	KinFaceW-I [25]	76.1	71.8	78	84.1	77.5
Nandy and Mondal [8]	Siamese Convolutional Network	FIW [22]	68.74	62.53	67.95	69.84	67.66
Yan and Wan [10]	Attention Network	KinFacew-I	77	77.6	83	86.5	81
		KinFaceW-II [25]	92.5	88.3	91.4	94.1	91.6
Fang et al. [2]	Pictorial Model	Own created data set	-	-	-	-	66.49
Liu and Jian [11]	Status aware projection learning	KinfaceW-IKinfaceW-II [25]	84.3 82.4	75.1 72.4	72.4 75.8	81.5 74.2	78.3 76.2
Yan [13]	D-CBFD	KinfaceW-IKinfaceW-II [25]	77.679.0	71.6 74.2	74.1 75.4	79.5 77.3	75.6 78.5

TABLE 18.3

Kinship Image Datasets

Dataset	Format	Size	Resolution
Cornell KinFace [2]	Image	150 pairs	100 × 100
UB KinFace [24]	Image	200 groups	89 × 96
KinFaceW [25]	Image	533 pairs	64 × 64
	Image	1,000 pairs	64 × 64
Family101 [26]	Image	14,816 images	120 × 150
TSKinFace [27]	Image	1015 tri subject	64 × 64
FIW [22]	Image	656,954 pairs	–
UvA NEMO smile [28]	Video	1,240 videos	1920 × 1080

Network (CNN) is the most impressive form of ANN architecture. It is primarily used for pattern recognition, and feature extraction tasks. In this chapter, we focused on different CNN architectures and the use of CNN for kinship verification. Due to some constraints, like the availability of homogeneous datasets in different environments, kinship verification is still a big challenge. Initially, researchers work with facial images but also currently operate on attributes like voice, smile, and disgust expressions. Kinship verification has lots of real-world applications, like finding missing children, constructing a family tree, etc.

References

1. Chang C.-C. and Lin C.-J., "LIBSVM: A library for support vector machines," *ACM Transaction on Intelligent System and Technology*, vol. 2, no. 3, pp. 1–27, Apr. 2011.
2. R. Fang, K. D. Tang, N. Snavely, and T. Chen, "Towards computational models of kinship verification," in *2010 IEEE International Conference on Image Processing*, 2010, pp. 1577–1580.
3. P. F. Felzenszwalb, D. P. Huttenlocher, "Pictorial structures for object recognition," *International Journal of Computer Vission*, vol. 61, no. 1, pp. 55–79, 2005.
4. A. Chergui, S. Ouchtati, J. Sequeira, S. E. Bekhouche, and F. Bougourzi, "Kinship verification using BSIF and LBP," in *2018 International Conference on Signal, Image, Vision and Their Applications (SIVA)*, 2018, pp. 1–5.
5. F. Bougourzi, S. E. Bekhouche, M. E. Zighem, A. Benlamoudi, A. Ouafi, and Taleb-Ahmed A., "A comparative study on textures descriptors in facial gender classification," in 10me Confrence sur le Gnie Electrique. April, pp. 1–4, 2017.
6. S. Albawi, T. A. Mohammed, and S. Al-Zawi. "Understanding of a convolutional neural network," in *2017 International Conference on Engineering and Technology (ICET)*. IEEE, 2017.
7. K. Zhang, Y. Huang, C. Song, H. Wu, and L. Wang, "Kinship verification with deep convolutional neural networks," in Proceedings of the *British Machine Vision Conference 2015*, 2015, pp. 148.1–148.12.
8. A. Nandy and S. S. Mondal, "Kinship verification using deep siamese convolutional neural network," in *2019 14th IEEE International Conference on Automatic Face & Gesture Recognition (FG 2019)*, 2019, pp. 1–5.
9. F. N. Iandola, S. Han, M. W. Moskewicz, K. Ashraf, W. J. Dally, and K. Keutzer, "SqueezeNet: AlexNet-level accuracy with 50x fewer parameters and <0.5MB model size," arXiv preprint arXiv:1602.07360, 2016.
10. H. Yan and S. Wang, "Learning part-aware attention networks for kinship verification," *Pattern Recognition Letters*, vol. 128, pp. 169–175, Dec. 2019.
11. H. L. Liu and C. Jian, "Kinship verification based on status-aware projection learning," in *IEEE International Conference on Image Processing (ICIP)*, 2017, pp. 1072–1076.
12. S. Mahpod and Y. Keller, "Kinship verification using multiview hybrid distance learning," *Computer Vision and Image Understanding*, vol. 167, pp. 28–36, Feb. 2018.
13. H. Yan, "Learning discriminative compact binary face descriptor for kinship verification," *Pattern Recognition Letters*, vol. 117, pp. 146–152, Jan. 2019.
14. X. Wu, E. Boutellaa, M. B. Lopez, X. Feng, and A. Hadid, "On the usefulness of color for kinship verification from face images," in *2016 IEEE International Workshop on Information Forensics and Security (WIFS)*, 2016, pp. 1–6.
15. Q. Duan, L. Zhang, and W. Zuo, "From face recognition to kinship verification: an adaptation approach," in *2017 IEEE International Conference on Computer Vision Workshops (ICCVW)*, 2017, pp. 1590–1598.

16. Y. Li, J. Zeng, J. Zhang, A. Dai, M. Kan, S. Shan, and X. Chen, "KinNet: fine-to-coarse deep metric learning for kinship verification," in Proceedings of the *2017 Workshop on Recognizing Families In the Wild – RFIW '17*, New York, New York, USA, 2017, pp. 13–20.

17. E. Dahan and Y. Keller, "SelfKin: self-adjusted deep model for kinship verification," *arXiv preprint arXiv:1809.08493*, pp. 1–11, 2018.

18. I. Önal Ertuğrul, L. A. Jeni, and H. Dibeklioğlu, "Modeling and synthesis of kinship patterns of facial expressions," *Image Vis. Comput.*, vol. 79, pp. 133–143, Nov. 2018.

19. X. Wu, E. Granger, T. H. Kinnunen, X. Feng, and A. Hadid, "Audio-visual kinship verification in the wild," in *2019 International Conference on Biometrics (ICB)*, 2019, pp. 1–8.

20. E. Boutellaa, M. Bordallo Lopez, S. Ait- Aoudia, X. Feng, and A. Hadid, "Kinship verification from videos using spatio temporal texture feature and deep learning," *arXiv Prepr. arXiv1708.04069*, 2017.

21. H. Yan and J. Hu, "Video-based kinship verification using distance metric learning," *Pattern Recognition*, vol. 75, pp. 15–24, Mar. 2017.

22. J. P. Robinson, M. Shao, Y. Wu, and Y. Fu, "Families in the wild (FIW) Large-Scale kinship image database and benchmarks," in Proceedings of the *2016 ACM on Multimedia Conference – MM '16*, New York, New York, USA, 2016, pp. 242–246.

23. A. Chergui, S. Ouchtati, J. Sequeira, S. E. Bekhouche, and F. Bougourzi, "Kinship verification using BSIF and LBP," in *2018 International Conference on Signal, Image, Vision and their Applications (SIVA)*, 2018, pp. 1–5.

24. S. Xia, M. Shao, J. Luo, and Y. Fu, "Understanding kin relationships in a photo," *IEEE Transactions on Multimedia*, vol. 14, no. 4, pp. 1046–1056, Aug. 2012.

25. J. Lu, X. Zhou, Y.-P. Tan, Y. Shang, and J. Zhou, "Neighborhood repulsed metric learning for kinship verification," *IEEE Transactions on Pattern Analysis and Machine Intelligence*, vol. 36, no. 2, pp. 331–345, Feb. 2014.

26. R. Fang, A. C. Gallagher, T. Chen, and A. Loui, "Kinship classification by modeling facial feature heredity," in *2013 IEEE International Conference on Image Processing*, 2013, pp. 2983–2987.

27. X. Qin, X. Tan, and S. Chen, "Tri-subject kinship verification: understanding the core of a family," *IEEE Transactions on Multimedia*, vol. 17, no. 10, pp. 1855–1867, Oct. 2015.

28. H. Dibeklioglu, A. A. Salah, and T. Gevers, "Like father, like son: facial expression dynamics for kinship verification," in *2013 IEEE International Conference on Computer Vision*, 2013, pp. 1497–1504.

19

Machine Intelligence-Based Approach for Effective Terrorism Monitoring

Riyazveer Singh, Sahil Sharma, and Vijay Kumar

CONTENTS

19.1 Introduction

Terrorism has provoked various sets of humanity in the foulest manner—the mutilation of individuals and obliteration of assets, both private and municipal, impacting the development of a country. Nifty coercions—from cyberattack, radicalism, and illegal migration—have aggravated the encounters with internal defense and external security. Outdated methodologies and adhoc fragmentary-based tactics are not vigilant enough to retort to new threats, hindering state security by generating ambiguities. Through the commencement of the internet, web data has developed enormously, encompassing data about radical incidents, terror actions, and intuitions of terrorists. This information from open-source domains and social media becomes a treasured resource for considering and tapping the operations of terrorists. To check these activities, national security agencies monitor the activities of persons of interest and trace them based on information collected from various sources. Conventional methods are not adequate to tackle such attacks. There can be multiple sources of structured, semi-structured, and unstructured data like websites, social media, news websites, and blog sites. A lot of challenges lie in identifying a proper location for a military/defense base. It is not only the primary target of the terrorist forces but also a gateway to take control of a particular territory. For a country, even though military power is prowess, the need for strategic planning and assistance for identifying an efficient location for a military base cannot be fulfilled unless a proper statistical prediction model is derived. Though a lot of machine learning algorithms for army base selection exists, the proposed algorithm will help arrive at a conclusive model, which will predict a suitable location for a military base, using an extensive process called Rival Check Cross Correlator (RCCC) with the help of already existing kNN algorithm.

The main objective of this solution is:

> By using machine learning-based techniques, security officers and defense personnel become more vigilant in building a 360-degree profile of persons of interest by collecting his data from various online and internal sources, presenting his links with incidents they are involved in (relatives, organizations, etc.).

19.2 Proposed Solution

Contour building of a person ensues in the subsequent method:

1. Information from interior report bases made through field majors is extracted. In our result, we have made model incidence and cross-examination intelligence. We can select from PDFs, word documents, images, and powerpoints.

2. Peripheral data from websites are scuttled iteratively. Information from RSS feeds of news websites is mined. Network crawling works by indexing web pages, and then indexing the pages for rasping. Hyperlinks for any websites are scuttled, and seclusion between section and actual article pages transpires. Once the article pages are found, we can scrape the article from the webpage. The above process happens iteratively until all relevant data are fetched [1].

3. Exterior data from social networking sites like Twitter and Instagram are also extracted to collect details about a person's social linkages and behavior [2].

   3.1. Twitter: Handler/keyword is fed as an input to the system, and then we generate top tweets, unique tweets, popular hashtags, word cloud, followers, followings, and sentiment analysis of tweets as output.

   3.2. Instagram: Keyword (either username or hashtag) is fed as an input to the system and all posts, photos, videos, likes, and comments are generated as output. After that, we find top posts by applying normalization and binning the values of likes, comments, and timestamps.

4. Natural language processing, along with co-referencing, is used on the extracted data to understand its semantics. Pre-processing like lemmatization, sentence tokenization, stop-word removal, noise removal, etc. is done during data cleaning. Named-entity recognition (NER) and Parts of Speech (POS) tagging is done to extract entities and understand linguistic features from sentences. Sentences are broken into noun chunks

to apply morphological transformations. Custom dictionaries and training have been done to obtain weapon names, incident names, and organization names. Co-referencing is a neural network-based technique that is applied to understand the contextual meaning and links between various mentions of entities [3–5].

5. Face detection and recognition happens on multiple images coming from the web as well as internal sources [6–8].

   5.1. Face Detection: Face is detected based on key features present in the image. Training is done on 10,000 images, and CNN is applied to build a model that identifies key features as vectors and creates a bounding box around all possible faces present.

   5.2. Face Recognition: Once a face is detected in the image, the next step is finding whose face it is. Recognition is a supervised learning problem. The feature vectors of the database are given as training data with personalized labels (for the person of interest at least one front pose with the right quality is needed). With this data, the model is created and saved.

19.2.1 Prediction

When a new image is processed from the web, faces are first detected, and the prediction process runs on these images.

19.2.2 Audio Processing

Audio clips are also an important source of data for building information about a person of interest. Voice recognition is similar to face recognition; deep learning is applied. In these voice prints, the **ivec** vector is created as training data. The voice recording of a particular person for a minimum of five minutes is needed for the training. When the new audio clip comes, it is converted to an **ivec** vector, and then the classification algorithm is applied [9,10]. Spark is used to distribute computing and make the application run faster across different nodes of the cluster. The processed data is put in HBase Tables that have leveraging capabilities of NoSQL database with fast retrieval. In searching, Solr, which offers a full-text search capability, is used. By using our solution, the customer can easily track a person of interest and get his full details, including data from his relationships. Linkages are built between internal and external data that will give in-depth insight and better analytics to visualize the person, entity, and incidence of interest. Figure 19.1. describes the architecture diagram of our solution. Data is collected across the web, news sites, and social media [11,12].

19.3 Proposed Work

In the proposed system, historical data is used for the learning algorithm. Any efficiency tracking algorithm will consist of ancillary aspects of proponents and opponents. The learning algorithm in the system will separate the learning process based on those aspects. In calculating military base location, the two rival variables will be effectiveness and

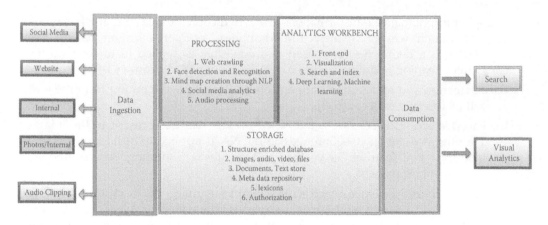

FIGURE 19.1
Arrangement plan of our projected explanation [15].

ineffectiveness. The learning algorithm conducts learning for those two competing variables. After the learning model is built, the results from these are sent to a Rival Check Cross Correlator (RCCC) for collinearity. Here, the correlator is a hypothetical machine or model that takes the results of the two-training data and performs the rival check analysis to eliminate the multicollinearity between rival variables.

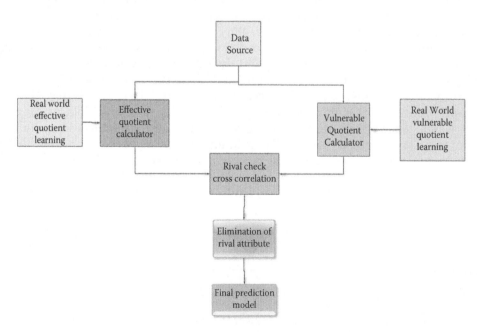

FIGURE 19.2
The representative of contending check cross correlator [13].

19.3.1 Description

This chapter illustrates the number of ways multicollinearity between rival variables can be minimized. Any supervised classification algorithm can be used to perform learning but kNN algorithm is used for this military base scenario. This methodology involves a step-by-step algorithm to perform the analysis. The process of finding a military base involves a prominent factor called effectiveness. In other words, effectiveness is the parameter that measures the extent to which the base can operate effectively.

19.3.2 Algorithm for Rival Check Analysis

The algorithm for performing the competitive check analysis involves three stages.

STAGE-1: Effective quotient learning from real-world historical data.

STAGE-2: Vulnerable quotient learning from real-world historical data.

STAGE-3: Rival Check Cross Correlator.

STAGE-1: Effective quotient learning from real-world historical data.

STEP 1: Real-world historical data collection regarding the military/army base.

STEP 2: Component analysis on the variable is performed to identify driver variable.

STEP 3: Driver variable is fed into the Effective Quotient Calculator (EQC).

STEP 4: EQC performs supervised classification on the variables.

STAGE-2: Vulnerable quotient learning from real-world historical data:

STEP 1: Real-world historical data collection regarding the military/army base.

STEP 2: Component analysis on the variable is performed to identify the driver variables.

STEP 3: The driver variable is fed into the Vulnerable Quotient Calculator (VQC).

STEP 4: VQC performs supervised classification on the variables.

STAGE-3: Rival Check Cross-Correlation

STEP 1: The outputs of the EQC and VQC are compiled and structured.

STEP 2: The outputs are fed into the Rival Check Cross Correlator (RCCC).

STEP 3: The RCCC performs multicollinearity analysis on the data.

STEP 4: RCCC checks for multicollinearity in the data.

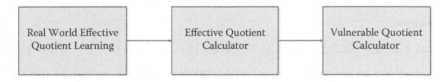

FIGURE 19.3
Identification of EQU driver variables [13].

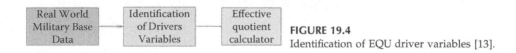

FIGURE 19.4
Identification of EQU driver variables [13].

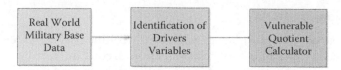

FIGURE 19.5
Identification of VQC driver variables [13].

   i. If multicollinearity exists, eliminate the particular combination of variables.

  ii. Otherwise, add them to the actual effectiveness list and concentrate on the next combination.

19.3.3 Algorithm of Rival Check Cross Correlator

```
EQC: Effective quotient combination
VQC: Vulnerable quotient combination
For (i from 0 to eqc.length)
{
For (j from 0 to vqc.length)
{
If(eqc.i has vqc.j)
{
eliminate (eqc.i);
j + +;
}
Else
{
add (eqc.i);
j + +;
}
}
I + +
```

19.4 Rival Check Correlator Eliminates the Intersecting Combinations

The common blend between two rival parameters has been abolished by the rival check cross-correlator output.

FIGURE 19.6
The output of Rival Check Cross-Correlator [13].

19.5 Application Specific Illustrations

This particular model was generic but was exclusively designed to deal with critical applications such as military base identification. The illustrations of implementing this model with the application are given below.

19.5.1 Driver Variables

Observations and Fields of Fire (OFOF), Concealment (CON), Weather (WTHR), Terrain Type (TERTYP), Avenue of Approach (AOA), Altitude from the Sea Level (ALT), Precipitation (PRP), Distance from Border (DFB), Visibility Radius (VR), Wind (WIN), Number of Breaches (NOB), Number of Past Infiltrations (NOPI), Number of Natural Barriers (NOBR) [13].

The table depicts the values of driver variables mentioned above as calculated by EQC, VQC, and Rival Check Cross-Correlation (RCCC), respectively. The sufficient military base and vulnerable military base combination calculate the value of driver variables by K-Nearest Neighbor Technique (KNN); the algorithm for rival check cross-correlation given above gives the final EQC. The final EQC provided by RCCC is clean and distinct.

TABLE 19.1

Values of Driver Variables as Calculated by EQC, VQC, and Rival Check Cross-Correlation

Driver Variables	Effective Military Base Combination (Calculated by kNN)	Vulnerable Military Base Combination (Calculated by kNN)	Rival Check Cross-Correlation Analysis Output
Observations and fields of fire (OFOF)	OFOF:100–120	OFOF:75–100	OFOF:100–120
Concealment (CON)	CON: 55–75	CON: 25–35	CON: 55–75,
Weather (WTHR)	WTHR: CLEAR	WTIIR: CLOUDY	WTHR: CLEAR
Terrain type (TERTYP)	TERTYP: MOUNTAIN	TERTYP: DESERT	TERTYP: MOUNTAIN
Avenue of Approach (AOA)	AOA: 15–20	AOA: 100–105	AOA: 15–20
Altitude from the sea level (ALT)	ALT: 2500–2600 ft	ALT: 100–200 ft	ALT: 1000–1100 ft
Precipitation (PRP)	PRP: 70–80	PRP: 40–50	PRP: 40–50
Distance from Border (DFB)	DFB = 30–60 km	DFB = 10–30 km	DFB = 30–60 km
Visibility Radius (VR)	VR = 1–7 km	VR = 1–7 km	VR = 1–7 km
Wind (WIN)	WIN: MEDIUM	WIN: HIGH	WIN: MEDIUM
Number of Breaches (NOB)	NOB = 120–140	NOB = 220–240	NOB = 120–140
Number of Pasts Infiltration (NOPI)	NOPI = 50–60	NOPI = 100–110	NOPI = 50–60
Number of natural barriers (NOBR).	NOBR: 60–70	NOBR: 20–30	NOBR: 60–70

19.6 Conclusion

The final prediction output of the rival check cross-correlator (RCCC) will now consist of the effective quotient in its purest form. The multicollinearity with the vulnerable quotient is completely excluded [14], giving a clean and distinct model. As the rate of terror incidents increase, it is a critical time when we need an AI-based solution to control such incidents and track the persons who are committing these crimes. Hence, we have proposed a solution that will help national security agencies in building a person's profile and monitoring it from various angles. Tracking a person of interest can be done through his phone number, passport details, bank account number, friends' and relatives' names, audio clippings, and photos. Full text search capability is provided to look at data in their most granular forms. Our solution utilizes the power of AI and deep learning — efficient in both accuracy and speed. The capabilities of web crawling, natural language processing, face detection, recognition, and voice detection make our proposal manage multidimensional real-time challenges. As persons of interest can have various avatars on social media and multiple information from different sources, authenticating valid [15] details becomes a major challenge. In the future, we will make our program handle these scenarios as well.

References

1. Mahto D. K. and Singh L., "A dive into Web Scraper world," *2016 3rd International Conference on Computing for Sustainable Global Development (INDIACom)*, New Delhi, 2016, pp. 689–693.
2. Paul P. V., Monica K. and Trishanka M., "A survey on big data analytics using social media data," *2017 Innovations in Power and Advanced Computing Technologies (i-PACT)*, Vellore, 2017, pp. 1–4
3. Cambria and White B., "Jumping NLP curves: a review of natural language processing research [review article]," in *IEEE Computational Intelligence Magazine*, vol. 9, no. 2, pp. 48–57, May 2014.
4. Patten T. and Jacobs P., "Natural-language processing," in *IEEE Expert*, vol. 9, no. 1, pp. 35, Feb. 1994.
5. Clark K. and Manning C. D., "Deep reinforcement learning for mention-ranking coreference models." arXiv preprint arXiv:1609.08667, 2016.
6. Parua, S., et al. "Determination of feature hierarchy from Gabor and SIFT features for face recognition." *Second International Conference on Emerging Applications of Information Technology (EAIT), 2011*. IEEE, 2011.
7. Dalal, N. and Triggs B., "Histograms of oriented gradients for human detection." *IEEE Computer Society Conference on Computer Vision and Pattern Recognition, 2005. CVPR 2005.* Vol. 1. IEEE, 2005.
8. Kazemi V. and Sullivan J., "One millisecond face alignment with an ensemble of regression trees." *Proceedings of the IEEE Conference on Computer Vision and Pattern Recognition*, pp. 1867–1874, 2014.
9. Dumpala S. H., Panda A. and Kopparapu S. K., "Improved I-vector-based speaker recognition for utterances with speaker generated non-speech sounds." arXiv preprint arXiv:1705.09289, pp. 1–5, 2017.
10. http://voicebiometry.org/.

11. Li Y. and Guo L., "An active learning based TCMKNN algorithm for supervised network intrusion detection", vol. 26, pp. 7–8, 2007.

12. Shlens J., "A tutorial on Principle Component Analysis", arXiv preprint: 1404.1100, pp. 1–12, 2014, https://faculty.iiit.ac.in/~mkrishna/PrincipalComponents.pdf.

13. Av, J. K., Bharathi, A., Kumar, V., Ku, T. and Balaji, N. S., 2017, February. "Rival check cross correlator for locating strategic defense base using supervised learning." In *2017 2nd International Conference on Computing and Communications Technologies (ICCCT)* (pp. 420–423). IEEE.

14. Agre G. H. and Mahajan N. V., "Keyword focused web crawler," *2015 2nd International Conference on Electronics and Communication Systems (ICECS)*, Coimbatore, 2015, pp. 10891092.

15. Singh, D. and Singh, D., "360-degree profiling and social linkage analysis of persons of interest." In 2018 *IEEE Punecon*, pp. 1–4, Pune, India, IEEE.

20

Utilizing Artificial Intelligence to Design Delay and Energy-Aware Wireless Sensor Networks

Ranjana Thalore, Vandita Vyas, Jeetu Sharma, and Vikas Raina

CONTENTS

20.1 Introduction: Wireless Sensor Networks

Plenty of motes are set out all over a precise terrain in a Wireless Sensor Network (WSN) [1]. The sensor nodes in the network are designed to sense, collect, and transmit to the base station. In a WSN shown in Figure 20.1, monitoring of substantial parameters in a terrain is done by the sensor nodes collectively. Lately, WSNs are being utilized to realize factual, tactical, medical, and smart applications [2–7]. WSNs are best suited for the regions where presence of humans is unsafe or impossible due to properties like the ability to self-organize, ease of deployment and unattended performance.

The idea of WSNs was proposed in the early 1970s by the US military. Afterward, many theories, research projects, and applications have begun. The advancement of WSNs [8] can be divided into several stages. The development of sensor network prototypes with point-to-point transmission in 1970 can be recognized as the first generation of sensor networks. The Defense Advanced Research Projects Agency of USA launched Distributed Sensor Network Program (DSN) in 1979 as one of the prototypes. From 1980s to the 1990s, there was an improvement in the processing and communication capabilities of sensor nodes that made them work together in a network with the advancement of technologies like microelectronics, wireless communication, network transmission. At the end of the 20th century, WSNs caught the attention of a wide range of areas such as the academe, military, and industry (Figure 20.1).

20.1.1 Artificial Intelligence-Based WSNs

Artificial intelligence is an important and interesting topic in all research areas. AI or machine learning are important in WSN because dynamic environments change over time and sensor nodes are used to monitor these changes; sensor nodes adapt and operate efficiently. Data is sometimes gathered in unreachable locations that might be considered dangerous and unpredictable, so self-calibrating network is essential. AI algorithms are used by researchers as an approach to SDN (Software Defined Network) to utilize them in SDWSN as well. Researchers have recently considered using AI in SDWSN save energy and improve routing and security. There are two approaches to implementing AI mechanisms within Wireless Sensor Networks (WSNs). According to the first approach, designers have a global objective to be accomplished—both the agents and the interaction mechanism are designed by the multi-agent system. In the second approach, a set of self-interested agents are constructed by the designer that evolves and interacts in a stable manner, in their structure, through evolutionary techniques for learning. Supervised and semi-supervised algorithms work wonders when it comes to network security using machine learning techniques. With the application of SDN to WSN to create SDWSN, there seems to be a need for efficient and reliable network security, and with machine learning techniques, the network can be secured and able to learn patterns that future network attacks and threats. This enables the defense mechanism to adapt to the new threats. Machine learning techniques can also assist the network with an improved response time.

20.1.2 Basic Elements of Wireless Sensor Networks

A WSN consists of three elements: sensors, observers, and sensing objects [9]. A WSN serves as a communication link between sensors and observers. The fundamental functioning of a WSN includes sensing, data collection, data processing, and distribution. A WSN can achieve a great sensing task and support with a group of sensor nodes that have limited resources and performance. Each sensor node can serve as a data router and could dynamically search, locate, and restore connections with other sensor nodes.

20.1.2.1 Sensors

A sensor node (Figure 20.2) consists of a sensing unit, a processing unit, a transceiver, and a power unit that provides the electrical power to all subsystems. With a battery of merely 0.5 mAhr, it is adroit to execute computational and transceiver's concerns. The batteries should be wisely used as reviving the batteries is difficult because of ecological or cost limitations. Power consumption by the communication subsystem for a sensor node is 100 times more than computational tasks. Architectural repressions, energy exhaustion, error lenience, channel, and constitution should be evaluated and cautiously selected to elongate the life of sensors.

20.1.2.2 Observers

Wireless sensor network customers who query, collect, and use sensed information actively or inactively are referred to as observers. An observer can be a human being, machine, or other equipment. The sensed information is analyzed before any decision is made by the observer.

20.1.2.3 Sensing Objects

Targets such as animals, tanks, soldiers, chemical plumes, etc. an observer is interested in are referred to as sensing objects. Sensing objects are represented as a digital characterization of physical, chemical, or biological events that include object movement, temperature, humidity, pressure, chemical concentration, and so on. A WSN can sense a range of targets within the communication region of the network (Figure 20.2).

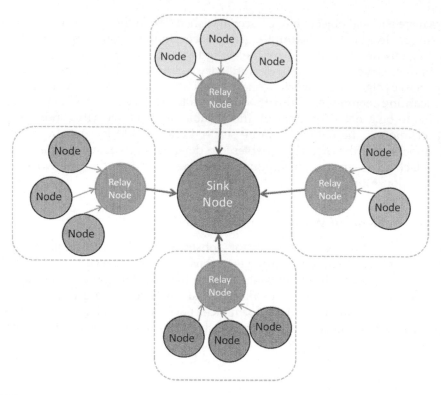

FIGURE 20.1
A wireless sensor network.

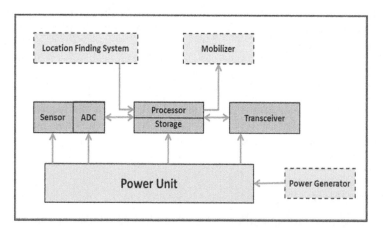

FIGURE 20.2
A wireless sensor node.

20.1.3 Features of Wireless Sensor Networks

A WSN is considered as a self-organizing network composed of varied sensor nodes that can communicate with each other wirelessly. The WSN is a collection of many low-cost sensor nodes deployed in a region under monitoring. The sensor nodes coordinate with one another to sense, collect, and process data of sensing objects within the network coverage forward it to observers. The wireless communications network is not the only similarity among WSNs, but they also have their own recognizable features [9] explained below.

20.1.3.1 Application-Related

Information from the physical world is obtained by WSNs through sensing the physical properties of various objects. The need for network systems varies according to different applications. This leads to variation in different hardware and software platforms and communication protocols. To attain reliable and efficient system objectives, the network design should be related to the specific application.

20.1.3.2 Data-Centered

A WSN is a function-oriented network; the WSN is tasked to collect sensed information from various sensor nodes and aggregate, and extract information and communicate it to users.

20.1.3.3 Large-Scale Distribution

WSNs are deployed in a large area. The quantity and density of sensor nodes are directly proportional to the variation in the area. The areas monitored by WSNs are usually difficult to reach, which makes maintenance of WSNs a tough task. Therefore, sturdiness and fault-tolerance are important properties of a WSN.

20.1.3.4 Dynamic Topology

The topology of a WSN may change dynamically for many reasons. For example, a new sensor may join or leave the network; a sensor node might be mobile; a sensor node may be set to alternate between active and sleep status to save energy, or a sensor node might break down and die due to unpredictable reasons. With these changes in network topology, a WSN should be able to self-adjust and reconstruct.

20.1.3.5 High Reliability

WSNs are usually deployed in unattended areas, making maintenance a difficult or impossible task. So, sensor nodes need to be stable, fault-tolerant, and versatile for extreme environmental conditions. Also, it is important that sensor nodes are provided with privacy and security mechanisms to prevent information from being stolen and damaged.

20.1.3.6 Self-Organization

There are uncertain factors in the physical environment of WSNs. For example, the geographic location of sensor nodes can't be located accurately; some sensors may die out due to energy exhaustion or another reason; environmental impact affects the accuracy of the forecast; or some network environment emergencies are irresistible. The situations above require sensor nodes to be self-organized.

20.2 Applications of Wireless Sensor Networks

Many researchers claim that WSN technology will aid existing areas of application and may bring new ones to existence. The actual sensing and actuating properties of a sensor node play a crucial and primary role in developing applications (apart from the need for cheap, easily programmable, and potentially long-lasting sensor nodes). Popular physical parameters like temperature, humidity, pressure, vibration, mechanical stress, visual and infrared light, chemical sensors, etc. can be integrated into the sensor node of a WSN.

Many kinds of applications can be constructed based on sensing and actuating properties of a sensor node by combining computational and communication abilities.

20.2.1 Military Applications

A WSN can be used in military areas like equipment monitoring, battlefield surveillance, object targeting, searching, and monitoring for attack sources [10], etc. Many international institutions are involved in wartime military research.

Smart Sensor Web (SSW) [11] is a web-centric WSN centered on a blend of sensor information. SSW conveniently provides situational awareness to fighters. It focuses on providing real-time information to soldiers regarding weather, imagery, objects, mission planning, etc.

Mines might be viewed as unsafe and out of date later and might be supplanted by many dispersed motes that will recognize an intrusion of unfriendly units, making the prevention of intrusion the responsibility of the defense system. An application related to this scenario, developed by the University of Virginia is presented in [12].

The Ohio State University has also demonstrated a project titled "A Line in the Sand" [13] that refers to the deployment of 90 nodes that can detect metallic objects. The final objective was the tracking and classification of moving objects with substantial metallic content (vehicles of armed soldiers and civilians was ignored by the system).

20.2.2 Environmental Monitoring

Another significant classification of applications is "environmental monitoring". The utilization of nodes to enhance the environmental conditions inside buildings has distracted the American Society of Heating, Refrigerating, and Air Conditioning Engineers (ASHRAE). WSN was deployed in an office building at Pacific Northwest National Laboratory, Richland, Washington to examine the advantages and drawbacks of wireless technology in the operation of Heating, Ventilation, and Air Condition (HVAC) systems [14,15].

Sensor networks may also be useful after an earthquake. Civil engineering research has demonstrated that the assessment of structures based on vibrations is possible [16]. Based on this observation, sensor nodes can be included inside cement blocks during construction or attached to structural units. The recording of vibrations during the life of a building can function as the identity of the building.

Outdoor monitoring is another huge area of applications for WSNs. One of the most illustrative examples is the deployment of a WSN of 32 nodes on Great Duck Island (GDI) [17]. The network was used for habitat monitoring. The sensors used were capable of sensing temperature, barometric pressure, and humidity. In addition, photoresistors and passive infrared sensors were used to monitor the natural environment of a bird and its behavior to changes in climate. Some nodes were installed inside the nests to detect presence, while the remaining were deployed in the surrounding area. The sensed information by sensor nodes is aggregated and passed through a gateway; the information is available on the internet. This application gives a case to monitor the utilization of a heterogeneous, multi-level network.

Research, with respect to habitat monitoring, has likewise been led by Wang, et al. [18,19]. The nodes that have been utilized amid these experiments are not size optimized (PDAs) and they control acoustic signals. Here, the accentuation is on exploiting the computing capabilities of a node, contrasting input and reference signal. In that way, a node utilizes more of its resources.

20.2.3 Health Applications

WSNs can also be beneficial to health science and the health care system. Intel's research worries about the problems of senior citizens [20]—cognitive disorders like Alzheimer's disease—can be examined and controlled at initial stages using WSNs.

In Portland and Las Vegas, Intel is carrying out a research where sensor nodes are used to record actions like taking medication, visitor details, etc., reminding senior citizens, indicating the real behavior of a person, or detecting an emerging problem. Intel and the University of Washington conducted a related research that uses RFID tags to observe patient behavior and record the frequency of their touching on certain objects. A display helps the caregiver extract information about the sick person carefully, without hurting their feelings. Finally, sensor nodes can also play an important part in studying the behavior of children. For example, the aim of the study reported in [21] was to analyze children behavior, by monitoring sensors inside toys.

20.2.4 Home-Automation

The hasty increase in usage and dependence on smart devices prompts the need to interconnect them. Present systems tender in home automation.

The link quality of WSNs in home automation may be unbalanced because of shadow fading. The Link-State-Aware Routing for Wireless Sensor Network in Home Automation (LSAR-WSNHA) [22] algorithm is proposed to design an appropriate routing algorithm to improve the packet delivery ratio and reduce delay. However, the deployment pattern of WSN affects the performance of the proposed method. The LSAR-WSNHA routing algorithm helps engineers deploy the sensors for the real-world home automation network.

The author in [23] elucidates a method to provide a low-cost Home Automation System (HAS) using Wireless Fidelity (Wi-Fi). The concept of the internetworking of smart devices is crystallized. A Wi-Fi-based WSN is designed to monitor and control environmental safety and electrical parameters of a smart home. The user can have perfect control over the devices via the android application based Graphical User Interface (GUI) over a smartphone. This system costs about INR 6000 or USD 100 for large-scale implementation.

Lakshya Gourav Moitra, et al. [24] have shown the integration of a cooling system with the cloud. Iris nodes are used to monitor and control room temperature. The Low-Energy Adaptive Clustering Hierarchy (LEACH) algorithm is used to improve energy efficiency. This system was tested with an Earth Air Tunnel (EAT). The system shows the adaptable nature of WSN, keeping in mind the low power consumption and reliable data transfer. This tested system provides a pollution-free environment as it uses earth's geothermal energy for cooling and not CFC-based cooling systems.

20.2.5 Industrial Applications

Inventory control is a key problem for big companies. Management of resources like pieces of equipment, machinery, different types of products, etc. can be a big mess, and since companies have branches globally, the problem can even be bigger. The use of RFID tags and WSNs is believed to be an impressive way to achieve resource tracking.

Intel research deploys a network to monitor the vibrations in semiconductor fabrication equipment [25, 26]. More particularly, the purpose is to detect the faulty parts that need any repairing or changing, by evaluating their "vibration signature".

Helsinki University of Technology [27] carried out research using the "weC Mini Mote" of Berkeley in paper production. The rolls used for paper drying are fitted with sensor nodes. These sensors act as temperature sensors and help control the heating rolls.

Deployment of sensor nodes in households can also benefit electric energy systems. This kind of scheme is investigated in CITRIS [28].

20.3 QoS Parameters

The quality of a service is closely related to the type of service for a network. Conventional quality of service requirements includes parameters like bounded delay, tolerance to latency [29], bandwidth of transmitted data, etc. In some cases, packets are required to be delivered occasionally while others need high reliability; some find delay as an important parameter.

20.3.1 Network Lifetime (NL)

The network lifetime of a sensing element network depends on the quantity of battery consumed when information is transmitted between sensing element nodes and sink for a specific amount of time (simulation time).

20.3.2 End-to-End Delay

The packet traversal time from the source node to the destination node is measured in terms of end-to-end delay. The initialization of active/sleep cycles of sensors at different adaptive instants is a prime cause of delay. It also accommodates the time consumed for optimum path selection, computation, and scheduling.

20.3.3 Throughput

The means of successful bits transmitted per second acquired by the destination is called throughput. Its approved unit is packets/bits per second.

20.4 Literature Review

The configuration for network setup and the available resources for a WSN are decided by the deployment plan of the network. This makes deployment planning a key parameter in deciding the performance of the network. A lot of research has been done to enhance the network performance during its operation by optimizing the MAC protocols [30] and routing protocols [31] but even the best blend of MAC and routing protocols cannot attain the required performance for the network if it is not properly configured. For example, if the installed sensor nodes are inadequate, or if there are deficiencies in network architecture, the network performance and network connectivity between deployed nodes will be vitiated, resulting in a non-operational network.

The optimized deployment of sensor networks is one of the most significant issues in this area. Therefore, most recent research is focusing on improving the network performance by optimizing the deployment plan. The WSN deployment approaches are categorized into two kinds: random deployment and deterministic deployment. In random deployment, nodes are deployed and handled in an arbitrary manner; in deterministic deployment, nodes are deployed in a planned manner, directing more efficiency in terms of aimed network properties.

20.4.1 Random Deployment

In random deployment, the sensor nodes are placed randomly to minimize the cost; the density of deployed sensor nodes is non-uniform in the area under monitoring. Random deployment of WSNs is required in practical applications where the terrain is unapproachable, or a dense network is needed.

Vales-Alonso, et al. [32] addresses a problem when the deployment area is too close or too separated; proper coverage becomes a major issue. An optimization model is proposed by spreading sensor node clusters over a target area using Gaussian random distribution. Multiple tests are done in real scenarios to optimize the sensor nodes to be deployed.

Mulligan and Ammari emphasized coverage in WSNs—the types of coverage—and its relation to lifetime and connectivity [33]. Various available techniques for evaluating the best and worst coverage scenarios are reviewed. Also, a survey of some deployment algorithms used to attain connectivity and coverage is presented.

Akewar and Thakur [34] presented a survey of deployment approaches that focus on mobile sensors in a network. The issues, like energy consumption and obstacle adaptability, are discussed. The authors focused on the classification of deployment algorithms based on

Artificial Potential Field and Computational Geometry techniques. Chen, et al. [35] classified the deployment algorithms as random, incremental, and movement assisted.

Apart from 2D deployment methods, researchers have also made efforts towards 3D deployment. For example, in [36] the authors considered the effect of sensing and communication ranges of a sensor node over the network connectivity in a randomly deployed 3D WSN.

Ishizuka and Aida [37] proposed a distributed algorithm in a random deployment-based 3D homogeneous WSN to achieve k-connectivity but the system requires complex and uneconomical hardware to reach the expected outcome.

20.4.2 Deterministic Deployment

WSN applications have encouraged sensor node deployment at predefined locations in a specific pattern. The deployment pattern and the locations can be optimized in terms of predefined network parameters and practicability of the location itself. This type of deployment serves more appropriately in WSN applications by improving network lifetime and reducing connectivity problems.

Wang and Kutta [38] investigated a detection problem in WSNs for a mobile intruder. K-connected nodes are assigned to sense the intruder to perform a successful detection. It is observed that a deterministic deployment scheme does not necessarily outperform its random counterpart.

Boubrima, et al. focused on a deployment approach for a WSN with low cost and independent sensor nodes aimed at the spatiotemporal domain of sensing [39]. The paper contributes to the design of an integer linear programming model that calculates sensor deployment by considering connectivity and coverage of pollution under varying weather conditions.

Khalfallah, et al. [40] proposed a new 3D Underwater Wireless Sensor Network Deployment scheme to detect solids in rivers. The objective is to minimize the number of deployed sensors in a target area and ensure the required connectivity and Quality of Monitoring (QoM).

De, et al. [41] presented a relative study of three different deployment algorithm and their performances. The algorithms are compared based on performance parameters like coverage, uniformity, connectivity, present computation time, and the absence of randomly placed obstacle.

20.5 Random and Deterministic Deployment Approaches

20.5.1 Network Model 1: Optimization of ML-MAC Protocol

The energy competency of IEEE 802.15.4 is augmented by employing the ML-MAC technique. The mechanism [42] is riveted on the improvisation of QoS parameters of a WSN. Motes are agreed to be coordinated to design a routing tree using AODV routing [43] mechanism. The MAC design of IEEE 802.15.4 pursues the mutated carrier sense multiple access with collision avoidance (CSMA/CA) contention-based technique (Figure 20.3).

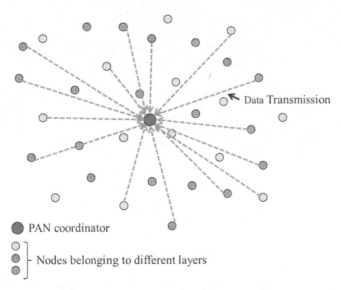

Data Transmission

● PAN coordinator

○
◐ } Nodes belonging to different layers
●

FIGURE 20.3
Layer architecture in WSN.

In a densely deployed sensor network, it often happens that multiple nodes are sensing and sending the same data from a region to the base station or PAN coordinator. This will either result in data duplicity or the data won't reach the sink due to collisions. This, in turn, results in more energy consumption of the nodes and the PAN coordinator. To reduce this energy wastage, ML-MAC divides nodes into several groups called layers. All the nodes in the network (except the PAN coordinator) are randomly assigned to these layers so that the whole geographic region of interest is in the range of nodes of each layer. Figure 20.3 shows the distribution of nodes in a different layer and the data transmission to the PAN coordinator.

In this technique, nodes from only one layer are active for communication purposes while others are completely off. To implement the technique with L layers, the scheduling of nodes in the network is done in a way that nodes from the first layer are contributing to communication and nodes in remaining $(L - 1)$ layers subsist in a sleep state. This procedure will establish substantial network energy as if E were the energy consumed without the concept of layering, and the overall energy exhausted by layering will curtail by a fraction of (E/L), where L is the number of layers taken for simulation. Also, this technique promises a reliable data transmission from the source node to the sink as fewer nodes contend for the medium at a time, resulting in reduced collisions.

20.5.1.1 Design Procedure

Let $\{n_1,\ n_2,\ n_3,\ \ldots\ldots, n_N\} \in N$ be the set of all nodes present in the sensor networks. These nodes are divided into S subnets where each subnet is further divided into L layers with $N/(S \times L)$ nodes in each layer. Thus, each subnet has around N/L nodes. Let $N_1,\ N_2,\ N_3,\ \ldots\ldots, N_S$ represent the number of nodes in each subnet. For simplicity, without affecting the complexity of the network, we can assume that

$$N_1 = N_2 = N_3 = \ldots\ldots = N_S \qquad (20.1)$$

Since there must be a PAN coordinator or sink in each subnet to collect data from the region covered by the corresponding subnet, the first node of each subnet is a PAN coordinator.

Let us consider subnet 1 with N_1 nodes, where n_{11} is set as PAN coordinator. Then, the remaining $(N_1 - 1)$ nodes can be divided into L layers with $(N_1 - 1)/L$ nodes in each layer. Similarly, for subnet S with N_S nodes, node n_{S1} is the PAN coordinator, and the remaining $(N_S - 1)$ are divided into L layers with $(N_S - 1)/L$ nodes in each layer. Therefore,

$$\begin{aligned}
\{n_{11}, n_{12}, n_{13}, \ldots\ldots, n_{1N1}\} &\in N1 \\
\{n_{21}, n_{22}, n_{23}, \ldots\ldots, n_{2N2}\} &\in N2 \\
\{n_{S1}, n_{S2}, n_{S3}, \ldots\ldots, n_{SNS}\} &\in NS
\end{aligned} \qquad (20.2)$$

The above set of equations shows the distribution of network nodes into different subnets.

The start and stop time of different nodes in any subnet depends on the layer the node is assigned to. Let us consider subnet S to explain multi-layering. $\tau1, \tau2, \ldots\ldots, \tau L$ are the allotted time durations for network layers, such that $\tau1 < \tau2 < \ldots\ldots < \tau L$. The total simulation time of the network is the sum of active durations for all layers (i.e.,)

$$\tau_S = \tau_{ON(L1)} + \tau_{ON(L2)} + \ldots + \tau_{ON(LL)} \qquad (20.3)$$

During the simulation of scenario, first $(N_S - 1)/L$ nodes of Sth subnet are active for $\tau ON(L1)$ duration given as

$$\tau ON(L1) = \tau1 - 0; \quad \tau1 > 0. \qquad (20.4)$$

where 0 represents that the network started at 0th second.

Similarly, the next $(NS - 1)/L$ nodes are active for $\tau ON(L2)$ duration given as

$$\tau ON(L2) = \tau2 - \tau1; \quad \tau1 < \tau2. \qquad (20.5)$$

And lastly, $(NS - 1)/L$ nodes of the subnet are active for $\tau ON(LL)$ duration given as

$$\tau ON(LL) = \tau L - \tau(L - 1); \quad \tau(L - 1) < \tau L. \qquad (20.6)$$

This procedure of operation of nodes is followed in all subnets, forming a complete network. This type of operation saves a lot of unnecessary power consumption in areas with dense node deployment.

20.5.2 Network Model 2: 2D AND 3D Wireless Sensor Networks

The preeminent aspiration of the network model [44] is to analyze the fruition of IEEE 802.15.4 for 2D and 3D terrains, maintaining identical simulation parameters for each. The simulations are accomplished employing the QualNet version 6.1 simulator. The scenarios are simulated with a ponderously arranged network.

20.5.2.1 Simulation Setup

The two simulations with 500 sensors are referred to where the sensors are positioned ambiguously over a terrain of 100m × 100m area for the 2D and a 100m × 100m × 50m area for the 3D terrain.

Figure 20.4(a) and (b) show scenarios in QualNet 6.1 for 2D and 3D networks respectively with 500 nodes divided into four sub-nets. Both scenarios are simulated for 1500 seconds.

(a)

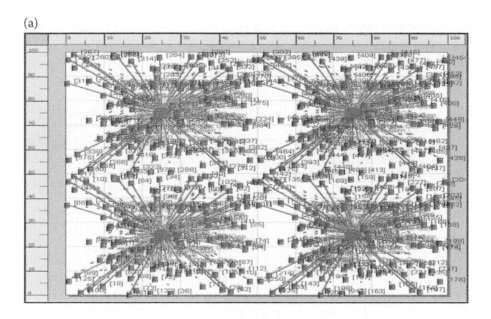

(b)

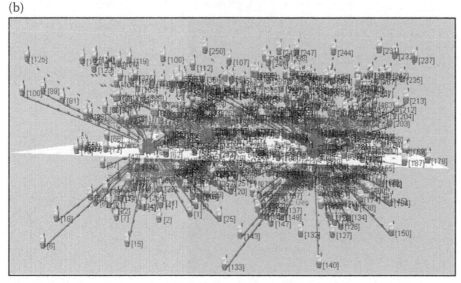

FIGURE 20.4
(a) A two-dimensional (2D) network scenario using IEEE 802.15.4 in QualNet 6.1 simulator. (b) A three-dimensional (3D) network scenario using IEEE 802.15.4 in QualNet 6.1 simulator.

20.5.3 Network Model 3: Random and Deterministic Deployments

20.5.3.1 Relay Node Problem

This section considers the general relay node problem of a sensor network—all nodes are given the same initial battery capacity. The relay nodes are selected among the network nodes based on coverage and residual battery capacity; the selection is random for coverage [45] of a particular area in the network. Figure 20.5 describes a general diagram of a relay node, depicting the function of a relay node as a data generator and data router [46].

The relay node placement in a WSN has been studied with three types of sensor deployments: *random, grid,* and *circular.* The arrangement of the network using the three deployment strategies above is shown in Figure 20.6.

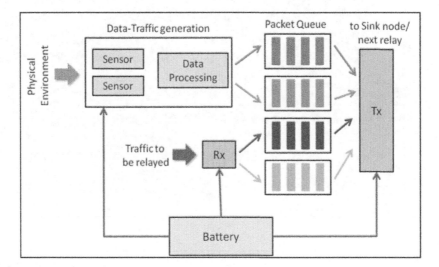

FIGURE 20.5
Diagram of a relay node.

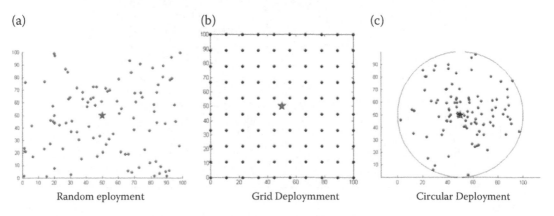

FIGURE 20.6
Node placement in a WSN using three deployment strategies.

Let us consider r as the communication range for the sensor and relay node, where $r > 0$. In addition, consider a set $S = \{s_1, s_2, ..., s_i\}$ of i sensor nodes on the XY-plane (2D plane), out of which $R = \{r_1, r_2, ..., r_m\}$ is the set of relay nodes in the network that performs routing of the sensed data. The remaining $p = i - m - 1$ nodes performs the sensing of any activity in the network. The sensing nodes are represented by a set $N = \{n_1, n_2, ..., n_p\}$. The goal is to select relay nodes in a way that the sensor nodes are fully connected to the sink node.

The following terminology is considered. Let s and d be the two points on the Euclidean plane, then $[s, d]$ denotes the line joining the two points and $||sd||$ denotes the Euclidean distance between s and d. The communication between two sensor nodes or two relay nodes, or a sensor and a relay node, is possible only if $||s_is_j|| \leq r$. The nodes s_i and s_j are called *neighbors*.

For the proposed technique LR-MAC, the simulation area is kept constant for all three deployment strategies. Also, the number of layers and the number of relay nodes in each layer are the same. The difference is in the allocation of relay nodes to various layers.

20.5.3.2 Random Deployment

Here, i sensor nodes are deployed randomly on the XY-plane (Figure 20.6(a)). Out of the i sensor nodes, m relay nodes are selected randomly from the whole network so (m/L) of them can route data from all the p sensor nodes that perform sensing. To execute LR-MAC for random deployment, the total simulation time, T_{sim}, is divided into L time slots so that each group of (m/L) relay nodes can route data for the respective (T_{sim}/L) duration (Figure 20.6).

20.5.3.3 Effective Deployment (Grid)

Here, i sensor nodes are deployed on the XY-plane in a grid pattern (Figure 20.6(b)) to validate the performance of the LR-MAC protocol for several types of scenarios. Out of i sensor nodes, m relay nodes are selected from the whole grid network so that (m/L) of them belong to one group of square grids. To execute LR-MAC for effective (grid) deployment, the total simulation time, T_{sim}, is divided into L time slots so that each group of (m/L) relay nodes can route data for respective (T_{sim}/L) duration from all the p sensor nodes that perform sensing.

20.5.3.4 Effective Deployment (Circular)

i sensor nodes are deployed on the XY-plane in a circular pattern (Figure 20.6(c)). Out of i sensor nodes, m relay nodes are selected from the whole grid network so that (m/L) of them belong to one group of concentric circles. The radii of concentric circles are given as $(D/L, 2*D/L, 3*D/L, ..., L*D/L)$, where D is the radius of the whole wireless personal area network. To execute LR-MAC for effective (circular) deployment, the total simulation time, T_{sim} is divided into L time slots so that each group of (m/L) relay nodes can route data for respective (T_{sim}/L) duration from all the p sensor nodes that perform sensing.

20.6 Simulations and Result Analysis

20.6.1 Network Model 1: Optimization of Ml-Mac Protocol

The empirical formula is obtained using observations from QualNet through MATLAB. The objective is to enable the WSN designer to choose various parameters with simple calculations. The results for Network Lifetime, Average End-to-End Delay, and Average Throughput from QualNet 6.1 simulator are used in MATLAB to calculate the values of these parameters using the second-order empirical formula given by

$$X = aD^2 + bD + c \qquad\qquad (20.7)$$

where a, b, and c are constants; X may be Network Lifetime (NL), Average End-to-End Delay ($d_{end-to-end}$), or Average Throughput (Th); and D is the node density in the network given as

Node Density = Number of Nodes/(Terrain Area × Number of Layers)   (20.8)

The root mean square error, calculated as the difference between observed values obtained with the formula, indicates the effectiveness of the estimators.

The variation in Network Lifetime (in days) for one, three, five, seven, and nine layers in optimized ML-MAC at various node densities is shown in Figure 20.7(a). The value of residual battery capacity obtained from simulations—after running the scenario to a full battery capacity of 200 mAhr to the respective simulation time for each protocol—is used to calculate network lifetime. The results show that lifetime of the network while using five, seven, and 9nine layers increases (linearly) with node density; three layers increase non-linearly (Figure 20.7).

The performance of average end-to-end delay for various layers at different node densities is shown in Figure 20.8(b). The results show that the average end-to-end delay with one layer or no layer is exceptionally low compared to three, five, seven, and nine layers. The reason is that an increase in the number of layers in a network decreases the number of nodes—this results in an increase in the distance of some nodes from the PAN coordinator, introducing more delay for the data. However, since we are considering network lifetime as a primary attribute, the delay may be ignored. With five layers, the delay is almost constant for the network, while it varies non-linearly for three, seven, and nine layers.

20.6.2 Network Model 2: 2D and 3D Wireless Sensor Networks

This subsection presents simulation results for 2D and 3D scenarios and compares performance parameters like network lifetime, throughput, delay, and packets dropped based on results obtained from QualNet 6.1 simulator.

Figure 20.8(a) shows the comparison of Network Lifetime (in days) for 2D and 3D scenarios. Expiration of a node in the network might make it operational or not depending on the role played by the node in the network, making network lifetime an important metric. It can be defined as an interval of time, starting with the first transmission in the WSN and ending when several active nodes for sensing information fall below a threshold. Network Lifetime is calculated using values from simulations after running the scenario to a full battery capacity of 500 mAhr with the

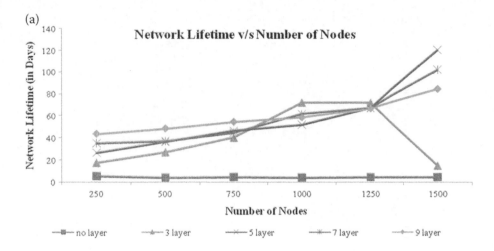

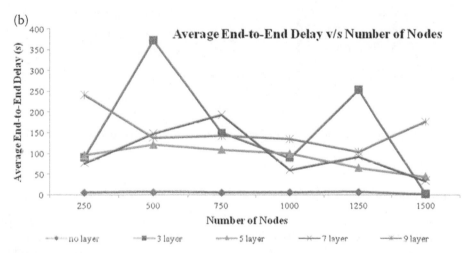

FIGURE 20.7
(**a**) Variation of network lifetime with node density. (**b**) Variation of average end-to-end delay with node density.

respective simulation time. The results indicate more practical results for a 3D scenario.

Figure 20.8(b) shows a comparison of average end-to-end delay for the two scenarios. It can be defined as the time taken by a packet to travel from a source node to a destination node. End-to-end delay includes the delays caused by retransmission, route discovery, propagation, processing, and querying. IEEE 802.15.4 performs better with a 3D scenario than a 2D scenario.

20.6.3 Network Model 3: Random and Deterministic Deployments

The parameters considered for the three deployment strategies using the LR-MAC technique are kept constant for all simulations to equally judge the performance.

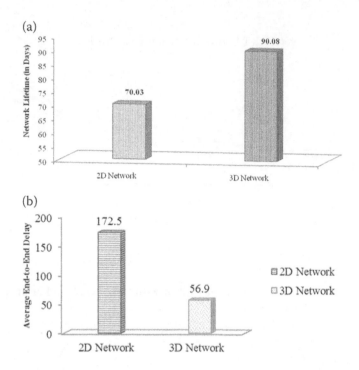

FIGURE 20.8
(a) Comparison of network lifetime for 2D and 3D networks. (b) Comparison of average end-to-end delay for 2D and 3D networks.

20.6.3.1 Effect on End-to-End Delay

Figure 20.9(a) shows the effectiveness of the LR-MAC protocol to reduce the end-to-end delay in the network. In a sensor network, end-to-end delay is due to channel access failure, data transmission delay, number of hops, and contention access periods. It is observed from the graph that the effect of LR-MAC protocol is random in nature for various deployment strategies; it increases the delay for grid deployment while reduces the delay for circular and random deployment strategies.

20.6.3.2 Effect on Network Lifetime

Network Lifetime (NL) is the most crucial design parameter for a wireless personal area network. NL is directly associated with the energy efficiency of the network. In the QualNet network simulator, energy consumed by the network during simulations is provided in terms of residual battery capacity (R_{bat}). The average battery (B_{avg}) provided to each sensor node in the network is given as:

$$B_{avg} = (((m + 1) \times 400) + (p \times 200))/i \qquad (20.9)$$

Thus, after a time T_{sim}, the battery consumed (B_{cons}) by the network is given as

$$B_{cons} = B_{avg}\text{-}R_{bat} \qquad (20.10)$$

(a)

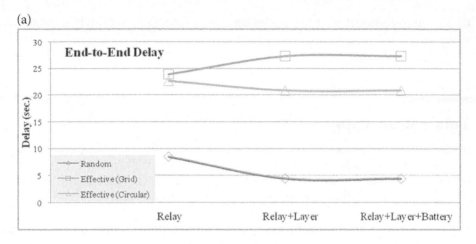

(b)

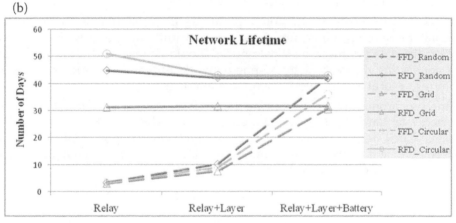

FIGURE 20.9
(a) Effect of LR-MAC on end-to-end delay for various deployment strategies. (b) Effect of LR-MAC on network lifetime for various deployment strategies.

Therefore, the network lifetime (NL) can be given as

$$NL = (T_{sim} \times Bavg) / B_{cons} \tag{20.11}$$

Figure 20.9(b) shows the variation of network lifetime for both types of devices in the network viz. RFDs and FFDs. As observed from the graph, there is a significant improvement in the network lifetime of relay nodes for all the three deployment strategies (since LR-MAC techniques deal with the relay nodes only), while RFDs (sensing nodes) remain unaffected. It is clearly observed that without the LR-MAC technique, the network falls since all FFDs (relay nodes and PAN) die out. The use of LR-MAC and enhanced battery capacity of FFDs increases the network life to five times. Figure 20.9(b) provides the average network lifetime of the network considering both RFDs and FFDs. The network lifetime increases linearly for all deployment strategies. The improvement in network lifetime happened because a major portion of the supplied battery was consumed by relay nodes in a short lifespan which was overcome by introducing layering for relay nodes—two-thirds of the relay nodes can switch themselves off while the remaining one-third work.

20.7 Future Road Maps

A Wireless Sensor Network can be optimized by using principles, algorithms, and applications of Artificial Intelligence. Future developments in WSN must produce powerful and cost-effective sensor nodes to extend the applicability of WSN in various research areas. Some of the issues that can further be investigated:

- The performance for divergent sink placement like center, corner, or a randomly selected location in a sensor network field can be tested.
- WSNs are especially useful for applications like health monitoring, wildlife habitat monitoring, forest fire detection, and building controls. To monitor a WSN, the data produced by sensor nodes should be reachable. This can be done by connecting the WSN with existing network infrastructure such as the global internet, a local area network, or private internet.
- Time synchronization in WSN bring the clocks of the sensor nodes together for a perfect (standard) clock. To bring these clocks together, the skew and drift of the nodes' clock need to be managed. To design a lightweight, fault-tolerant, and energy-efficient protocol with minimal energy consumption is the main challenge for time synchronization in WSN.

References

1. Akyildiz I. F., Su W., Sankarasubramaniam Y., and Cayirci E., "A survey on sensor networks," *IEEE Communications Magazine*, vol. 40, no. 8, pp. 102–114, Aug 2002.
2. Cannon P. S. and Harding C. R., "Future military wireless solutions," Ch. 8 in Wireless Communications: The Future, Webb W., Ed., John Wiley & Sons, 2007.
3. Stuart E., Moh M., and Moh T. S., "Privacy and security in biomedical applications of wireless sensor networks," in *First International Symposium on Applied Sciences on Biomedical and Communication Technologies*, Aalborg, 2008, pp. 1–5.
4. Akhondi M. r., Talevski A., Carlsen S., and Petersen S., "Applications of wireless sensor networks in the oil, gas and resources industries," in *24th IEEE International Conference on Advanced Information Networking and Applications*, Perth, WA, 2010, pp. 941–948.
5. He T., Gu L., Luo L., Yan Ting, Stankovic J. A., and Son S. H., "An overview of data aggregation architecture for real-time tracking with sensor networks," in *Proceedings20th IEEE International Parallel & Distributed Processing Symposium*, Rhodes Island, 2006, pp. 8.
6. Stattner E., Vidot N., Hunel P., and Collard M., "Wireless sensor network for habitat monitoring: A counting heuristic," in *37th Annual IEEE Conference on Local Computer Networks – Workshops*, Clearwater, FL, 2012, pp. 753–760.
7. Hussain S., Schaffner S., and Moseychuck D., "Applications of Wireless Sensor Networks and RFID in a Smart Home Environment," in *Seventh Annual Communication Networks and Services Research Conference*, Moncton, NB, 2009, pp. 153–157.

8. Chee-Yee, C, Kumar S. P., "Sensor networks: evolution, opportunities, and challenges," *Proceedings of the IEEE*, vol. 91, no. 8, August 2003, pp. 1247–1256.

9. Jin H. and Jiang W., Eds., Handbook of Research on Developments and Trends in Wireless Sensor Networks: From Principle to Practice, IGI Global; 2010 February 28.

10. Winkler M., Tuchs K. D., Hughes K., and Barclay G., "Theoretical and practical aspects of military wireless sensor networks," *Journal of Telecommunications and Information Technology*, pp. 37–45, 2008.

11. Paul J. L., "Smart Sensor Web: Web-based exploitation of sensor fusion for visualization of the tactical battlefield," *IEEE Aerospace and Electronic Systems Magazine*, vol. 16, no. 5, pp. 29–36, May 2001.

12. He T., et al., "Energy-efficient surveillance system using wireless sensor networks," in *Proceedings of the 2nd International Conference on Mobile Systems, Applications, and Services, ACM*, June 2004, pp. 270–283.

13. 20The Ohio State University. (2003, August 20). A Line in the Sand [Online]. Available: http://www.cse.ohiostate.edu/siefast/nest/nest/nest_webpage/ALineInTheSand.html

14. Kintner-Meyer M. and Brambley M. R., "Pros & cons of wireless," *ASHRAE Journal*, vol. 44, no. 11, pp.54–59, November 2002.

15. Kintner-Meyer M. and Brambley M. R., Wireless Sensors: How Cost-Effective Are They in Commercial Buildings? PNNL-SA-36839.

16. Rytter A., "Vibration-based inspection of civil engineering structures", Ph.D. dissertation, Department of Building Technology and Structural Engineering, Aalborg University, Denmark, 1993.

17. Mainwaring A., Polastre J., Szewczyk R., Culle D., and Anderson J., "Wireless sensor networks for habitat monitoring", in *Proceedings of the1st ACM International Workshop on Wireless Sensor Networks and Applications*, Atlanta, GA, 2002, pp. 88–97.

18. Wang H., Elson J., Girod L., Estrin D., and Yao K., "Target classification and localization in habitat monitoring," in *Proceedings IEEE International Conference on Acoustics, Speech, and Signal Processing*, Hong Kong, 2003, pp. IV-844-7, vol. 4.

19. Wang H., Estrin D., and Girod L., "Preprocessing in a tiered sensor network for habitat monitoring," *EURASIP Journal on Applied Signal Processing*, vol. 4, pp. 392–401, 2003.

20. http://www.businessweek.com/magazine/content/03_34/b3846622.htm Aug 25, 2003.

21. Srivastava M. B., Muntz R. R., and Potkonjak M., "Smart kindergarten: sensor-based wireless networks for smart developmental problem-solving environments," in Proceedings of the 7th annual international conference on Mobile computing and networking, July 2001, pp. 132–138.

22. Xu J., Li X., Ding Y. and Chen Y., "A comparative study of the link-state-aware routing in typical wireless sensor network models for home automation," in *36th Chinese Control Conference (CCC)*, Dalian, 2017, pp. 8890–8894.

23. Vikram N., Harish K. S., Nihaal M. S., Umesh R., Shetty A., and Kumar A., "A low cost home automation system using Wi-Fi based wireless sensor network incorporating internet of things (IoT)," in *IEEE 7th International Advance Computing Conference (IACC)*, Hyderabad, 2017, pp. 174–178.

24. Moitra L. G., Singh A., Deka M., and Joshi J., "Energy efficient smart cooling system using WSN," in *13th International Multi-Conference on Systems, Signals & Devices (SSD)*, Leipzig, 2016, pp. 424–429.

25. http://www.intel.com/research/exploratory/heterogeneous.htm.

26. Holmes I. A., "Making maintenance invisible," *AB Journal*, pp. 49–53, Sep. 2004.

27. Blomqvist E. and Koivo H. N., "Security in sensor networks – a case study," in *12th Medical Conference On Control and Automation (IEEE)*, Kusadasi, Turkey, 2004.

28. Rabaey J., Arens E., Federspiel C., Gadgil A., Messerschmitt D., Nazaroff W., Pister K., Orena S., and Varaiya P., "Smart Energy Distribution and Consumption: Information Technology As An Enabling Force," *White Paper*, 2001 [Online]. Available: https://www.semanticscholar.org/paper/Smart-Energy-Distribution-and-Consumption%3A-as-an-Rabaey-Arens/87be34558e6c9da8098de522e893f64322bd0a52.

29. Asada G., Dong M., Lin T. S., Newberg F., Pottie G., Kaiser W. J., and Marcy H. O., "Wireless integrated network sensors: low power systems on a chip," in *Proceedings of the 24th European Solid-State Circuits Conference*, 1998, pp. 9–16.

30. Khan S., Pathan A. S., and Alrajeh N. A., Eds., Wireless Sensor Networks: Current Status and Future Trends, CRC Press, April 21, 2016.

31. Kumar N. and Singh Y., "Routing protocols in wireless sensor networks," in Handbook of Research on Advanced Wireless Sensor Network Applications, Protocols, and Architectures, IGI Global, 2017, pp. 86–128.

32. Vales-Alonso J., Parrado-García F. J., López-Matencio P., Alcaraz J. J., and González-Castaño F. J., "On the optimal random deployment of wireless sensor networks in non-homogeneous scenarios," *Ad Hoc Networks*, vol. 11, no. 3, pp. 846–860, 2013.

33. Mulligan R. and Ammari H. M., "Coverage in wireless sensor networks: a survey," *Network Protocols and Algorithms*, vol. 2, no. 2, pp. 27–53, 2010.

34. 21Akewar M. C. and Thakur N. V., "A study of wireless mobile sensor network deployment," *International Journal of Computer and Wireless Communication*, vol. 2, no. 4, pp. 533–540, 2012.

35. Chen J., Li S., and Sun Y., "Novel deployment schemes for mobile sensor networks," *Sensors*, vol. 7, no. 11, pp. 2907–2919, 2007.

36. Ravelomanana V., "Extremal properties of three-dimensional sensor networks with applications," *IEEE Transactions on Mobile Computing*, vol. 3, no. 3, pp. 246–257, 2004.

37. Ishizuka M., Aida M., "Performance study of node placement in sensor networks," in *Proceedings of 24th International Conference on Distributed Computing Systems Workshops*, 2004, pp. 598–603.

38. Wang Y. and Kutta A., "Joint and simultaneous k-sensing detection in deterministic and random sensor networks," in *IEEE 26th International Parallel and Distributed Processing Symposium Workshops & PhD Forum*, Shanghai, 2012, pp. 1506–1511.

39. Boubrima A., Matigot F., Bechkit W., Rivano H., and Ruas A., "optimal deployment of wireless sensor networks for air pollution monitoring," in *24th International Conference on Computer Communication and Networks (ICCCN)*, Las Vegas, NV, 2015, pp. 1–7.

40. Khalfallah Z., Fajjari I., Aitsaadi N., Rubin P., and Pujolle G., "A novel 3D underwater WSN deployment strategy for full-coverage and connectivity in rivers," in *IEEE International Conference on Communications (ICC)*, Kuala Lumpur, 2016, pp. 1–7.

41. De C., Rane A. D., and Prabhakar N., "A comparative study on performances of sensor deployment algorithms in WSN," in *39th National Systems Conference (NSC)*, Noida, 2015, pp. 1–6.

42. Manju, R. Thalore, and Jha M. K., "Optimized ML-MAC for energy-efficient wireless sensor network protocol" *Proceedings of Confluence-2014 5th IEEE International Conference on The Next Generation Information Technology Summit*, September 25–26, 2014.

43. Perkins C., Royer E., and Das S., "Ad hoc on demand distance vector (AODV) routing," IETF RFC No. 3561, July 2003.

44. Thalore R., Khurana M. and Jha M. K., "Performance comparison of 2D and 3D Zigbee wireless sensor networks." *Springer International Conference on ICT for Sustainable Development*, July 3–4, 2015, pp. 215–222,.

45. Akhlaqand M., Sheltami T. R., "Coverage, connectivity and communication (C3) protocol method for wireless sensor networks," U.S. Patent 9148849, September 29, 2015.

46. Thalore R., Jha M. K., and Bhattacharya P. P., "A layered relay-medium access control (LR-MAC) protocol for wireless sensor networks," in *Recent Patents on Computer Science*, vol. 10, no. 3, pp. 255–264, 2017.

Index

Note: *Italicized* page numbers refer to figures, **bold** page numbers refer to tables.